PENGUIN BOOKS

STEAL THIS URINE TEST

Abbie Hoffman was an American dissident for more than a quarter of a century. In the early sixties he was involved in community organizing, Ban the Bomb activities, and the civil rights movement in the South. He was one of the most visible opponents of the Vietnam War, and he shot to national prominence as a result of the Chicago Conspiracy Trial. He spent most of the 1970s as a fugitive, remaining, however, politically active. As "Barry Freed," he led Save the River, a grassroots battle to defeat an engineering project on the St. Lawrence River. During the 1980s he was active in opposition to U.S. policy in Central America. In 1987 he, Amy Carter, and thirteen others were acquitted of illegal-trespass charges growing out of efforts to block CIA recruiting on campuses. Abbie Hoffman died in April 1989.

Jonathan Silvers attended the University of Pennsylvania and has written extensively on politics and culture. He lives in New York City.

Also by Abbie Hoffman

Revolution for the Hell of It
Woodstock Nation
Steal This Book
Steal This Book: The Sequel (unpublished)
Vote! (coauthored)
To America With Love (coauthored)
Soon to Be a Major Motion Picture
Square Dancing in the Ice Age

Steal This Urine Test

Fighting Drug Hysteria in America

ABBIE HOFFMAN
with Jonathan Silvers

 PENGUIN BOOKS

PENGUIN BOOKS
Published by the Penguin Group
Penguin Books USA Inc.,
375 Hudson Street, New York, New York 10014, U.S.A.
Penguin Books Ltd, 27 Wrights Lane, London W8 5TZ, England
Penguin Books Australia Ltd, Ringwood, Victoria, Australia
Penguin Books Canada Ltd, 10 Alcorn Avenue,
Toronto, Ontario, Canada M4V 3B2
Penguin Books (N.Z.) Ltd, 182–190 Wairau Road, Auckland 10, New Zealand

Penguin Books Ltd, Registered Offices:
Harmondsworth, Middlesex, England

First published in Penguin Books 1987
Published simultaneously in Canada

10   9

LIBRARY OF CONGRESS CATALOGING IN PUBLICATION DATA
Hoffman, Abbie.
   Steal this urine test.
   Bibliography: p.
   1. Drug testing—United States.   2. Drug testing—
Government policy—United States.   I. Silvers, Jonathan.   II. Title.   III. Title: Urine test.
HV5823.5. U5H64   1987   362.2'9386   87-12093
ISBN 0 14 01.0400 3

Printed in the United States of America
Set in Caledonia and Century Schoolbook

Dedicated to the workers of America,
who have nothing to lose
but their jobs.

Nothing so needs reforming as other people's habits.
—Mark Twain, *Pudd'nhead Wilson*

The Vial of Contents

Introduction to Independence

All my political friends have advised me not to write this book. They felt taking any position on drugs would lead to problems, dredging up the cocaine bust, now fourteen years old, but still a vulnerable wound. And *that*, in turn, could hurt my credibility as a critic of government policy. "Let sleeping drugs lie" was the general tone of advice. It would be a lot safer writing about my environmental protection battles over the past nine years, or my trips to Central America, the subject I most consistently address at lectures and rallies. Publishers love the idea of a book on how Amy Carter, myself, and thirteen others have just beaten the CIA in a Northampton, MA, trial. Even a book about the seven-year underground odyssey, a result of the cocaine arrest, would be a lot safer.

But my twenty-five-year chosen role as an American dissident, by definition, means that I have often had to reject the advice of well-intentioned friends and follow the dictates of my own conscience.

Politically, there are no points gained writing about drugs today unless you are willing to slam them. With the passing of the sixties and the hedonism of sex, drugs, and rock 'n' roll, the American Left has developed a puritanical streak almost as rigid as the Religious Right. The Black Political Caucus in Congress will probably scorn this book right along with the TV evangelists, in the same way that Women Against Pornography have adopted the Meese Commission pornography report as truth about sex. Neither side

1

in the debate would recognize that drugs are being scapegoated in an attempt to avoid making badly needed social and economic changes in a disintegrating society.

Norman Mailer warned me, "Let the fascists have dope, it's time to draw the wagons round and carefully choose the liberties we still have enough time to defend." Ironically, we had this discussion while he introduced me to "the drug of defeat"—Scotch. We drained a bottle of the finest defeat available while mourning the passage of Enlightenment.

It's been years since I could properly be called a "drug experimenter." I used recreational drugs in the sixties, but I just don't feel the same enthusiasm for the subject as I did when I was younger. I have gone on to other things, resisting pressure to challenge or champion the matter. This neutral position has been scorned by friend and foe alike, who feel I must repent, be born again, even if it means compromising the truth as I perceive it.

There are Brownie points to be won by loud, firm atonement. But all renunciations, even sincere ones by people I know and admire—like Grace Slick and Dennis Hopper—seem misused and oversimplified by the media. The famous public renunciations look like cartoon confessions extracted under threat. They have the tone of fifties movies in which "Communists" confessed to being traitors on bended knees before someone's mother or priest.

This book is not "preachy." It does not beat the drum for or against drugs. It does not cry out for legalization, the passing out of free dope, or threaten to fill the reservoirs in Chicago with LSD. In the drug section (Part I), I simply apply what I've learned over the years to introduce complexity and sensibility into an area dangerously misunderstood. What you will read is an insider's viewpoint on drugs, not dogma chiseled in stone. Every line should be prefaced, "In my opinion."

What are these opinions? I believe society would be best served by abandoning the reigning turbulence and moving to a calmer plateau from which we could engage in drug education, research, and treatment programs with a decent chance of success. It's easier to work on solutions without people shouting in your ear.

Without minimizing the problem of drug abuse, our attention should focus on equally serious problems, such as poverty, homelessness, unemployment, and inadequate medical care. I don't believe we can cope with drug abuse on a meaningful scale until we are willing to tackle these more general and pressing issues.

I'm confident our healing community can come up with sound, workable strategies for all who need help, not just those who can afford it. However, I'm pessimistic about the chance that sane reasoning has against fundamentalist blind faith. Our scientific knowledge has increased dramatically in the past decades, but unfortunately the power brokers ignore this evidence, preferring to keep society as a whole in the dark ages. They offer stiffer punishments as the *only* solution.

On the one hand, this book is meant to be philosophical about drugs. On the other, it is meant to be precise, political, and activist on urine testing. *This is a call to arms against a ritual that has nothing to do with drug abuse and a lot to do with controlling citizens.*

My suspicions were aroused in 1982, when on a prison work-release program I was subjected to constant, random urine testing. Because of actual drug use and/or faulty tests, a lot of inmates regularly flunked. The guards used the test results as blackmail, judging social behavior to be more important than actual drug use. Those who conformed to the warden's image of the model prisoner were not punished for positive results, while those whose spirit of resistance had not been broken were.

My own case was unique. I was the most famous inmate on a work-release program in New York's history, and an unrepentant troublemaker to boot. The press had drawn incredible attention to my case and conservative legislators were using it as an excuse to abolish the entire work-release program. The *Daily News* front page screamed, "ABBIE WALKS!" noting parenthetically "The Pope Goes Home." (This was the biggest free job-wanted ad imaginable.) I saw it as my activist duty to defend this humane prison program with every act.

Offered several high-priced jobs, which under the rules I could have taken, I chose instead to work on a near-voluntary level as a drug-abuse counselor, returning to prison after each work day. I was meticulous about obeying the no drugs or alcohol rule, but on two occasions I flunked the urine test anyway. I refused to buckle under to lies. Threats of court suits, extensive publicity, and a demand for confirmatory testing were sufficient to scare the guards into ignoring the results. Beyond this, I began a campaign to enlist inmates, cheated out of privileges by a bogus test, in a court challenge against the screening process. I had lined up two of the best lawyers in the country (Gerry Lefcourt and Michael Kennedy) and felt a dozen plaintiffs were needed to make the proper challenge. No more effort than signing the suit was required; no inmate would have to pay a penny. But out of more than one hundred men, not a single one was brave enough to join the suit, and challenge the system. Remember, these are men who boast the lifestyle of the tough, macho con, ready to fight all comers. A bluff when it really counted.

Knowing something stinks in the system changes nothing. People have to be willing to stand up and be counted. Injustice is transformed into justice only when people at critical points in their lives are willing to risk the consequences, go for freedom, and Just Say No.

If not for these experiences, and the proliferation of the procedure, I would never have felt the urge to write about or even think this much about drugs.

Reading this book, I hope you get a sense that drug testing is the most tangible manifestation of Big Government policies aimed at destroying civil liberties that took decades to achieve. Already, close to 30 million Americans are being subjected to some form of chemical testing, and that number is expected to triple within five years.

This book asks a lot of the reader. Although I tried making the language accessible to the layperson, at various times you will need to be part scientist, part lawyer, part sociologist, as well as constant philosopher. Above all, I ask you to *think*.

Those of you who are new to my books might best start with Part II, where you will find more than you ever wanted to know about urine testing, more than is available in any other source. You will learn that manufacturers admit the tests are imperfect. You will see how margins of error are being badly misused to disgrace and fire complete non-drug users. Libertarians concerned about privacy will learn that a urine screen gives the Government or the Boss a complete chemical profile of everything in your body—information that you should quite rightly feel is none of their damn business. You will learn how a pseudo-scientific testing/surveillance industry with strong assistance from the Reagan administration mushroomed overnight into a billion-dollar-a-year business, how these bladder spies have struck gold in urine, forcing people to give testimony against themselves and submit to unlawful searches and seizures. It will certainly surprise you to learn how widespread urine testing has become. You can follow the court battles over constitutional issues, and watch Congress, as usual, stand with its hands in its pockets.

With no hesitation whatsoever, this book gladly offers the most up-to-date advice on beating the tests. It also provides information to educate your friends, fellow workers, and politicians on how to resist and organize against mass screening before the practice becomes a permanent fixture in all our lives.

If you choose to read about urinalysis first, you should then return to the beginning and read the drug section. I hope by then you'll be so outraged over urine testing that you'll give some serious thought to what is being said about drugs, drug abuse, and hysteria—even some extra thought to politics, media, power, human values, and how things happen and don't happen in our society.

I've deliberately avoided all profanity and rhetoric in the text, because I want this book to have a chance with readers who have honest concerns about their jobs and might be turned off by my "media image." I have also done this so as to reach parents confused and frustrated when it comes to getting information they can trust about drugs and abuse. I have done this, I hope, without compromising what I believe to be truth, justice, and the democratic values of my country.

Abbie Hoffman
Northampton, Mass.
Patriots' Day
April 19, 1987

PART I

Drugs

1.

Knee Deep in Hysteria

Let's get something straight at the outset. This book is pro-choice, pro-civil liberties, and antitotalitarian—American values as old as the Declaration of Independence. However, given the controversial nature of drugs, drug testing, and the prevailing political climate, it may well be mistaken as being pro-drug. That's because virtually everything the average citizen sees on TV or reads in the newspapers on the subject is a combination of irrelevant nonsense and disinformation posing as antidrug knowledge. Anyone who disputes these watered-down factoids, as I do in this book, gets lumped with the deviant opposition.

The major institutions in our country produce, through mutual interests, a National Party Line (NPL) on any number of social issues. Defining this National Party Line would take several pages. Suffice it to say that the NPL is the modern American gospel, dictating rights and wrongs. Deviation from its scripture conjures up the label "heretic."

The NPL on drugs dictates which drugs are morally acceptable and which are not. It also determines which users are socially acceptable and which are stigmatized outlaws. Narrow focus and strict categorization preclude meaningful debate on the topic. It is no different than, say, the NPL on Communism or God. An NPL emerges when a deliberative body, such as the U.S. Congress, reaches virtually unanimous agreement on an issue that is philosophically not so clear-cut. In other words, at some point adherence to blind faith, rather than scientific objectivity or common sense, becomes the criterion for judging someone's viewpoint. God is great, communism is evil, drugs do the work of the devil. End of the debate. An NPL thrives on simplicity. If an issue gets *too* complex, there can be no instant consensus. Once the NPL is set in place, few people are brave enough to venture into the issue's complexity or perhaps even challenge the accepted dogma.

This consensus is rigid, bigoted, simplistic, and ultimately counter-productive to the treatment of drug abuse. It tries, by demanding strict obedience, to impose the moral and ethical values of the Enforcers on all citizens. This National Party Line is neither left nor right, but totalitarian in nature. Listen to the words of R. C. Cowan, writing in our most respected conservative forum, *The National Review* (April 29, 1983): "Our drug warriors (some fifty programs and agencies in the last seventy-five years) are an enormous, corrupt international bureaucracy that has been lying for years." Unfortunately, there are very few critics on either side of the spectrum willing to challenge the shibboleths regularly accepted as truth.

It is a National Party Line filled with hysteria and hypocrisy, using fear and intimidation, a policy which, if history has taught us anything, is doomed to failure. This approach to drugs reflects the general wave of fear encouraged by the Reagan administration and its supporters: the welfare monster eating up all our tax money; crime in the streets; AIDS-ridden homosexuals molesting our children; the Evil Empire creating beachheads on our continents; the persistent terror of losing the nuclear arms race. This general hysteria manifested itself most strongly in the summer of 1986, when citizens of Fortress America could no longer visit Europe for fear of "world terrorism." The odds of being on a hijacked plane were lower that season than of drowning in your own bathtub. But rationality and the European tourism industry could no more compete with the fashionable hysteria of that summer than facts could shield Americans from the next season's fashionable bogeyman—the Drug Menace.

Drugs, naughty drugs, of course, have been a perennial favorite among pushers of hysteria. They symbolize the seven deadly American sins: laziness, violence, promiscuity, theft, godlessness, disrespect, and chaos. But nothing in memory seems to match what took place in the fall of 1986, during the national political campaigns.

Virtually every politician, from Jesse Helms to Jesse Jackson, advocated some kind of mandatory drug testing. Pierre DuPont, Republican presidential candidate from the state of DuPont (i.e. Delaware), demanded that every teenager pass a urine test before getting a driver's license. The First Lady suggested the death penalty for dealers. Even an enlightened Senator like John Kerry (D-Mass.), who expressed doubts about "the accuracy of such tests, questions of privacy, and the potential for misuse by employers," felt compelled by the omnipotent power of the NPL to vote against common sense and in favor of a Senate Commerce Committee bill calling for mandatory testing in the public-safety sector.

Moving from the absurd to the ridiculous, politicians urged the use of the military to "seal off the borders" from drug smugglers. A low estimate of what it would take to do this effectively might be three million soldiers. Not only would such a program cost billions of dollars, but were it to be implemented, it would soon be seen as be nothing more than a futile gesture. For example, drug abuse is a growing problem in East Germany, where authorities maintain that the chief crossing points for illicit drugs are the checkpoints at the Berlin Wall. Even if such a naive anti-importation policy could ever be implemented in the U.S., it would simply lead to the domestic production of more powerful synthetic drugs, no more expensive or complicated to produce than the imports. (See Chapter Three, "Common Everyday Myths About Drugs.")

That fall, nothing less than a "War on Drugs" was declared. But as we will quickly see, it was a war at conflict with itself, with truth becoming the first casualty. Typical of the initiatives of the Actor-in-Chief, it was a war only in the symbolic sense, complete with all the trappings—the uniforms, the "combat footage," the body counts, and, of course, the hundreds of millions of dollars spent. Like the long and difficult war we fought two decades ago in Southeast Asia, it seems the more the authorities claim we are "winning," the worse the battles get—and the stronger the enemy grows.

Let's take a look at the front lines of this so-called War on Drugs.

Here is an excellent opportunity to begin chipping away at the National Party Line. During one week in the month preceding the 1986 election, the news media were flooded with stories about an upcoming "secret" raid on a major Bolivian cocaine laboratory by U.S. troops. Military preparations, along with official statements, were fed to the public for five days running, even before the helicopters left for the jungle. The notion of a major cocaine lab that could produce millions of dollars worth of "devil powder," the nerve center of an enemy with whom we are at war, must have seemed to the public, with such exaggeration, more fitting a description of the laboratories at Los Alamos.

Back to reality. A "major" cocaine lab is usually no more than a few thatched huts, some with large, gas-operated stoves upon which sit a half dozen restaurant-size aluminum cooking pots, and a few sheds to store coca leaves. A second smaller hut stores the rather primitive additives, such as lime, used to extract the active ingredients from the leaves. There are also living and eating quarters for a dozen workers, lots of guns (this is, after all, a dangerous business), a well-camouflaged trail leading to an airstrip. Such is the humble reality of a "major lab"; a "minor lab" is a Bolivian family doing the whole process in their kitchen. (They might, incidentally, be using Bolivian money to kindle the flame, since that currency right now is considered the most worthless in the world.)

While the week of hoopla and ballyhoo preceding the invasion certainly gave ample warning to the lab workers to disassemble and disperse into the jungle, a process that would have taken about two hours, the workers chose instead to leave the labs undisturbed.

Why? Under the rubric "international cooperation" was hatched a virtual conspiracy that must have included the highest officials in Bolivia and the U.S., the armies of both countries, and major cocaine traffickers. They decided to put on a show that would dramatize to the world that Ron Reagan, Ed Meese, and the gang were "really" serious about *this* War on Drugs. As opposed to Nixon's "Operation Intercept" or any of the dozen other initiatives we've waged over the past quarter century. Leaving aside emerging reports from the Kerry Senate Commission that the Contras are smuggling cocaine into the U.S. on Southern Air (i.e., CIA) planes, (reminiscent of the well-documented Southern Air, i.e. CIA, heroin-running during the Vietnam War—see *The Politics of Heroin in Southeast Asia* by John McCoy), the major lab bust was, in reality, a staged fantasy in the War on Drugs.

When a deliberate fantasy is devised by Enforcers with great power, it is a good rule of thumb to suspect that something else is afoot. Troops in jungle camouflage, bearing automatic weapons, zooming in on Huey helicopters, may *look* like a war on drugs, but looks are the limit of this symbolic confrontation.

Another scenario on the front lines concerns the apprehension of "kingpins," and what are routinely called "the largest drug busts on record." The following story could be told about other illegal drugs, but cocaine or, to be precise, its more concentrated version—crack—is currently the media's hot epidemic, so let's stay out on the cocaine trail.

In February 1987, Carlos Lehder, a thirty-seven-year-old Colombian, was extradited to Miami with great sound and fury, identified by the Drug Enforcement Agency (DEA) and the news media as allegedly responsible for most of the cocaine on the streets of America. Peter Jennings, on ABC-TV's "Nightly News," associated Lehder with 80 percent of the illegal shipments to the U.S. Now, before we start passing out medals, let's apply some minimal knowledge of cocaine trafficking and a little common sense.

Cocaine dealers can realize tremendous profits from a relatively small amount smuggled into the world's largest seller's market. Most of the trade is still in the hands of free-lancers. Everyone, from an ambitious family trying to break out of poverty in Baranquil, Colombia, to a caper-oriented "ring" of preppies at one of America's most fashionable academies, Choate, tries his or her luck. Certainly there is a measure of control by organized, ruthless, and extraordinarily rich criminals, but a more likely kingpin might be a sixty-year-old Bolivian general, because it takes a lot of guns, murders, and political power to rise to the top echelon of smuggling.

Every six months or so, the DEA and the media parade a new and more powerful kingpin. Even more regularly, some prosecutor in our country holds a press conference announcing another "largest drug bust on record." If any serious statistician or investigative journalist used his brain and a calculator, it could be easily "proved" that over the past four years, we have eliminated more than 400 percent of the drug supply for all users in America. In other words, capturing a "kingpin responsible for 80 percent of the cocaine" or making the "largest drug bust in history," or adding bigger numbers to the body count (arrests) may be nothing more than propaganda ploys to justify the expense of the war on drugs. Ironically, after all the DEA's "successes," the problem keeps getting worse and worse.

In March 1987, the U.S. Congress Office of Technology Assessment released figures showing that cocaine imports rose from an estimated sixty tons in 1984 to one hundred-thirty tons in 1986. Heroin imports over the same two-year period rose from four to six tons. Meanwhile, federal spending to combat drug importation more than doubled, from $400 million in 1981 to over $820 million in 1986. Once again, the reality of the drug situation was laid bare: in the fifty years of an Enforcer-controlled drug policy, there is absolutely no evidence proving that increased federal expenditures for so-called "get tough" policies have any impact on supply. Neither do domestic crackdowns seem to matter. New York State special narcotics prosecutor Sterling Johnson compares these efforts to "digging a hole in the ocean." His office claims that the price of a kilogram of cocaine dropped from $60,000 in 1981 to between $17,000 and $25,000 in 1986. Such a dramatic drop could only occur because of a substantial increase in supply.

The other end of the War on Drugs, the resolution end, has an equal number of staged plays. Lambasted for her extravagances during Ron's first term (recall the presidential china, a refurbished White House, and several thousand-dollar only-to-be-worn-once gowns), the First Lady was anxious to shed her Marie Antoinette image. She scanned the *New York Times* Neediest Cases for appropriate causes. Fighting drug abuse was available, and she grabbed it. Let them eat cake, but not coke. Let's take the most famous scenario: Nancy Reagan's visit to the rehab center, where victims of the war on drugs are "cured" of their addictions. The highpoint of the visit is the moving testimonies of former addicts, no different from sinners confessing at a Jimmy Swaggert revival meeting. Who is not going to be moved by a sixteen-year-old black kid, tears streaming down her cheeks, talking about her awful life with drugs, the wonderful people at Sunrise Village, and her determination to stay cured, to stay drug-free, by "just saying no"?

The centerpiece of the "just say no to drugs" campaign is the superficial ease of miracle treatment. Like its counterpart being played out in the Bolivian jungle, it too is deceptive. It is deceptive in two ways. The "cure the victim" morality play ignores drug abuse as a serious, complex, deeply rooted illness that is extremely difficult to remedy even on a long-term basis. *The Consumers Union Report on Licit and Illicit Drugs*, considered by many experts as the most complete study of drug addiction, reports a recidivism rate as high as ninety percent among "reformed" addicts.

In other words, chances are nine out of ten that within a few years, the "cured" patient will be back on the same drug or will have switched to another, more harmful addiction. There is much medical evidence that our rehab centers have concentrated for too long on the symptom—i.e. the drugs—and not enough on treating individuals. The more we learn about drug abuse the more we discover that it is an illness as dificult to cure as diabetes, cancer, heart disease, or any serious psychiatric illnesses. Indeed, some recent evidence suggests that substance abuse probably is a symptom of deeper psychiatric illnesses (such as anxiety or depression). In other words, contrary to popular mythology, drugs don't take people, people take drugs.

On the mass educational level, the same problem of oversimplification persists. Telling serious drug abusers to "just say no" has about the same effect as telling serious depressives to "just cheer up." It oversimplifies and masks the real clinical problem.

The other hoax being perpetuated by Nancy's well-orchestrated sideshow to Ron's action-packed war is the charade that government "really" cares about drug abuse. If that were true, there would be enough facilities to accommodate at least the many victims of drug abuse who *voluntarily* seek treatment. Daily, however, thousands trying to enter rehab centers get turned away for lack of space and funds. Worse, rejection from treatment centers leads many addicts to desperate acts, including suicide.

In the fall of 1986, the peak of the drug hysteria, strange things began happening. Twelve-year-old kids were praised as heroes for turning in their parents, reminiscent of the Hitler Youth days; PTAs called for random strip searches in high schools; rock 'n' roll was again being scrutinized in congressional hearings for references to drug use; professional athletes were forced to squeal on teammates, then publicly confess and parrot the National Party Line on television. Unconstitutional restrictions on travel, with strong components of racism, mushroomed in popularity. Police on the George Washington Bridge set up roadblocks, tying up traffic for hours, hunting for suspected drug users. In Fort Lauderdale, police stopped motorists daily, distributing cards saying "WARNING: You Are Entering a Dangerous Area Known for Drug Sales."

The media was far from being a passive, objective observer of this phenomenon. To the contrary, it fueled the flames with sensationalism. *Newsweek* and *Time* devoted five cover stories to drugs from March to November 1986. *Newsweek,* in one dose of hyperbole, compared the drug crisis to "the plagues of medieval times." The CBS News documentary, "48 Hours on Crack Street," earned the highest ratings for a documentary in the past five years. NBC Nightly News, in the seven months preceding the election, ran 429 segments on drugs, a record sixteen hours of air-time. Throughout this media onslaught, criticism of the government's anti-drug policies was virtually nonexistent. That, free speech lovers, is what you call a National Party Line!

All this and more reflected, and still reflects, the kind of hysteria this country has not seen since the fifties' "crackdown on communism." National talk shows and the weeklies ate it up and presented "all sides" of what was essentially a one-sided debate. Then came the urine test, a ten-dollar mass surveillance device. Some members of Congress, bidding for re-election, actually challenged their opponents to urine test-offs. Some form of drug testing was being demanded for nearly the entire population as the linchpin of the War Against Drugs. The urine tests became to the drug hysteria of the eighties what the loyalty oath was to the Red Menace of the fifties. In both cases, cooperation with a simple but meaningless and degrading ritual offered "proof" of good, productive citizenship.

That's the way it was in the fall of 1986: the public was so hyped up that polls identified drug abuse as the number-one concern of the voters. A *USA Today* poll showed 77 percent of Americans felt this way, and the poll was echoed throughout the media as accurate.

Imagine, drug use the number one concern in a country that is rapidly losing its industrial base to runaway corporations and foreign competition; that has just become the largest debtor nation in the world; where budget and trade deficits zoom out of control; where 200,000 farmers are going bankrupt each year; where Wall Street scandals are reported weekly; where 34 million people live below the poverty level; where more than 3 million go homeless; where 9 million are out of work; where supply-side polarization is causing the middle class to vanish; that is panicked by, but not about to cure, AIDS; where the Office of Technology Assessment predicts that within ten years half our drinking water will be contaminated with toxic chemicals; where schools are churning out functional illiterates; where roads and bridges are falling into dangerous disrepair; where a rising tide of racial terrorism, exemplified by incidents in Cummings, Georgia, and Howard Beach, Queens, threatens gains made during the past quarter century; where an entire generation of young people seems to be growing up without hope; and where the potential for nuclear obliteration haunts us all.

Clearly the priorities are wrong.

In the midst of these hazards, somehow a problem in which the annual fatalities number only in the hundreds (a very small number when compared with fatalities related to any of the major legal drugs) was blown totally out of proportion. The voters somehow nominated drug abuse number one on the list of social ills, and, I'm ashamed to say, 80 percent of my fellow Americans agreed that urine tests were a good way of stopping it. (Incidentally, that's roughly the same percentage that favored loyalty oaths back in 1953—a percentage, I would guess, that also held true among the public three centuries ago, when tests for witches were popular in Salem.)

Of course, it was campaign time, so Democrats and Republicans engaged in a "can you top this?" verbal duel over drugs. Issue-hungry candidates thought up the most outlandish things they could say or do to show they were tougher than their opponents on drugs. No one, needless to say, was tougher than the Cowboy himself, Ronald Rambo Reagan. The voters did not exactly exert free will in elevating drug abuse to the top of the social-problem heap. They were simply carrying out by rote the instructions of this strong father-figure.

Polls showed that Reagan was the most popular President of the century, even more popular than FDR. Reagan was playing a yuppie version of Juan Perón, pushing a hard-working, drug-free, entrepreneurial culture, while Nancy, as his Evita, cared for the poor, helpless losers. The two campaigned tirelessly to push these lopsided priorities. More to the point, the Reagan administration, by committing us to "wiping out this evil scourge," used the fight against drugs as a litmus test of patriotism: who among us was brave enough to "just say no" to the Reagans and demand a return to fair play?

Reagan was out to protect "traditional family values." This, mind you, from a divorced man who never goes to church, whose daughter publicly lampooned him in a novel, whose son, a contributing editor to *Playboy*, had made a big splash by pulling down his pants on "Saturday Night Live," and who claims he has no time to see many relatives, including his own grandchildren. These were "traditional family values" Hollywood-style, with scripts and special effects.

Well, politics, like football, is a game where the ball takes funny bounces. Within weeks, even days, after the elections, the Great Communicator was exposed as either the worst liar, the biggest bungler, or the dumbest President ever. The critics were too stunned to figure out which. Who would have guessed that he would suffer the greatest drop in presidential popularity (20 percent) ever recorded in a single month? The "Teflon presidency" had now turned to cellophane, and all could see that the Emperor had no clothes.

Throughout his reign, Reagan had sworn on a stack of Bibles that he would never do business with terrorists. Who would have guessed that one of those Bibles was already on its way to Iranian "moderates"? Then came revelations and confessions that for eighteen months we had been trading arms in hopes of getting hostages released. After threatening our allies not to trade with Iran, an "outlaw" country, it was revealed that millions, perhaps even a billion, dollars worth of arms had been sold to none other than the Ayatollah Khomeini himself. All this skirting of our laws, the will of Congress, and the defiance of public opinion was done in service of Reagan's obsession with controlling the destiny of Central America.

That deceit exists in high places is not a new lesson. Certainly we must have learned at least this from Watergate. But what a great hoax Reagan perpetrated. He had us convinced that here was the Leader of the Free World, who, though he may have made mistakes here and there, was really a sincere man who believed what he said. Go tell that to the dead Marines in Lebanon and the dead civilians in Tripoli. While Reagan and the CIA were misinforming the world that Libya was chiefly responsible for terrorist acts such as the bombing of the Marine barracks in Lebanon, he not only knew the culprit was Iran, he was secretly supplying weapons of death to its arsenal.

While the scandals of Reagan's foreign policies occupied the headlines, the misinformation and broken promises of his domestic policies will be seen in the battered society he leaves in his wake. The major pledges Reagan made for domestic programs in the campaign of 1986 were all broken within weeks after the elections. Whether over the issue of aid to the elderly, student loan programs, or cuts in deficit spending, the Reagan administration had with all deliberate speed gone back on its campaign word. A pledge in October 1986 to support the $20 billion Clean Water bill, desperately needed for the health of our country, was changed to a veto only weeks after the election.

But easily the biggest bluff of all was Reagan's "sincerity" on drug abuse. As election day drew near, the President claimed that fighting drug abuse would be the number one priority for the remainder of his term. "We seek," he said, a "drug-free generation."

Congress, trying to stay even with the Gipper, passed the $3.96 billion Anti-Drug Abuse Act. It was the fifty-fifth federal anti-drug action in eighty years. On October 27, 1986, Reagan signed it, saying, "The American people want their government to get tough and to go on the offensive and that's what we intend with more ferocity than ever before."

Not three months later, Reagan, preparing his 1988 fiscal budget, cut nearly $1 billion from the anti-drug budget. Funds for enforcement, which this book certainly would not endorse, nevertheless were cut a drastic 60 percent. Public service education campaigns lost $250 million. The cruelest blow was the recommendation that absolutely no federal money be spent on drug treatment programs. "It's so phony and pitiful and, let's face it, this is why people have a cynical view about politics," said Congresswoman Barbara Kennelly (D-Conn.). "It's absolutely unconscionable, terrifyingly stupid," said Senator Alfonse D'Amato (R-NY). "If it's such an epidemic, why the cutbacks?"

And that, in a nutshell, is the reality of Ronnie's War on Drugs and Nancy's concern for the victims of drug abuse. Far from being part of the solution, they became an intricate part of the problem. Worse, the damage they did to our values, our knowledge, our priorities, our sense of hope will take decades to correct.

2.

Drugs Are As American As Apple Pie

I really have to laugh when I hear politicians and preachers shout about "wiping out all drugs in America." I laugh because they would have an easier time trying to wipe out electricity. Contemporary America is arguably the most drug-ridden culture in the history of the world. Exactly how "drugged" it is depends on one's perspective.

A drug is defined in Talber's *Cyclopedic Medical Dictionary* as "any substance that when taken into the living organism may modify one or more of its functions." To narrow this vague description, it may be helpful to state at the beginning that we are not talking about extremes—food on the one hand and poison on the other. Our drug domain includes the vast category of substances in between. Some of these substances are considered illegal, but the overwhelming majority are not.

Understand that *legal and illegal are political, and often arbitrary, categorizations; use and abuse are medical, or clinical, distinctions*. Science evolves before politics, and its evolution is less haphazard, less fraught with punishment and stigmata. What's illegal today might be legal tomorrow—and vice versa. As our historical references demonstrate, political attitudes, punishments, and laws change quite rapidly.

Putting a wholesale stamp of illegality on a drug, or attempting a prohibition, often has just the opposite effect as what was intended—increasing curiosity to try the prohibited substance. Rebelling against authority has been considered by psychologists as one of the motivating forces behind illegal drug use. The primary effects of any ban seem to be: inconsistency in quality; a (slight) difficulty in purchase; and an enormous increase in the cost of the prohibited drug. In a trade known for lawlessness, laws of supply and demand still dictate the dynamics of the market. This is what attracts organized crime to the selling end and breeds random individual crime on the purchasing end. This criminal element becomes another serious social problem. Not only does the user sometimes take on society's label as "criminal" and act accordingly, he or she is exposed to a subculture filled with violence of the worst kind. The world of *Scarface* does exist.

Virtually anything requiring a prescription can be found listed in the voluminous *Physicians' Desk Reference (PDR)*. It is an annual publication which gets thicker every year, currently listing about 300,000 different drug products. This is the ammunition the doctor has at his battle station, firing away as he chooses. Choosing *not* to prescribe means not supporting one of the country's biggest industries—and disappointing the patient's expectations. We are conditioned early on that a doctor's visit is worthless unless we leave with prescriptions. No one believes fruit juice, rest, and aspirin alone are worth $50 a visit.

The *High Times Encyclopedia of Recreational Drugs* is the most complete catalogue of illicit, or outlawed, drugs available. Not as useful for a doorstop as the PDR, it lists only 5,000 different substances. Some, like marijuana, are very old; marijuana can be traced back 12,000 years in human history (see *Marijuana: The First 12,000 Years* by Dr. Ernest L. Abel). Others are as new as the inspiration of the garage scientist.

Both sources barely hint at *all* the drugs available to the consumer. Over-the-counter, off-the-shelf potions by the thousands are also used, and abused, by the public. Heavily advertised remedies and pseudo-remedies create the notion of instant cure and instant relief. It's a very American concept—immediate satisfaction, one that has even influenced so many of our personal relationships.

Far from being a purely contemporary practice, drug taking goes back to the times before the first Europeans set foot on this continent. Authorities on the colonial period such as Barbara Melosh,

Curator of Medical Science at the Smithsonian Institution, and Dr. Peter Wood, Medical Historian at Duke University, maintain there is evidence that more than two hundred natural psychedelic drugs were cultivated among indigenous Indian tribes. Stimulants, depressants, antipain remedies of all sorts were derived from bark, leaves, wild plants, berries, anything that grew wild. Religious rituals went hand in hand with the general pharmacology of the tribe. According to Rayna Green, Director of the American Indian Programs at the Museum of American History in Washington D.C., Indians used tobacco, or *nicotiana*, only in a mixture with barks and leaves, and primarily for ritual purposes. "It was the white man," she said, "who decided to smoke it pure, who cultivated the most potent forms and made smoking common practice." Other natural substances, used both for medicinal purposes and to achieve an altered state of consciousness, arrived early on these shores as part of the African and Caribbean slave trade.

Certainly, by the time the leaders of the American Revolution got around to writing the Declaration of Independence in the late eighteenth century, drug use had proliferated. Constitutional experts have still reached no consensus as to what Thomas Jefferson meant by "the inalienable right to life, liberty, and the pursuit of happiness" —especially that last item. All agree that he at least had in mind the rights of the individual being protected from a powerful enforcement-prone government. But no expert has concluded that the Founders felt obligated to protect the general public from the mind-altering substances which were all around them. This isn't to say they approved of intoxication or getting stoned. The Founders didn't feel it was an overwhelming concern, and controls were limited.

Dr. Alfred Young of Northern Illinois University, a leading Jeffersonian scholar, told me: "Borrowing from the tradition of common English law, the Founding Fathers put privacy at the highest level of values. 'A man's home is his castle' influenced all their thinking. The urine tests and all modern invasions of privacy would have horrified them."

Given the task of inventing a nation, drugs and enforcement were not very high on their list of social problems. That's not to say substance use and abuse didn't exist. As Barbara Melosh states,

"We can assume there was widespread use of every sort of natural drug available." We can deduce the early lawmakers' attitude of *laissez-faire* or ambivalence because it took more than a century to consider outlawing any of these extremely old-fashioned drugs.

Experts who study the usage of opium and cocaine derivatives at the turn of the present century (just prior to their prohibition), claim that although the price was relatively cheap and the supply plentiful, the ratio of use to abuse did not differ significantly from that of today. The same can be said of marijuana prior to its being outlawed in 1937, or of LSD prior to 1966. I remember asking the late Dalton Trumbo, one of the blacklisted Hollywood Ten and a thirties activist, if the old Left was into marijuana. "Hell, we're so old, we smoked it when it was legal," he replied.

Perhaps getting high was not one of the rights the Founders protected by "the pursuit of happiness," but libertarian attitudes still prevailed. Although some states came down hard on sodomy, no scholars have discovered any state laws restricting what we would call drugs. George Washington, typical of Virginia planters, grew hemp, which is marijuana. For the most part, this material was used to make rope, but there's no record of anyone being arrested for smoking the rope, or any other substance. Since fields sometimes caught fire, and the acrid fumes entered the lungs, people must have known something was happening. Benjamin Franklin, the most widely traveled and exotic experimenter of the group, probably used opium to check a painful kidney stone problem. Now, the fact that Ben experimented with drugs or was a sexual libertine for most of his life is not exactly highlighted by the DAR or the Bicentennial Commission. Enforcers write history faster than they can write laws. What we read in our grade-school textbooks is, obviously, a watered-down and slanted version of history. A thought-control mechanism. To question the "official version" of history, you must do some extra digging. You must rebel.

For example, you rarely read about the drugs that proliferated in America in the nineteenth century. But some historians say the U.S. had more drug addicts per capita in the second half of the nineteenth century than it does today. Mark Twain was a big cocaine fan. Buffalo Bill, Kit Carson, and other legendary western heroes smoked, drank, and ate just about everything the Indians did. Peyote use was common. Opiates were readily available to the general public: doctors prescribed them, made their own concoctions, and pushed them directly, while drugstores sold them over the counter. Hundreds of medicines containing opium or its derivatives—with names like Ayer's Cherry Pectoral and Godfrey's Cordial (a mixture of opium, molasses for sweetening, and sassafras for additional flavoring)—were available in grocery and general stores. Opium was the poor man's high: narcotics were much cheaper than liquor in those days and were generally considered safer.

Couldn't get to the store? No problem. The Sears & Roebuck catalogue offered a two-ounce bottle of laudanum—opium doused in alcohol—for eighteen cents, or two dollars for one and a half pints. As for the kiddies, well, children should be seen and not heard. There were plenty of patent medicines for them, too, with names like Mistress Winslow's Soothing Syrup, Mother Bailey's Quieting Syrup, and Kopp's Baby Friend. They all contained opiates. At the giant 1876 Centennial Exposition in Philadelphia, a Turkish hashish stand "to enhance the Fair experience" was very popular. Dr. John Morgan, Professor of Pharmacology at Mt. Sinai School of Medicine, estimated that 5% of the population was physically dependent on over-the-counter opiates.

Doctors prescribed opiates for pain, cough, diarrhea, and dysentery. In fact, the nineteenth-century doctor prescribed morphine the way doctors today give out tranquilizers—with a shovel. One 1880 textbook listed fifty-four diseases that could be alleviated with morphine injections. Morphine was even given to alcoholics, in the belief that it was better to be hooked on narcotics than on alcohol. (This practice continued in the rural South until narcotics prohibition got serious in the late thirties.)

Interestingly, the demographics of users back then differed greatly from users today: they were largely female, mostly white, and mostly in their forties. Women users, outnumbering men by nearly three to one, were an easy target for addiction—first, because opiates were prescribed for menstrual and menopausal discomforts; and second, because it was thought unwomanly to be seen drinking liquor in public, or to have it lingering on your breath. So while husbands were in town chuckin' 'em down at the local saloon, the wives were back home demurely taking their opium. Smoking cigarettes, as the Virginia Slims folks like to remind us, was considered unfeminine. Fortunately for their lungs' sake, the wives hadn't "come a long way" yet.

It was all legal back then: opium was being imported, and morphine was then being extracted and manufactured from it. Opium poppies were also grown inside the U.S., in places like Vermont, New Hampshire, Connecticut, Florida, and Louisiana in the East, and in California and Arizona in the West. They were often home-grown, no more difficult to raise than the colorful spring varieties in my own flower garden. Over time, a few states took it upon themselves to ban opium. Congress couldn't pass any antidrug legislation until the 1906 Pure Food and Drug Act, and didn't register the first all-inclusive drug act until 1942 with the Narcotics Control Act.

I can still remember, as a child, seeing official licenses to distribute opium and coca leaf products in my uncle's pharmacy and even later on the wall of my father's medical supply company in the late forties.

The federal role in enforcement began in earnest in 1937, with the appointment of Harry Anslinger to the Federal Bureau of Narcotics (FBN) and federal enactment of the Marijuana Tax Act. This was barely three years after the repeal of alcohol prohibition. Anslinger was the first drug czar of this country, and he helped direct much of the subsequent propaganda. Viewing the movie *Reefer Madness* will give you a glimpse into the narrow mind of Czar Anslinger.

One strong Anslinger supporter was William Randolph Hearst. His yellow-journalism newspapers ran numerous antidrug (especially anti-marijuana) stories with strong racist overtones. These articles were read into the *Congressional Record* as fact. Larry Sloman, in his book *Reefer Madness,* quotes Anslinger testifying before Congress: "Most of the marijuana smokers in the U.S. are Negroes, Mexicans, and entertainers." An interview with Anslinger's close friend Dr. James Munch revealed that the Drug Czar hated jazz, which he labelled "satanic music." According to Dr. Munch, Anslinger believed that the combination of jazz and marijuana caused white women to have sex with Negroes.

Surprisingly, the strongest lobbyist for the autonomy of Anslinger's agency was J. Edgar Hoover. Wishing to preserve the pristine image of the FBI, Hoover realized that drugs and police corruption went hand in hand. Other supporters included many of the legal drug, tobacco, and alcohol industries, who benefitted economically from the repeal of the prohibition on booze and the imposition of prohibition on now-outlawed drugs. Incidentally, the American Medical Association campaigned against making marijuana illegal, since so many doctors had been using marijuana-based medications.

The chief benefactor of all these laws was organized crime, which during the years of alcohol prohibition had developed a sophisticated system of smuggling, production, marketing, distribution, and bribery. The principal loser was the taxpayer.

One major difference between the nineteenth century and now was in how society treated narcotics users. They were not considered a social menace a hundred years ago, and there was little outcry for prohibition. Moral sanctions against opiate use were rare—addicts weren't fired from their jobs, people didn't divorce or turn in addicted spouses, and families weren't split up, with kids placed in foster homes. In short, there was no attitude problem toward addicts such as we have today; drug users continued to function—erratically, perhaps—in society. Today the opiate user is ostracized, resulting in the formation of an outlaw subculture cut off from society.

Getting from permissive to restrictive took some imagination on the part of the Enforcers. In arguments for the prohibition of narcotics, racism was extremely prevalent. The first anti-opiate ordinance was drafted in 1875, in San Francisco, where the target of the Enforcers was oriental opium dens; Chinese were accused of using such dens to trap white women into slavery. In the early twentieth century, during the congressional debate that led to the Pure Food and Drug Act of 1906, boll weevil congressmen from the South claimed that cocaine made blacks lust for white female flesh and also made them impervious to bullets. A Southern sheriff testified how he had to "change from .32-caliber to .38-caliber bullets in order to kill niggers crazy on cocaine." (See *Drugs and Minority Oppression* by John Helmer.) Anti-marijuana campaigns

came of age in the thirties in part because it was a "Mexican habit."
It's no coincidence that there was a strong concurrent sentiment
to "drive Mexicans back across the border." During efforts to increase the funding and scope of anti-drug legislation in the fifties,
through the Kefauver Committee on Organized Crime, it was clear
that the targeted users were young urban blacks.

Various legal and moral tactics have been used throughout the
century. The attitudes of the police against hippies during the
sixties was a new form of cultural prejudice. There was no mistaking
the vicious hostility "flower children" elicited from police just by
their presence. Little due process or civil rights were observed in
thousands of drug busts and frame-ups. Drug enforcement was the
easiest way of destroying a counterculture which was allegedly
breeding revolution. In 1969 alone, 400,000 arrests for marijuana
possession were made.

Biases, moral and political, continue to divide the country.

Contemporary evidence of extensive use of drugs can be found
on the shelves of any convenience store. Nicotine is responsible
for 200,000 to 300,000 deaths a year, *a hundred times more deaths
than from all illegal drugs combined.* And it is not only legal, but
is *encouraged by the government in the form of farm subsidies.*

Nicotine, incidentally, is the *only* drug where the overwhelming
majority of its users are clinically considered to be addicts. Use
and abuse are virtually synonymous where smoking is concerned.
Surprisingly, the *New York Times Magazine* recently ran an excellent article, "Nicotine: Harder to Kick Than Heroin." I suspect
this was hard for *Times* readers to believe, because of strong class
prejudice against heroin. But there is little medical argument with
this point. A psychiatrist at Rockefeller University in 1967, after
examining and testing heroin addicts, reported: "Cigarette smoking is unquestionably more damaging to the human body than
heroin." Subsequent studies over twenty years have confirmed
this.

It is extremely difficult to determine how widespread the use
of illegal drugs or the misuse of legal drugs is, especially in a time
of hysteria, when "no" is a much safer answer on a questionnaire
form or in a phone survey. There is no area, with the possible
exception of the arms race, where cooked statistics are so blatantly

used to justify budget requests as with drugs. Still, both the Enforcers and those championing a more liberal policy toward drug use agree that the number of users is in the millions. The latest National Institute of Drug Abuse figures (for 1985) claim that 62 million Americans have tried marijuana, and 18 million had smoked it in the month of the survey. About 22 million have tried cocaine, 5 to 6 million within the month. Nearly 2 million have used hallucinogens. These are large figures, indeed, but they are dwarfed in comparison to the misuse of prescription drugs, alcohol, and cigarettes. At least 100 million Americans drink alcohol regularly.

The percent of *misuse* is even more difficult to determine, although a general estimate has been placed at 14 percent of all drug use. Also, nearly 70 percent of drug misuse has been attributed to prescription drugs.

Alcohol, as controversial as heroin, is our second biggest killer drug—120,000 annual fatalities. Readily available in thousands of different forms, it is a drug that destroys lives across the whole fabric of society. It affects the alcoholic's family, friends, and co-workers. (See Chapter Three, "Common Everyday Myths" for all comparison fatality figures.)

Experts claim the new, popular teenage craze today is crack, though crack is hardly new; people have smoked cocaine for a few thousand years. It is, however, more stable (less affected by humidity, temperature, and sunlight), inexpensive (cut with more additives than cocaine), and easier to smoke in this form (which makes it more dangerous).

But I suspect an "epidemic more severe" than crack and not being talked about at all is the widespread use of easily accessible wine coolers. Promoted on television as if they were harmless soda pop, these wine coolers contain approximately as much alcohol as beer and wine. Bartles and Jaymes are more than just homespun philosophers pushing soft drinks; they are responsible for getting the next generation plastered to the gills.

Alcohol is a distant second to the popularity of nicotine among the young. Most kids who smoke started before they were thirteen! According to the *New York Times Magazine*, the average smoker needs 70,000 hits a year. That's what you call a chimney, not a human.

Sugar, caffeine, and chocolate are additional substances that if misused, or used by the wrong individuals, can be bad for one's health. Although legal, all three are pharmacologically considered drugs.

Then there is a whole class of readily available substances, rather benign in nature and not generally thought of as drugs, which can be used as if they were drugs. When I was young, sniffing model-airplane glue was a popular way to fool around, and equally popular was a movement to ban the substance. In prison, sniffing shellac fumes from a pail is a common—though not very exotic—way of getting high. Morning glory seeds became so popular during the sixties as a mild hallucinogen (you have to eat loads of them) that the large seed companies were forced to coat the seeds with a bitter substance so it wouldn't taste good. Nitrous oxide, or laughing gas, a most interesting drug, is sort of legal: if you buy a can of certain aerosol whipped creams, hold the can upright, slowly bend the nozzle, and deeply inhale the gas propellant. You can open the bottom of the can with an opener later to get the yummy cream. Ha! Ha! Even nutmeg can be used for more than just food seasoning. If you live in a rural wooded area, there are probably dozens of wild things that if brewed, stewed, or eaten raw will alter your state of consciousness, even produce hallucinations. If you really love New York, Wild Man Steve Brill's botanical tours of Central Park are becoming a popular attraction. He will happily point out the natural highs growing wild in Central Park, but this is strictly an educational expedition. "I show all kinds of mushrooms," he says, "edible, poisonous, and hallucinogenic." The Department of Parks frowns upon consumption of park flora and fungi, so be forewarned.

Drugs are everywhere in our society, readily accessible and often used or abused. A wine made out of dandelions in Mississippi, a fraternity house brew at the University of Minnesota which relies on sweat-laden athletic socks as its chief ingredient—the ingenuity of Americans knows no limits when it comes to getting high.

New drugs enter the market continuously. Like Brooke Shields's blue jeans, these very chic substances are referred to as "designer drugs." Most just have initials that mean nothing or correspond

to a rock group. But the most popular one is termed "Ecstasy."
The reason I say "termed" is because many of us suspect that
Ecstasy is several different drugs grouped under one name, that
it is a derivative of MDA, which is also suspected of being a class
of drugs rather than a single substance. It is hard to keep a listing
of the names of all the new drugs coming on the market, let alone
their molecular structure. The Haight-Ashbury Free Medical Clinic,
easily the best chronicler of new drugs, will by the time this book
is published have seen abusers of many "1987" drugs. The 1988
models promise to be more varied.

The movement to outlaw certain drugs is sometimes as old as
some of the drugs themselves. Of course, no law can be made
banning a drug that precedes the invention of the drug itself. In
order to make a drug illegal, there has to be a period preceding
its illegality when the drug was legal.

Now, making drugs illegal is a tricky process. Lawmakers trying
to outlaw cannabis, for example, would have as tough a time as
committees trying to decipher rock music if only words were involved. There are probably a thousand or more words to describe
grass, pot, or its current slang expressions—"smoke" in the North,
"dube" in the South. That's also a problem in reverse: there could
be many drugs with just one name. A law making "Ecstasy" illegal
just wouldn't sound right.

Banning drugs means banishing specific molecular structures.
Governments can and do legislate against a molecular structure,
but any creative science-minded pusher can rearrange some of the
molecules, and presto—you've got yourself a custom-made high
that produces just about the same high as the outlawed one. Only
the new molecular structure isn't illegal, because even the fastest
lawmakers in the world can't outrace shifting molecules.

Lately, politicans are trying to isolate and outlaw a rather narrow
range of molecular structures. The Enforcers, being just as faddish
as drug users, have their own top ten, headed by whatever is that
year's "epidemic drug of the year." Thirty years ago it was marijuana. Twenty years ago it was LSD. Then STP. Then heroin.
Then cocaine. Then angel dust (PCP). Then crack. Tomorrow it
will be Ecstasy or Adam. Then probably Bazuco—a cheaper, more

stable version of crack. Something is always just around the corner, ready to be the new "in" (as in hip) and "out" (as in epidemic) drug.

The Law tries to keep informed, and the users try to keep ahead. Fifty years ago, the cat-and-mouse game was alcohol, and if we were to look at other countries and their cultures, we could find periods where coffee or cigarettes were considered the most evil substances. It's all part of the same cycle. Enforcers have been working overtime to try and suppress one thing or another since the beginning of time, and with extremely poor results. The only real consistency has been the zealots' ability to label someone else's notion of pleasure illegal. Uniforms, badges, guns, budgets, and bribes have also been pretty consistent.

Remember the concept that every illegal drug has to have a prior period when it was legal. The reverse is also sometimes true, with *legal* drugs having had a prior period of illegality. It's possible to trace this back to the source of humanity: "In the beginning there was a substance; and some took that substance and got high. Others took that substance, and didn't get high. Then arose someone who partook of that substance, and got sick, or had an awful time."

Now who do you think got up and said, "Hey, that's illegal!"? It certainly wasn't the ones getting high. They were having too much fun. Those feeling nothing probably said, "Why bother? It's no big deal." No, it must have been the one(s) having a bad trip.

Forerunners of the modern-day Enforcer in effect passed a judgment that said, "if you're getting high, you're now an outlaw, because you're outside the laws we've just created." From that first bad primeval trip, and from subsequent definitions of legality, things kept getting more and more confusing.

Fundamentalists say that drug taking is a crime against God and nature, although I'm sure what they really mean is a crime against the Protestant ethic, since pleasure can't be put in a savings account or postponed to the hereafter. Dr. C. Creighton, a British physician, concluded in 1903 that the Bible is filled with many drug references. "Honeycomb," "honeywood," and "calamus" are thought to be pot. The manna that fell to the wandering Jews in the desert is now thought to have been pollen in a windstorm—and it probably contained ergotine, an active ingredient in LSD. David and Solomon were often downing exotic libations of one sort or another. There probably were a lot of nasty drugs in Sodom and Gommorah, though a more benevolent God might have tried something other than incinerating all the inhabitants. There were surely a lot of drugs at the Tower of Babel: not only were the people talking in all sorts of different tongues, they were also talking from different states of altered consciousness, since by that time there were many different substances floating around the marketplace.

Let me make another, more modern, point. In 1956, James Olds discovered that electricity, if transmitted through electrodes implanted in a particular area of the cortex, can get rats high. (It wasn't Olds that discovered it, rather the laboratory rats he tested. The rats told Doctor Olds they were high. What can I say, lab rats have big mouths.) Dr. Olds himself never tried his means of pleasure, and I don't blame him. My only experience in taking electricity turned out to be a bummer. That was the time I grabbed two live wires and had this incredibly bad trip. It was so bad that for many years I considered starting a social movement to ban electricity.

What do you think is the most efficiently run corporation in America? If you answered IBM, you were operating on yesterday's information. Today, Merck Co., Inc. is considered by the Wall Street crowd to hold that position. Merck pumps out chemicals by the thousands. For the politicians, this presents no problem, because legal drug manufacturers contribute greatly to campaign war chests. However, for the clinician concerned about drug addiction, most of these drugs can be misused and abused. Drug companies make their money on overprescribing, not underprescribing. They advertise heavily and give free samples. I can't tell you how many Celtics games I've had to see surrounded by boring hospital supply buyers, riding the payola wagon of my father's medical supply company.

When the AMA, joining the fall 1986 hysteria, called on physicians to report drug abusers to the police, anyone knowledgeable in the field must have had a good laugh. The *New England Journal of Medicine* believes that as a group, doctors have the highest abuse level in the country.

When it comes time to define what is a good or bad substance, the dictionary is of little value. Like laws and history, the dictionary is also written by the Enforcers. The original Enforcer in this thought-control sector was Noah Webster. He was a Puritan, and if the Puritans ever got their hands on history, they would surely take out all the sex, drugs, and rock 'n' roll—and the real Benjamin Franklin, too. No surprise that Webster, rigid prude that he was, tried to remove all hints of earthly pleasure in his original dictionary.

Attorney General Edwin Meese, today's leading Enforcer of morality, is descended from a long line of Puritans. Meese is not only tough on drugs, but he is also tough on sex, which his blue-ribbon commission virtually equated with violence. Puritan Meese, before he was Attorney General, was the district attorney of Alameda County in California, where he had a chance to come down hard on the sixties hippies and radicals of Berkeley. (Ronnie was governor at the time.) Puritan leaders are somber, righteous types who believe their pogroms of repression and suppression are the will of God. Casual sex and drug-taking are activities indulged in by, well, savages. Throughout history, attempts have been made to isolate or exterminate the heathens—for their own good.

Psychotherapist Anne Wilson Schaef, in her current book *When Society Becomes an Addict*, argues that our nation as a whole is exhibiting all the symptoms traditionally attributed to the individual addict. She postulates an "addictive system," which, among other things, denies reality, needs to control everything around it, and employs other habitual mechanisms—like lying and compulsive stimulation—to "feed its habit." Schaef demonstrates the wafer-thin line between addiction and obsession—claiming our culture is hooked on work, sex, and money—the Yuppie Triad.

Not all mood-altering drugs are alien to the body. Science has isolated chemicals in the brain called *endogenes*, which affect our moods and state of consciousness. Apparently, they can trigger themselves or be triggered by a variety of externally induced substances, but the point is, they are already inside us all.

Long ago, when I was a clinical psychologist at a mental hospital, one of our clients was an air swallower. Air swallowers gulp air and force it into their stomachs rather than their lungs. They do this, they say, because it makes them feel high, probably through over-oxygenation of the blood system. It's a very dangerous practice, since on occasion the stomach will burst like a balloon. Fortunately for the Enforcers, ever ready to outlaw a new substance, air swallowers are not very common. Which is just as well—it's rather difficult outlawing air.

Bulimia, an illness which causes the sufferer to go on enormous food binges followed by self-induced vomiting, leads to dehydration and rapid weight changes. Unlike air swallowing, it is fairly common but an equally dangerous malady. It leads to no "high," but satisfies a psychological desire.

For too long discussion about drug abuse and addiction has been substance-oriented. I am trying to point out the futility of this by showing how extremely benign substances, even air and food, can be abused. This is not to say heroin, barbiturates, coffee, chocolate, and Afrin nose sprays offer similar risks, but rather that looking at individuals and their relationships to drugs will tell us much more about the nature of illness. Hopefully, this will lead us to more fruitful research and treatment programs.

And to conclude our discussion with a note on recreational drugs, here's a quote from a study by the advertising agency D'Arcy Masius Benton & Bowles reported in the *New Republic* (3/23/87). The report, "Fears and Fantasies of the American Consumer," surveyed 1,552 U.S. households, asking them to identify their primary source of pleasure and satisfaction. Surprisingly, "drugs are four times as popular as grandchildren as a source of pleasure and satisfaction to the average American." So if we have to say no to drugs, which apparently make a lot of people happy, what are we supposed to say to our grandchildren when they call collect!?

I'll hold by my initial premise, that drugs are as American as apple pie, that in reality they surround us and comprise us. Virtually all Americans, with the exception of a few Christian Scientists and scores of hypocrites, ingest quantities of drugs. Drugs are an integral part of our long history, and will inevitably play an even greater role in our future. To deny this fact is to deny reality.

3.

Common Everyday Myths About Drugs

The Billion-Dollar Bust

The monetary value of illicit drugs—always publicized in the media when yet another "biggest drug bust in history" is reported—boggles the mind. In no other area of economics are figures so readily distorted.

Let's say, for example, that 500 pounds of cocaine are seized after it has crossed the border and is in the importer-wholesaler's house. The price the dealer paid for that very large quantity would be about $1 million, or $2,000 per pound. This represents the lowest price and highest product quality.

Enter the narcs. The public has been fed an elaborate story of keen-eyed border patrols, coordinating efforts with local, state, and national enforcement agencies. Month-long stakeouts, round-the-clock surveillance. Ha! Someone in Bolivia, Colombia, or stateside probably had a grudge or wanted to cut down on competition and made a single phone call to a desperate agency, the tip-off, a favor which may be returned in kind. "Hello, Rodriguez, this is the DEA. Tuesdays from three to five P.M. are all yours." "*Gracias, compañero.*"

A smuggler for a major Colombia cocaine cartel testified before Congress that he "donated" $10 million to the CIA for the Nicaraguan Contras. "The cartel figured it was buying a little friendship," he said.

Now, one of "the biggest busts in history" is about to unfold.

Since Geraldo Rivera has brought a camera crew and promised two minutes on the evening news, the Enforcers put on an extra good show. It's supposed to look like "Miami Vice," and it does. Only this is the real thing!

As to price, for some strange reason that one-million-dollar shipment has miraculously and immediately become worth a billion! Wow!

Here's how it happens. If the bust never took place, the 500 pounds, which was originally at 96 percent purity, would be immediately doubled (stepped on, cut, etc.) at the wholesaler's with a look-alike additive, usually an Italian baby laxative (the reason why many coke users do extra number-twos in the toilet). These 1,000 pounds are distributed in single-pound units for about $10,000 each. That's now $10 million. Each pound at the distributor's is doubled with more additive, reducing the purity to 24 percent of the original shipment. And these 2,000 pounds are subdistributed as one-ounce packages for $1,000 each. That's now $32 million, if the calculator is correct. But wait, we're not done yet! Street cocaine varies from 6 percent to 20 percent purity when bought in single-gram units or processed into crack. Let's just leave it at 24 percent purity. The price on the street: $100 per gram. There are approximately 907,200 grams in 2,000 pounds. Sell each gram at $100 a shot, you get an end price of $90,718,500. Make it an even billion, since most will be sold at less than 24% purity. A thousandfold increase! Not bad, considering that nothing has left the premises.

The day after the bust, the TV news will be trumpeting, "Major drug raid nets $1 billion in coke!" Isn't that amazing! Using this economic system, I can prove that a car you just bought for $10,000 is actually worth $500,000. But I'd have to break it down and sell each part separately to very desperate parts buyers in countries under economic embargo by the U.S. I couldn't sell in bulk, have any lost or unsold parts, or any overhead, travel or labor costs. And no middle people to take risks, do work, or make profit.

The rare newscaster adds the phrase "at street value" to the one billion. Some media outlets automatically halve all drug figures reported by the Drug Enforcement Administration or the local

DA's office. This is called responsible journalism. But all use some maximum potential street profit figure instead of the price *actually* paid by the dealer.

Why is it done this way? Here again, inflated numbers make everyone look good—the DEA, the local sheriff, the hard-working cop, the news team; even the apprehended dealer puffs up his chest a bit. Certainly his lawyers are happy, thinking they'll actually get their fees paid.

This hyper-inflation may seem harmless, but actually it is very counterproductive. A poor group of ghetto folks at home or in Latin America ("down there," as Mr. Reagan loves to say) sees those numbers and figures that smuggling is like winning the lottery. In the lottery you risk a dollar. In the drug trade, you risk about ten years in prison, or deportation if you are not naturalized.

One of the most depressing parts of being in jail or prison is to hear poor minority people talk about coping a "deal for a dime." A dime is ten years of your life, if you're caught. Life is that cheap. "I can do a dime on one hand!" is an expression commonly heard before plea-bargaining. I wonder how many readers can really appreciate poverty and prison and the forces that drive people to acts of despair.

Of course, one million is *not* one billion. The phrase "at street value" is gratuitous, since the real world of dealing never works the way it is thought to on a Washington bureaucrat's flow-chart. Dealers use a little and lose a lot. They get robbed. The substance deteriorates. There's counterfeit money. They must pay for protection (including police protection). Robberies and double-dealing are routine. (Whoever said there's honor among thieves was, of course, a thief.) The window opens and some of the stuff blows away. Coke makes dealers paranoid; they hear imaginary sirens and flush shipments down the toilet. They pay huge fees to lawyers, accountants, and bank officials laundering the profits. They contrive elaborate fronts to explain why they have no job but manage to drive a Mercedes. *Snowblind* by Robert Sabbag, an excellent journalistic account of dealing, says that after two years of not getting caught, every dealer has to be surrounded by guns. And many end up dead because the risks and profits are enormous—not as much as in selling illegal arms to Iran, but close.

Smugglers Can Be Nailed at the Border

Cocaine or heroin can illustrate further the futility of the "sealed border" discussed in Chapter One. The bipartisan Congressional Office of Technology Assessment claims that 130 tons of cocaine entered the U.S. in 1986. Cocaine is not produced domestically (too many big trees to get a very small amount of product), so that's the total annual supply. Many smuggled shipments are large plane loads, others a few pounds. Let's calculate smuggling methods. Assume that two suitcases could safely conceal twenty-six pounds. That means a mere 10,000 people carrying two suitcases each *could* import 1986's total volume. Actually, the true number of smugglers would be far less than 10,000, because the Big Players ship direct in much bigger bulk. For 1986's entire heroin supply, estimated at six tons, fewer than 500 individuals each carrying two suitcases could do all the smuggling. So could one medium-sized airplane.

About 300 million people a year pass through customs, and something in excess of 150 million tons of cargo annually enter our ports. Happy hunting!

Some things are just too bulky to be smuggled in traditional ways. Bundles of marijuana are dropped out of small planes during midnight runs over the Florida Keys. Nightly, hundreds of bales, resembling nothing so much as hay, splash down into the coastal waters, to be retrieved by chartered skiffs. What they can't find in the dark gets washed ashore with the morning tide, an economic boon to Key West's teenagers, who collect the stuff at dawn.

In the early seventies, American potheads got very nervous about the reliability of their supply. Paraquat sprayed on field crops was posing a health hazard, and although Nixon's 1972 Operation Intercept failed to stamp out Mexico's harvest, the potential for shortage was real. A "New Age" consciousness correctly saw paraquat as a harmful inhalant. Simultaneously, the Arab Oil Embargo led to a sharp decline in the economic stability of the nation. Inflation and unemployment soared. None of this was helped by large numbers of returning Vietnam veterans who were broke, rejected by society, and definitely pot-oriented.

These economic forces led to a re-evaluation of black-market importing policy. "Do it in America" became a slogan for all business, legitimate and otherwise. Today, the majority of marijuana consumed in the U.S.A. is homegrown. If California can challenge the French wine industry in quality and quantity in just a decade, imagine what outlaw American farmers with some Miracle-Gro, hydroponics, and computerized grow lights can do with a common weed. Today, NORML (the National Organization for the Reform of Marijuana Laws) claims marijuana is the nation's top cash crop; *Time* magazine can't decide if it's marijuana or soybeans. Sensimilla, the highest grade of pot, requiring extra care in cultivation, is supporting lots of small farmers. Reagan would be flabbergasted to learn that small farmers whom his pro-agribusiness policies have bankrupted have turned to growing pot for survival.

The moral (because every countermyth should have one) is that sealing off the borders guarantees two things: It raises domestic prices, and it increases the potency of the drug on the home market. Nice going, customs patrol!

Step Right Up and See Real, Live Heroin Babies

"Placental transfer of narcotics prior to and during labor is poorly understood, and the conclusions of experimentation are open to doubt," claimed Drs. Blinick, Wallach, and Jerez in "Pregnancy in Narcotics Addicts Treated by Medical Withdrawal" (*American Journal of Obstetrics and Gynecology*, December 1969). Apparently the amounts of drugs that reach the placenta are too minute to be measured by the best-known chemical methods.

This study was performed at Beth Israel Hospital in New York City. In one hundred consecutive births from heroin-addict mothers, not one baby was born a junkie, or required additional opiates to stay alive. Pediatricians today believe that the terrible physical condition of poor addict mothers leads their babies to show many *symptoms* of addiction, but not true dependency. Low birth weight or hyperirritability are associated with, but do not guarantee, addiction. Dr. Saul Blatman, the pediatrician overseeing the Beth Israel study, concluded, "Withdrawal symptoms [was] an unsatisfactory term, which we should eliminate."

This has been reaffirmed several times since the initial study. But don't expect to read about it in *Reader's Digest*. Pop culture and the NPL are saturated with exceptional events which prove their contention. If there is one heroin-addicted baby born for every 10,000 addict mothers, Enforcer collaborators will make this kid a star. Not even two-headed babies get as much ink.

Still skeptical? Check the methodology of any study doting on infant addicts. Was a control group of babies, born to equally poor, malnourished mothers who were *not* addicts, available for comparison? I doubt it. The unfortunate part of the myth is that unsophisticated doctors delivering babies of addicts will sometimes look at symptoms other than withdrawal and immediately prescribe small doses of opiates to "stabilize the baby's condition," forcing the baby into drug dependency.

One more point crucial to any study dealing with a controversial subject: *the law of selective funding and publishing is rarely broken*. If 100 studies are conducted to prove a given hypothesis and 99 say "no," but "no" doesn't fit the preconceived NPL, then the one that says "yes" gets the okay. Even if some "no" studies get published in scientific journals, the Enforcers will block their entry into the mass media. Tacit censorship is involved, or the data isn't considered newsworthy, a principle similar to a successful airplane landing not being considered news.

The Scare-of-the-Month Club

Unlikely, even impossible, stories often earn national reputations with the complicity of medical or scientific authorities. Doctors with very good credentials—who really should know better— often sacrifice methodology, or their findings get misused to boost propaganda. Tulane University research led to SCIENCE PROVES POT KILLS BRAINS headlines, a study later discredited. The thirties film *Reefer Madness*, made with "expert consultation," is an example of scientifically endorsed ignorance.

In the late sixties, a physician in Pennsylvania told the press that he had several patients go blind on LSD. Acid supposedly made them stare at the sun for too long without blinking. Excessive sunlight burned their corneas. Big press coverage! Later, he quietly confessed that he had been "mistaken." Oops. But little press!

A typical story in this category comes from the editors of *Playboy*, who after interviewing specialists claimed, "People on PCP are drawn to water but are unable to swim; many drownings result from PCP intoxication." (*Playboy*, 5/87, p. 150.)

My prejudices run against body drugs (i.e. stimulants and depressants), and PCP (phencyclidine) is high on my hate list. It produces very strange, often contradictory effects, serving as a stimulant and a depressant. In the early seventies it was manufactured as a human tranquilizer, but didn't work very well. Then it was tried on cows. Same results. I don't think PCP (commonly called angel dust) has any clinical supporters, human or animal. Nonetheless, that unqualified *Playboy* statement is alarmist. Perhaps one case of drowning was related to PCP, but to extrapolate such clearly superficial conclusions is science at its worst. PCP may inhibit motor responses, but it doesn't turn people into lemmings who automatically sink.

The viewpoint in *Playboy*'s survey, "Addiction and Rehabilitation: What We've Learned in 14 Years," continued in the same alarmist vein. It made several interesting points, and is semitough on urine tests, but it's very disappointing. Practically everyone using nitrous oxide, airplane glue, barbiturates, alcohol, and narcotics ends up dead. Just about everything is addictive, from No-Doz to Ecstasy.

Why does a libertarian, entertainment-oriented magazine like *Playboy*, a magazine which for years campaigned for a liberalized drug policy, feel compelled to print stuff like this? The *Playboy* editorial board has served notice to its staff that they have been much too lenient on drugs. *Playboy* had been put under serious economic pressure by Attorney General Ed Meese and his pornography commission. He personally requested several major magazine outlets to stop carrying "porn." Some biggies, like Southland, the parent of 7-11, capitulated. The "new" *Playboy* attitude on drugs became apparent in the fall 1986 hysteria, obviously to regain some credibility with the Enforcers and rack space. Subsequently, Meese said *Playboy* wasn't pornographic—another example of the pervasive power of the NPL.

The Counterculture Was Responsible for LSD

Dr. Albert Hofmann, a Swiss researcher, synthesized lysergic acid diethylamide in 1943, while experimenting with rye fungus.

From this humble grain came one of the most mysterious compounds of the twentieth century.

The first group to experiment with LSD in the U.S. was *not*, as pop culture would have it, the sixties hippies. Hollywood found the drug in the fifties, and it was quite the rage. Cary Grant attributed his "ability to stay young forever" to regular LSD trips, and other stars agreed. In May 1957, *Life* ran the first mass-media article praising psychedelic drugs as part of its "Great Adventure" series. A seventeen-page article celebrated the biochemical experience. In the early sixties, *Life* printed two cover stories on LSD. The first heralded acid as the new anti-aggression drug. The second featured LSD-influenced art, a breakthrough that "bombarded the senses." During this period, America's most famous publishing couple, Henry and Clare Boothe Luce, had several publicized LSD sessions with their friends. (It was still legal.) The Luces apparently had second thoughts later on. The March 25, 1966 *Life* cover story, "The Exploding Threat of the Mind Drug That Got Out of Control—LSD," is testimony to their doubts.

In 1972, when I interviewed Clare Boothe Luce, Grand Duchess of the Republican Right, I asked if she had changed her feelings about LSD. "No," she said, "but you don't want to overdo a good thing." In true aristocratic fashion, she regarded it as a substance that should remain exclusive to the sophisticated (i.e. her) circles.

The group that really got into acid in a big way was none other than your friendly Central Intelligence Agency. The U.S. drug treatment center in Lexington, Kentucky, performed many biochemical experiments on humans at the CIA's request. Once, seven men were kept on LSD for *seventy-seven days*, a dangerous experiment under the best conditions (*The Agency: Rise and Fall of the CIA*, John Ranelagh). (Don't try this at home!) In September 1977, Senator Ted Kennedy opened hearings into Operation MK-ULTRA, a CIA study "investigating whether and how it was possible to modify an individual's behavior by covert means." As part of the program, the CIA admitted employing prostitutes to spike the drinks of unsuspecting customers with LSD, who could then be observed, photographed, and recorded. Testing continued for years as subjects were guinea-pigged against their will for periods of up to eight days. Research into dosing large populations was tested on a limited scale. Acid hit lists included public figures such as former Egyptian president Gamal Abdel Nasser. CIA inspector general John Earman stated that "LSD had been tested on individuals at all social levels, high and low, native American and foreign." The U.S. Army also got into the act, testing thousands of soldiers without their knowledge. There were several hospitalizations, and in subsequent suits, permanent damage was shown as one unfortunate byproduct of Pentagon chemistry. (See Lee and Shlain, *Acid Dreams* for the complete story.) On June 24, 1987, the Supreme Court put its stamp of permission on these long-contested experiments. Justice Antonin Scalia, writing for the court, said such suits cannot be permitted because they would "require judicial . . . intrusion upon military matters and would disrupt the military regime." Justice William J. Brennan Jr., in dissent, likened the experiments to "human experimentation programs carried out by the Nazis."

Then the hippies got their curious little hands on the formula.

Pot Leads to Hard Drugs

Maybe so. But it's impossible to prove such a thing. In fact, it's a lot easier to prove that alcohol leads to heroin addiction, since more junkies had been weaned on alcohol. No one has a group of laboratory rats puff away on joints and then waits to see if they ask for some heroin. No one does it with people, either. Researchers ask addicts how they arrived at using drugs. The addict answers, "Well, like about three years ago I was doing some pot with the gang . . ." Before you know it, the researcher definitely "discovers" a cause-and-effect link. The addict knows what the interviewer wants to hear, probably believing the myth as well. The addict could have started the story with "When I was a baby, my mother fed me baby food with sugar in it . . ." Perhaps someday, a researcher will conclude that eating sugar leads to heroin addiction.

The scientific error here is called *sophistry,* false or deceptive reasoning. Here's an example of it. You stand at a bus stop all day and observe Bus A make a stop and leave. About ten minutes later Bus B makes exactly the same stop, and it too leaves. This happens 100 out of 100 times. What you have observed is that Bus B comes *after* Bus A. You have not proved that Bus A *caused* Bus B's arrival.

I can destroy the cause-and-effect hypothesis by walking back a block and slashing a tire on Bus B.

One personal observation here. Over the years, virtually all the marijuana dealers I ever knew hated heroin and would never consider selling it. Dealers tend to specialize. Passing out free samples in school yards to "hook" kiddies is more Enforcer mythology. The only ones that do this routinely (though no longer in school yards, I hope) are the big cigarette companies. If you don't believe this, walk over to Times Square and see which pushers are giving out free samples. The ones with the crinoline miniskirts and the four-color sandwich boards are not handing out illegal drugs.

Another point: except for very few illegal drug users, most users are defined as dealers under the law. Giving away and sharing is dealing. Buying one unit and selling half to make your unit free is typical and very illegal.

If you want the truth about pot, I've conducted a carefully controlled study of twenty people who were allowed to smoke one joint for the first time: 14 percent felt nothing at all; 3 percent could not get the cigarette lit before we ran out of matches; 83 percent said they were hungry, horny, and had intense cravings to be in Negril, Jamaica. Six actually quit work the next day, cashed in their IRAs (with complete disregard for tax penalties), and headed south. One, whose automatic banking card refused to work at five machine tellers, hijacked an airplane to Monterey Bay, walked, then finally crawled to Negril.

I've tried to publish this paper, but the National Institute of Health has warned the journals that this would present a national security problem. People more stable than myself, who worry about my career, urge me not to make a stink. "Things take time, politics change, be patient." They also ask why I would want to ruin a nice place like Negril by shooting off my big mouth.

The study went into the shredding machine last night. Now Negril and the national security will not be threatened. Whew! What a load off my mind!

Free Heroin Programs Are Failures

Fifty-three years ago, the British Government formally recognized heroin addiction as an illness. This meant that any physician of the National Health Service (NHS) could dispense heroin or any other opiate to addicts. The NHS recognized that addicts could function normally for prolonged periods if they received carefully monitored doses under medical supervision. What the program did best (and still does) is eliminate the connotations of "scum-criminal," unhealthy physical conditions addicts generally exhibit, illegal smuggling, and the enormously high crime statistics associated with the heroin culture. It freed hundreds of police for other work and diminished the threat of violence (the harsher the penalties, the easier the decision to shoot it out).

Prior to the program, heroin use in the U.K. was escalating at alarming rates. The NHS has since saved thousands of lives and has stabilized the total abuser population. Figures have lately shown the heroin-addict population to be inelastic, averaging about 2,000 per year. Not that there haven't been some rough periods. In the early sixties, Canadian, American, and other European addicts flocked to England specifically for free samples. With the influx from the West Indies and Africa of poor black immigrants in the mid-seventies, the rates again showed some increase. From time to time, addicts are caught getting extra medication to shoot or sell.

Restrictions have since closed many of these loopholes. Morphine and some methadone is now distributed instead of heroin. In 1968, dispensing was limited to clinics specializing in addiction diseases.

In the Thatcher era, the NHS has cut corners but stands intact, a hugh success. The Health Service Division of the Netherlands (the country with probably the most liberal drug laws in the world) reports similar success after short periods of stress. A recent expansion of the "drug culture" has caused certain Dutch politicians to raise doubts about several aspects of the program, but very few call for abolition. The program will improve and grow as intended. The same goes for Denmark and Sweden.

Yet since World War II, American "authorities" have consistently pronounced these European experiences to be failures. The media has never paid them much attention at all. When they first appeared to work, American Enforcer experts explained that these countries were mono-racial (i.e. no blacks), and similar programs couldn't work in a heterogeneous society. Waves of minority immigration in the sixties to these European nations has made this excuse pretty lame. Today, the U.K. and Netherlands are increasingly polyracial.

One conclusion is obvious: we are not being told the full truth (or even half-truths) about these programs any more than we are told the same about any free national health program. The American Medical Association is an integral part of the National Party Line, placing its restrictive policies above criticism.

Drug Education Campaigns Are Working

Big faces of born-again celebrities plastered on subway walls and TV screens threaten death for anyone stupid enough to try drugs. Hot lines, which collect some informative data, also heat up panic and fear. Consider a typical full-page ad in the *New York Times* sponsored by the Partnership for a Drug-Free America. A well-dressed, apparently successful "buppie" (black urban professional) scowls contemptuously above the words "The last thing an addict needs from you is understanding." It's geared to corporate executives, advising them to take a hard line with employees: "Get well or get out." The copy continues with hardball logic: "The threat of losing a job sometimes gets drug users into treatment." Sometimes it may. And sometimes they hang themselves from the world's insensitivity. The ad stresses that compassion should be avoided until users play by Enforcer rules. Exactly how is this educational? This ad is the first sell for a urine testing program, a not-so-free way to make America drug free. Nothing I've read shows that increasing the fear level will decrease the level of abuse or addiction.

In 1982, while working at the Veritas Therapeutic Community, I watched TV ads pushing the "Get High on Life" campaign, clearly aimed at inner-city minority kids. The problem, as I saw it, was that the ads pushed white middle-class suburban standards. How can you tell someone fatherless from birth, abused from infancy, housed in a rats' nest of a tenement without heat in the winter, undernourished, with twenty times the chance of going to prison than college, saddled with a 40 percent unemployment rate, to go out there and *get high on life?* Could you? It's another world, another language.

Okay. So I had an idea to make a public-service commercial that was anti-heroin, different from all others because it would use the addict's own language and not attack street culture. I would separate the bad from the good of New York inner-city street life. First I put together a glossary of addict language, picked up terms like "chillin' out" and "noddin' on the deuce." Next, I wrote a song in disco rap called "Ain't 'Bout Nothin'." I got Curtis Blow, the most popular rapper around, to record it, the Rock Steady Crew to break-dance around him, and Marty Perlmutter's Ghost Dance Productions to video and edit the piece professionally. Other friends designed a classy logo for the ad. "Veritas" is the Latin word for truth. The slogan I coined for them: "Veritas means no bullshit."

The trouble was, five years ago none of this was respectable. the piece aired on one local TV show called "Live at Five," because I agreed to a guest appearance only if they aired the spot. That was the only time you could have seen it. Every local station and national network rejected it. Some called it racist because no whites were in it (actually there was one, but he wasn't white enough). Others refused because you can't show an actual syringe on television. Executives complained about not understanding the language. My argument was that addicts didn't speak the "get high on life" language. The one-minute rock video stayed in the can.

Today there are some TV announcements that approximate the basic idea. I've yet to see one I thought as good. I was going to make another, stressing the strong relationship between child abuse and drug abuse when I realized that America wouldn't listen to this message either. You figure it out. By the way, any rehab center that wants to use this video with their own logo can have it. It's free, but you've got to make your own dub, change the logo, and hustle the networks. And you can't take one millisecond out. Ain't it the Veritas.

In spring 1987, researchers Paul Crnkovich, Tim Finnerty, et al. from Harvard Business School reported on the effectiveness of anti-drug commercials for the city of Boston. They studied the responses of fifty school kids, ages 10 to 16, to ads currently appearing on TV that deplore drugs. The study found that talking-head celebrities were ineffective because they lacked credibility. Kids sensed that they "say one thing but do another." A few kids actually laughed at the commercials. Others resented the wealth and condescension of the celebrities. They also resented being told how to act.

When asked what would make a strong anti-drug statement, the kids suggested real-life situations, segments of broken families and friendships resulting from abuse. One effective ad they helped create, for example, showed a teenage girl, expected to babysit, getting high with a friend while the unwatched baby fell out of the crib. Similar scenarios were shown to fifty other school kids who, as a group, responded much more favorably. (Unpublished study, reported on the Peter Mead Show, WBZ, Boston, 5/25/87.)

Drugs and Sports Don't Mix

"Why are sports teams against cocaine?" Dr. Mark Gold, director of the Fair Oaks Center, asked himself in the previously quoted *Playboy* survey of addiction. "Because it makes wide receivers drop the ball. We have linemen with judgment problems, defensive ends who try to pick up the opposing player, or a linebacker who tries on national TV to do a one-and-a-half somersault over a tight end."

Drug abuse is not merely present in major sports. It is an integral part of the game. Big-ticket sports are about money, winning, and pain. The last, but also the other two, require large amounts of a variety of drugs.

The word "hypocritical" seems to have been invented for this situation. While team owners are gleefully hopping on Baseball Commissioner Peter Ueberroth's bandwagon, drugs—*legal* drugs— are being pumped into their players in record amounts. Kevin McHale, of my hometown Boston Celtics, once remarked that as a rookie in the National Basketball Association, he was surprised to learn that most athletes played with an injury. Take a 180-pound wide receiver in the National Football League, at full extension, reaching to the sky for a pass reception. Immediately, he's whipsawed in opposite directions by two thundering 260-pound muscle machines. Repeat that two hundred times a year. Or take the most obvious example, a boxer being punched in the head with an arm as strong as a battering ram for an hour or so every few months for ten years. Prescription drugs help them heal and bear the pain.

Right off, you can see some element of hypocrisy when commissioners and owners talk about protecting the health of their athletes. To alleviate or mask the pain, powerful habituating drugs are used. To bulk up the muscle on the "machines," dangerous steroids are often illegally prescribed. To calm the thrill of victory and especially the agony of defeat, all sorts of tranquilizers, mood elevators, and antidepressants are doled out. To deal with the constant insomnia provoked by road schedules, sleeping pills are routine, as are uppers to get groggy players to early-morning field practice.

Columnist Mike Lupica of the *New York Daily News* noted the double standard applied to booze and drugs in sports. In one column, he called attention to the little-known case of California Angels pitcher John Candelaria, who in April 1987 was twice arrested for drunken driving. Candelaria was quietly placed on the team's disabled list for thirty days without a word from Commissioner Ueberroth. Lupica lists several sports figures, such as Earl Weaver, Mike Ditka, and Sonny Jurgensen, who were also stopped for driving while intoxicated, yet escaped punishment and public outcry. Meanwhile, someone like New York Mets pitcher Dwight Gooden, in trouble with cocaine, gets disgraced. (Crucified might be a better word.) "If you were driving last week in Anaheim [home of the Angels]," wrote Lupica, "who was more dangerous to you? Gooden or Candelaria, drunk behind the wheel?" (*N.Y. Daily News*, 5/24/87).

"Budweiser," Lupica wrote, "practically owns baseball." He could have pointed out that Anheuser-Busch Co. (Budweiser) and Phillip Morris' beer subsidiary the Miller Brewing Co. (Miller Lite) lobbied successfully to install the "TV Time Out" in all major money sports. Today, games are interrupted so we can watch ex-athletes in exotic locales slug beer. Fifteen minutes later, we get to watch a "Don't Do Drugs" commercial.

Cigarettes are also treated hypocritically. True, advertising is banned from television, but most ballparks and stadiums are plastered with cigarette billboards. Shea Stadium, for example, has a double-size Marlboro sign in dead centerfield. It gets a lot of airtime and Mookie Wilson (the Mets' outfielder) doesn't mention the Surgeon General's Warning after each catch. Cigarette advertising is generally the most profitable revenue-producer in game programs.

Lupica, Howard Cosell, and one or two other sports commentators are bold enough even to hint at the hypocrisy.

There is a legitimate argument about whether athletes use illegal drugs to a greater or lesser degree than other professional groups. The players' unions say no. Athletes have too short a playing span, too much to lose, and are too closely monitored. The owners and commissioners (who serve the owners) see it differently. When the spotlight shines, where do you think the owners would like it to point?

Wide receivers might drop the ball because of cocaine, says Dr. Gold. But it could also be that they are walking drugstores to begin with. And maybe they don't drop the ball at all. Just as licit drugs get the player back on the field or court, illicit drugs might contribute, well, *something*.

Lefty Driesell, long considered one of basketball's best coaches until Len Bias' death at the University of Maryland, made this exact point. Speaking at a conference at the University of Rhode Island on June 8, 1987, he was quoted as saying, "I'm a firm believer that if you know how to use cocaine, and use it properly, it can make you play better." As a student, Driesell had written his master's dissertation on cocaine as a performance-enhancing drug. Reaction to Driesell's presentation was fast and furious. No media outlet could allow such an opinion to go unchallenged. Experts were wheeled out by the truckload to lambast and ridicule Driesell. Not a single voice was allowed to dally on the complexity of the issue or to side with Driesell who felt he "had to be honest about his observations." Within a few days, the pressure proved too much and Driesell claimed he had been misquoted and began reaffirming the NPL. "Cocaine is horrible," said Driesell. (*USA Today*, 6/11/87)

In the 1985 NCAA basketball championships, one of sport's greatest upsets occurred. Mighty and unbeaten Georgetown, featuring Patrick Ewing, an eleven-point favorite, fell to underdog Villanova. Villanova's star point guard, Gary McLain, heavily into cocaine at the time, led his team to victory. In an interview with *Sports Illustrated* (3/23/87), he talked of other players on that Cinderella team doing coke and of the permissiveness of head coach Rollie Massimino. The Reverend John Stark, dean of students, had a heart-to-heart talk with Gary, but it changed nothing. The coke rumor was all over campus, but the schedule went on. "Sometimes I had played well on coke, sometimes bad," said McLain. "It didn't seem to matter."

The grapevine is ripe with stories of drug-enhanced performance. One California baseball player confessed he hit two home runs in one game while on LSD. One of football's greatest running backs, a few years ago, told anyone in listening range at parties how cocaine helped his game. You would be shocked if I wrote his name. No one tells stories like that today. Gary McLain's story ended in the tragedy of drug abuse. These anecdote incidents are not meant to build a case *for* cocaine use but only to debunk the simplicity of the Enforcer anecdotal arguments.

Dr. Gold has good reason to say that coaches get mad when wide receivers drop the ball. That's why abuser-athletes end up paying huge fees at Fair Oaks, where he practices. Someday it would be nice to read Dr. Gold's exposé of the *whole* world of drugs in sports.

This is not meant to diminish the tragedy of the drug-related deaths of Len Bias, Don Rogers (of the Cleveland Browns), and most recently, University of Texas-El Paso basketball player Hernell Jackson. Jackson died of cardiac arrest during a benefit game on May 2, 1987. Immediately, headlines appeared across the nation: "Cocaine kills another athlete." However, the following day Dr. Juan Contin, the medical examiner, said, "No final conclusion has been reached as to cause of death."

In the Bias case, original announcements claimed Bias had been a first-time cocaine user. Later, reports emerged that such behavior had been occurring for some time, apparently with the knowledge of the athletic department at the University of Maryland. Coach Driesell resigned in the scandal that followed.

Because I was raised as a semijock, today I am as ardent a sports fan as I was when my father first took me to see the Celtics. Sports is the ultimate in risk-taking and trade-offs. And there is incomparable grace and beauty as the best excel in extraordinary tests of human endurance and potential. Len Bias had all the right moves. He was a complete player with immense talent—possibly another Oscar Robertson. There is a lot to mourn, but the truth should not die with him.

Take Drugs and Die

As revealed by federal statistics, not an awful lot of people die because of illegal drugs when compared with fatalities from legal substances. Yes, any death which could have been avoided is regrettable, but the emphasis on illicit drug overdose is wildly exaggerated.

ANNUAL SUBSTANCE-RELATED FATALITIES

(Source: U.S. Bureau of Mortality Statistics and the National Institute of Drug Abuse, 1979 estimates.)

Substance	Estimated Deaths
Tobacco	200,000–300,000
Alcohol	30,000–130,000
Licit Drug Overdose	8,000–10,000
Illicit Drug Overdose	1,000–3,600

Figures such as these can only approximate actual fatalities since accidental, suicidal, and other concurring medical and environmental factors affect complete accuracy.

These figures might have changed slightly since 1979. But on an ABC-TV "Evening News" special report on drugs, Peter Jennings estimated fatality figures for 1985 as follows:

Tobacco	380,000
Alcohol	125,000
Illegal Drugs	3,500

Not a big difference at all.

Death by illegal drugs is much smaller than the general public would assume after weekly doses of hysteria.

In 1973, when I was busted for cocaine, the New York City

Coroner's Office listed nineteen deaths by cocaine overdose the previous year. Researchers interested in my case took a closer look. Fourteen of the cases had fatal bullet wounds, three suffered fatal knife wounds, one had jumped off a tall building, and the last accidentally ingested a half pound of cocaine. She had been a "mule" border crosser, hiding the coke inside a balloon which she swallowed, planning to excrete it when safe. Unfortunately, the balloon broke.

When I read the *Consumers Union Report on Licit and Illicit Drugs* (often cited by this book), the most startling discovery was that of the "Heroin Overdose Mystery." They clearly found that people who used heroin showed a high incidence of sudden fatality. But they were skeptical that these deaths were a *direct* cause of the drug itself. The study cites research paper after paper which indicate a heroin-use plateau effect, after which larger doses of heroin appeared to have little or no effect on the physiology. Addicts given up to nine times their normal dosage showed insignificant bodily damage or change:

> A conscientious search of the United States medical literature throughout recent decades failed to turn up a single scientific paper reporting that heroin overdose, as established by these or any other reasonable methods of determining overdose, is in fact a cause of death among American heroin addicts. The evidence that addicts have been dying by the hundreds of heroin overdose is simply nonexistent. (*Licit and Illicit Drugs*, Chapter 12, "The Heroin Overdose Mystery.")

There are *heroin-related* deaths, to be sure, but serum hepatitis and other infectious diseases (now including AIDS) seem to be the chief villains as addicts persist in using and sharing unsterilized needles. Tetanus, bacterial endocarditis, and tuberculosis were on closer examination found to be the actual cause of many "heroin deaths." And as in our research on New York City's few cocaine deaths in 1972, physical violence and suicide also contributed to fatality figures. The Consumers Union survey found the answer to the mystery "in the customs of the United States coroner-medical examiner system." Often the subjects are poor, limited autopsies are performed, and any suspicion by friends or the presence of drugs or drug paraphernalia is presumed sufficient evidence for the M.E. to list cause of death as overdose.

There are heroin overdoses, although perhaps *poisoning* is a more accurate term. The first signs are intense, exaggerated stupor followed by coma. Death can come in hours, usually from respiratory failure. Those hours are crucial; death can be easily prevented by administering an effective antidote—a narcotic antagonist known as nalorphine. This is no different from treatment of venomous snake bites. This isn't meant to minimize the dangers of heroin. It is one of the most dangerous substances around. But consider how blindly we label, mislabel, panic, shoot the system full of exaggerated fear to the point where victims and nonvictims believe no hope exists.

4.

Warning!
This Drug Is Dangerous

If it were humanly possible, I would place warning stickers on every illegal drug in existence—even those that don't yet have names. It would be an enormously difficult task and a ridiculous packaging problem as well. All illegal drugs and, admit it, all legal drugs are dangerous. Or to be more precise, all drugs have the potential to be dangerous, whether they are used for medication or recreation. *There are no intrinsically good or bad drugs, only good and bad ways of relating to drugs, good and bad choices for each individual.*

I could easily recommend many ways to "get high" without drugs—jogging, aerobics, hyperventilated breathing, and meditation, to name a few. Also, wild dancing or just spinning around out of control produces a giddy dizziness. The wilder the dancing and spinning, the longer the individual can learn to stretch and master the produced altered consciousness. One non-drug high that I experienced was through fasting, which I have done twice (for some unfortunate reason, I'm able to maintain the necessary discipline only in jail). On one nineteen-day fast, I experienced extrabody travel and visionary hallucinations similiar to an LSD experience. I also managed to lose 20 pounds, and my skin felt much "younger." It was one of the great experiences of my life, actually.

Drug users generally know about all these techniques, and still by the millions choose a short cut—they choose drugs. You could say that they are self-medicating, exhibiting exploratory behavior, succumbing to peer pressure, responding to inner biochemical needs, being self-destructive, or a dozen other explanations. Any theory—and there are many—should include an element of irrationality.

Anyone who has had a lengthy discussion about the scientific evidence connecting nicotine to lung cancer with a chain-smoker knows what I mean. There they sit, puffing away while nodding agreement at every key point. "Humans are, after all, human beings and not piano keys," wrote Dostoyevsky, meaning they are filled with and entitled to all sorts of irrationalities and idiosyncrasies.

Beyond the individual's right of choice, drugs have many beneficial aspects, just as they have dangerous potentials. If you just say the word "drug" quietly, shutting out the swirling din of hysterics, you can practically hear the word "good" emerge from its inner meaning. Drugs, including recreational drugs, have not served humanity that badly. I would not tell my own kids, or most kids for that matter, *never* to try drugs. I would tell them to get to know the limits of danger and the limits of pleasure or other benefits. I would tell them just what I tell you, the reader, or myself. Curiosity might have killed the cat, but without curiosity it would be a pretty boring ball of fur. Life is a process of risk taking. The more honest information that is shared about the risks, the less likely those risks are to produce serious injury. But there are few "free lunches." Drug-taking means a system of trade-offs.

No matter how vehemently the moralists protest, drug use is here to stay. The responsible emphasis should be on minimizing the dangers.

When you're doing a drug, no one but you can tell if it's a good or bad decision. The only relevant question is: do you know what you're doing? Are you in control of the situation? In this sense, drug education is no different from driver education. You can teach the rules of the road, the importance of having a sound vehicle, but basically the individual driver must decide to stay in charge.

Up until now, I have avoided drawing sharp dichotomies between drugs. Deliberately so, since distinctions are drawn to fit personal prejudices and sacrifice common sense. Enforcers, for example, draw very sharp distinctions between drugs meant to get you well and drugs meant to get you high. Just about everyone I know brings class prejudices to the subject. I certainly do. Most of my friends make all sorts of excuses for cocaine, Valium, and marijuana, but condemn heroin, PCP, and crack—drugs they really only know about through mythology since they have long since "left the streets." "New Agers" seem to feel that "natural" is good, "synthetic" bad, but there are countless substances in nature— cyanide, belladonna, arsenic, nasty-looking mushrooms with red dots—that can very quickly make you dead, which is also "natural."

Part of the National Party Line states that drugs are meant to get you well, and only authorized medical professionals should dispense them. But is it that simple? There are many instances when getting well, feeling good, and getting high are not so easy to separate. Take nitrous oxide (laughing gas). Some dentists use it to relieve pain, but it is also one of the cheapest, most enjoyable, and least harmful (unless you exclude plain oxygen) ways of getting high. It's been a perennial favorite of drug experimenters for centuries.

Maybe this is not the best possible example of a substance that gets you well and high simultaneously, but there are many others, from ether-liquid Valium mixtures and epinephrine, to codeine, vitamin B_{12} injections, and amyl nitrates. I don't know how anyone can take a pain killer like Demerol and not get high.

This sharp distinction by the Enforcers often breaks down in the doctor's office. In the minds of more "primitive" peoples, as well as among history's most renowned drug experimenters, this distinction crumbles. To get high is to feel good is to get well. William S. Burroughs, Allen Ginsberg, Aldous Huxley, Edgar Allan Poe, William Blake, and William James, among many others, have written brilliantly about their drug experiences. These authors were pros at using the drug experience to enhance their creativity. It gave them insight and vision.

I was recently on a panel where Hunter Thompson extolled and, indeed, demonstrated the virtue of several drugs. On another, Tom Robbins bluntly stated, "The symbol of the sixties should be a mushroom." He did not mean the kind Campbell uses in its soup.

Reading their work is nothing at all like listening to teenagers talk about drug experiences. Abusers can run off their personal list of drugs like a suburban housewife preparing her grocery shopping: "Let's see, I use to do eight Tuinals, four 'ludes, three uppers, and shoot smack twice a day. Then, like in June, I think it was, I got off the Tuinals, but switched to some barbs, some reds, and a few pocket rockets, which seem to do better. I agree, the smack's gotta go, but there's nothin' wrong with downers and speed—it's an incredible combination, and it gets me through the day okay."

This sort of chatter goes on endlessly, with the drugs and the dollars spent and stolen spinning like wheels on a slot machine. Somewhere between these experiences, between a Huxley on the one hand and very strung-out people in lots of trouble on the other, is your typical drug user. There is a continuum from the best possible use to the worst abuse. From enlightenment to death.

Interestingly, efforts to sharpen these distinctions between users and abusers were strenuously pursued by three prestigious U.S. Government panels during the seventies. The first was the 1972 Nixon-appointed Shafer Commission, probably the most rational fact-finding body in the past two decades to consider the subject. Perhaps ever! It recognized that "the use of psychoactive drugs is commonplace in American life." The Shafer Commission refused to accept the functional utility of the phrase "drug abuse."

> Drug abuse has become an emotional term that connotes
> societal disapproval and elicits a sense of uneasiness and
> disquiet. It is a term that changes meaning depending
> on time and place. According to one's society, his place
> on the continuum of human history, and his reason for
> using a particular drug, such use is regarded as either
> socially desirable or undesirable.

The report identified five categories of use:

- **Experimental**—short-term, nonpatterned trial use of one or more drugs, motivated primarily by curiosity or a desire to experience an altered-mood state.
- **Recreational**—occurs in social settings among friends or acquaintances who desire to share an experience which they

define as both acceptable and pleasurable. Recreational use is both voluntary, patterned, and tends not to escalate to more frequent or intense use patterns.

- **Circumstantial**—generally motivated by the users' perceived need or desire to achieve a new and anticipated effect in order to cope with a specific problem, situation, or condition of a personal or vocational nature. This category would include the use of stimulants for work-related tasks, and the use of sedatives or stimulants to relieve tensions or boredom.
- **Intensive**—drug use which occurs at least daily and is motivated by an individual's perceived need to achieve relief or maintain a level of performance.
- **Compulsive**—consists of a patterned behavior at a high frequency and high level of intensity, characterized by a high degree of dependency, such as with chronic alcoholics, heroin dependents, and compulsive users of barbiturates.

The report concluded that "the overwhelming majority of users of psychoactive drugs of all kinds are experimental, recreational or circumstantial and present little problem to either themselves or others. A much smaller group of users could be classified as intensive and the smallest group as compulsive."

The report of the Shafer Commission, a blue-ribbon panel selected by the President, and its 1978 successor (and confirmer) the Liaison Task Panel on Psychoactive Drug Use/Misuse, appointed by President Carter's Commission on Mental Health, read like radical underground documents today. The reports recommended the elimination of criminal penalties for personal possession and use of small amounts of marijuana. They found that legal substances such as tobacco and alcohol present a far more serious threat to individual health and society than most illegal substances; it recognized that the use of amphetamines and barbiturates rank with heroin use as a major social problem; and it downplayed the social costs of all illicit drugs in comparison to legal drugs.

The Shafer Commission (1972), the White Paper on Drug Abuse (prepared by the Domestic Council Drug Abuse Task Force for President Ford in 1975), and the Liaison Task Force Panel (1978) all placed very low priorities on cocaine. In 1975, the White Paper stated that "cocaine as it is currently used does not result in serious social consequences such as crime, hospital emergency room admissions, or death." Later, in 1978, the Task Force wrote that cocaine "does not seem to present a serious health threat to the individual when nasally inhaled in small amounts." (*Yearbook of Substance Use and Abuse*, Volume II, pp. 42–44.)

Nine years later, no government health official could keep their job if they agreed with any of this. I'm not even sure *I* would agree with some of the statements.

These insights and recommendations seem to have been swept away in just a few short years. The panels included many of the best medical minds in the country, yet their findings were ignored. Science has not drastically altered our knowledge of drugs in the few years since. What did change was the administration, which ignored the conclusions and proceeded as if we were back in the Dark Ages, where evil scourges haunted the darkened city streets preying on helpless youth. "A new broom sweeps clean," they say. Reagan brought a new bulldozer to the subject of drugs.

We are not concerned here with legalities or politics, only the nature of drugs. Let me say that drugs are all things to all people— that is, any drug can be beneficial in its *responsible* use, while the same substance can be deadly to the uninformed misuser, or to someone suffering from "drug abuse."

Let me suggest that *drugs themselves are only one portion of the drug experience*. The individual and the setting are equally important, as well as the mindset the person brings to the experience—what each person expects the drug to do for or to him or her. One has to also take into account what kind of drug, the dosage, strength, method of ingestion, and many other variables.

For example, heroin is more addicting than codeine; and heroin injected is much more addicting over time than if it's sniffed or smoked. It's better to eat opium than smoke it, because smoking puts it in the blood and brain much quicker, which makes the rush more intense and prone to abuse. Eating it almost forces you to use moderation: too much, and you'll eventually throw up. Snorting coke is more addicting than chewing coca leaves. But this rule does not necessarily apply to marijuana and hashish. When they are smoked, some inhibitor, biochemical or acquired, says enough.

There's a plateau effect. When they are eaten, the dosage is much harder to control; the effects range from mild euphoria to agonizing nausea. I wouldn't say don't eat Mrs. Sally's (name changed) special cakes in Negril, Jamaica. I will just tell you what she wisely told me. "If it ya furst time, mon, betta take half and wait till an hour to see if'n ya like mowa."

Responsible drug education seeks to save lives. It's not about saving souls; that's another department. Here is a perfect example of information considered *verboten* by the Enforcers' education program: dirty hypodermic needles contaminated with bacteria, viral infections including AIDS, and just plain unsterilized matter are responsible for more heroin-related deaths than the drug itself. European countries, all of which have more sensible drug policies than the U.S., have long recognized this and have made sterilized disposable syringes and needles nonprescription items. France, in January 1987, was the latest of several concerned about AIDS transmission to adopt this policy.

Well meaning as this effort is, it still doesn't recognize street culture. In real life, addicts have disposable syringes and often re-use and share them, especially when they are at a peak inebriation high and rationality has disappeared. Here is absolutely the best, cheapest, easiest explained way of saving scores of lives: IF YOU DO SHARE OR REUSE NEEDLES, take a small glass, fill it with common household liquid bleach. Flush the syringe twice in the bleach, then rinse the syringe twice in a glass of fresh water. Throw away the old bleach and water after each usage. Each time you shoot up, repeat this procedure. You'll have done a pretty good job of disinfecting the "works."

The U.S. Surgeon General, the National Institute for Cancer Research, and the Department of Health, Education, and Welfare have all recommended that marijuana be smoked only through a water pipe. The water filter reduces carcinogenic elements in the smoke by fifty percent. Unfortunately, since 1976, thirty states have outlawed such paraphernalia.

The only place I know encouraging the distribution of such life-saving information (they also actively distribute condoms on the streets) is the Haight-Ashbury Free Medical Clinic in San Francisco.

Individual experiences vary from person to person, as different as each person's culture and biochemistry. For example, one user may think a drug is a sexual stimulant; another reports just the opposite effect. Concurrent multiple effects in the same person are also not uncommon.

Environment can have a profound impact on the experience. Take a drug like sodium pentathol, a drug I can say got me very high indeed. Taking it from a happy-go-lucky family dentist about to pull a wisdom tooth was one easy way of getting over the pain (especially after the tooth was long gone!). That's quite different from taking a trip on sodium pentathol courtesy of the Argentine junta in the 1970s, and telling under torture every secret they want to hear. No matter how much evil is attached to a drug, it can still be used for good in the right situation and vice versa. I have my prejudices, but I can't honestly say that any drug has "morality" built in, one way or another.

So it's not just the drug itself we have to consider, but the internal and external environments of the person. Let's talk about what Enforcers hate to hear: using drugs responsibly. Drugs should not be used as a weapon, getting people to do things they would deeply regret. That's sick! Or as a macho initiation rite, to make a newcomer part of a gang. The Weather Underground thought using LSD would keep their hidden cells free from government agents. For the most part, it worked, but one agent took acid with them and later identified and helped apprehend fellow members. Using drugs is a matter of free choice. It's not for head games, power trips, or whatever your term is for toying with people's minds.

Drugs are, like most things, to be used with caution and moderation. Two shots of Jack Daniels will impair motor skills; ten shots will impair your ability to wake up. Drugs should be used intelligently, with a knowledge of their potential benefits and harm. You should not aim to "wipe out your brain," or "escape all memory," or "leave the planet." Sure, people use such terms poetically, but if you're serious, you could be setting the stage for a harmful experience. You've brought the wrong philosophy to the experience.

When I spoke of internal environments, I mean those self-generated chemicals known as endogenous secretions (endogenes). An example is endorphin, a chemical that reduces pain and induces euphoria. Meditation is said to trigger it. Runners get it flowing.

Dopamine, another endogene, is thought to send chemical messages to the brain that signal sexual and feeding sensations. There is some interesting research that suggests cocaine "imitates" dopamine—also, that it imitates norepinephrine, which signals impending danger. That might help explain the paranoid edge that accompanies excessive cocaine use. Serotonin, another internal drug, has been linked to depression. Too much seems to cause depression; too little can be correlated with manic behavior.

Naturally, all this biochemistry is new, very exciting, and still iffy. It's pretty clear that individuals with certain internal chemistries cannot handle certain drugs without taking an extra measure of risk. Hard-liners believe that *all* psychoactive drugs activate pleasure circuits in the brain that nature has ruled off limits. Once thrown out of kilter, malfunctioning circuits keep demanding more stimulation (i.e. drugs, addiction). Although this hardly explains why most people who use drugs do not become addicts, it has led to some pioneering work with nonaddicting chemicals that relieve the agony of withdrawal symptoms.

The major drugs fall into four basic categories. There's the natural stuff, which comes in its *crude* form. Examples are coca leaves, peyote, coffee beans, and opium poppies. The second form is a *refined* or *processed* drug, like morphine, coke, brewed coffee, and sugar.

Semisynthetic drugs involve changing the structure of the refined drug slightly, producing substances like crack, heroin, aspirin, and LSD. Finally, there are totally *synthetic* drugs, made entirely in labs, like Valium, PCP, and Seconals. Crude drugs are less toxic than their tampered forms—which means they are not as potent. In other words, if you decide to use drugs, you can make responsible decisions about the form you use. This proper choice gives you an edge in the trade-offs that accompany every drug experience.

Drugs should be taken in a setting that's not threatening, with a friend(s) you trust. That supportive surrounding is helped by a condoning culture. People drink in bars and smoke opium in dens.

This has been true for indigenous people throughout history. Taking yagé with the Cofan Indians in the headwaters of the Amazon is one thing; drinking the powerful brew on the L.A. Freeway on the way to a meeting is bizarre, dangerous—and you'll throw up on your new suit. In the sixties, when the counterculture was in bloom, lots of people nodded their heads and said, "It's okay what you're doing, 'cause I'm doing it too." It was a counterculture support system that is not that strong in the eighties, although in certain sections of any city, crash pads, communes, and a counterculture paper can be found. And the Grateful Dead hasn't taken a break in twenty years.

The very concept of responsible drug use drives Enforcers absolutely beserko. It's like discussing responsible sex education before marriage with Phyllis Schlafly. It defeats the whole purpose of encouraging abstention. It's because of folks like me "confusing" the young that prohibition breaks down. Fundamentalism, or having a moral code based on blind faith, is, shall we say, fundamental to the Enforcer mentality. Of all the knee-jerk "-isms" in the world, this one's probably killed more people, been responsible for more torture and imprisonment, and held back human knowledge more than any other.

We must move from considering drug abuse as a "sin" or crime to considering it as an illness, the worst form being "addiction disease." And no matter how sensible or humane this may sound, you must realize that what I have just said is still very much a minority view, muted in the onslaught of the fundamentalist crusade.

5.

Warning! This Person May Be Dangerous

With vast quantities of chemicals being consumed by millions of Americans, it's common sense to look at the different categories of drug use. Serious clinicians recognize classification as the first step in any cohesive study. The mass media conveniently avoids such distinctions. In the thirties, during the first major drug hysteria, a person had only to smoke one marijuana joint to earn the label "junkie." Not much has changed fifty years later. A professional athlete today admitting occasional cocaine use (after getting caught) gets lambasted as "an extremely sick person." He gets lumped in with, say, Dennis Hopper, who admitted to using $1,000 worth of cocaine a day for stretches. (He characterized this decline as, "going from *Easy Rider* to *Scarface*.") If everyone using illegal drugs, as well as those abusing legal drugs, were considered in need of treatment, every hotel and ballpark in America would have to be refitted as a rehabilitation center.

The Undifferentiated Continuum of Drug Use
The concept of the Undifferentiated Continuum of Drug Use is central to our discussion. It's an imaginary line spanning the spectrum of user personalities. The end points can be thought of as health and sickness, although this somewhat oversimplifies the complex nature of each individual. There are two primary distinctions. Free-choice risk-takers have no compulsion to take drugs. Not-so-free-choice risk-takers are dependent. At one extreme there

are the *enlightened*—that is, the people for whom drug consumption is a cathartic, enhancing creativity. Aldous Huxley, Gertrude Stein, and William Burroughs are only a few who made maximum use of the drug trade-offs. After the enlightened come *users*, the majority of consumers who find drugs pleasurable, consciousness-altering, or medicinal. *Drug dependents* (the habituated), meaning those who practice unconscious consumption as second nature, follow. *Allergics* are the next category, one that has been little studied. Then come *abusers*, the largest category, which consists of persons taking not-so-free-choice risks. (Occasionally the words "abuser" and "abuse" are used more generally.) *Addicts* are those who exhibit extremely hazardous consumption, where there is no creativity or pleasure, only compulsion. There are scores of subcategories in between.

You can get a better idea of the total user/abuser population by reading the chart. The figures are based on what you'd call an educated guess. In defining the total use population, some choices had to be made to make general points. Half of the drug-dependent group, where the biggest risk-taking begins, is on long-term medication prescribed by doctors. There are many more than 5 million people in this category, but several long-term medications do not have bad interactions with psychoactive drugs. The point is, if you are in a long-term program for any illness, you obviously have built up a trust relationship with your doctor and his or her advice. The allergic group is an arbitrary classification, since little research exists in this area. Allergics are individuals for whom a particular drug is harmful because of damaging metabolic or psychosomatic effects. Total alcohol consumption was halved to account for overlap with other substance use. Nicotine was excluded since use and abuse are uniquely close and impossible to distinguish between. Some abusers fall into the addict category while others lean toward drug dependency.

Pregnant women are not factored into the chart. Because of so much hormonal, enzymatic, and endogenic activity taking place inside a woman's body, drugs are not a good idea, especially in the third trimester. When in doubt, abstention or moderation makes common sense.

UNDIFFERENTIATED CONTINUUM OF DRUG USE

Free Choice Risk-Takers:

Enlightened	1 Million
Users	68 Million
Drug Dependents	3 Million
	72

Not-so-free Choice Risk-Takers:

Addicts	5 Million
Abusers	15 Million
Allergics	1 Million
Drug Dependents	7 Million
	28
Total	100 Million

These figures are estimates only.

Nicotine use/abuse is excluded.

Total alcohol consumption was reduced by half to
    compensate for overlap.

The Allergic category is somewhat arbitrary.

Drug dependency can be equated with habituation.

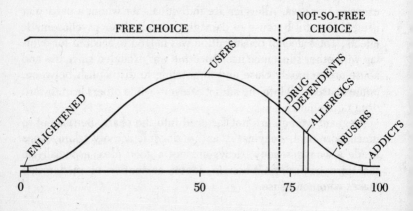

Assuming a normally distributed population, a bell curve would show the relative frequency of each drug-use category on the continuum. The categories are by no means exact, and show only relative frequency. "Undifferentiated" means there are no rigid categories. Adjacent personalities blend into one another.

Here's a personal example illustrating how categorization works. Since my initiation at age seven, I was a cancerette smoker, *habituated* to nicotine. Nineteen years ago, I quit smoking cigarettes. There were about thirty mind-wrenching days, automatic cigarette ticks, and a tendency to let my eyes follow any line of smoke from tail pipes or nearby smokers. Eventually the fantasies and cravings tapered off. I stopped completely and haven't yet resumed. Today, I would no sooner smoke a cigarette than a candle. Close friends, even one who quit with me in a buddy-reinforcement situation, had quite different experiences: "Not a day goes by when I don't think of lighting up upon waking or after sex or a good meal." At moments of great stress, some give in and puff their little resolutions away, demonstrating their addiction. *Addiction and habituation look very similar when the drug is used, and even share withdrawal symptoms.* The long-term picture is quite different. Habituation is broken more easily than addiction.

My guiding principle in quitting was to make an unconscious act conscious. Habituated users respond successfully to short periods (thirty days or less) of treatment and walk away from any drug if the cycle is broken. Even addictive personalities can develop or be taught coping techniques to lengthen their periods of non-use, limit the cravings. The trick is never to slide into unconscious behavior patterns. Be aware of each puff on each cigarette. Count yourself into consciousness and out of the pattern.

Clinical studies suggest that, for some, addiction fades or mysteriously stops as a person ages. However, in most cases it is long-term, probably lifelong. Free of treatment-center propaganda, true recidivism rates vary from 65 percent to 90 percent, depending upon the study and the drugs examined. Any in-house study claiming near-perfect "success"—0 percent recidivism—should be considered suspect. Reliable follow-up is difficult and costly, given the noncompliance and mobility of former treatment participants.

Reality: Out of Business

True addiction, the most serious form of abuse on the continuum, is a small category, but five million is still a lot of people. From the newspapers, you'd think it comprised 90 percent of all usage. Distortions are common, especially if celebrities are involved. Drug-*related* deaths are reported as drug-*caused* deaths (see "Common Everyday Myths About Drugs," Chapter Three). In everyday gossip about addicts or bad experiences, stories of serious abuse get told and retold because they are more dramatic and also because they toe the National Party Line. *A minority of sufferers have a disproportionately high impact on the full range of drug usage.*

Addiction prejudice isn't restricted to the tabloids. The scientific community can be equally biased. Medical journals, conferences, and "experts" invariably discuss addiction while excluding "popular" use. Research grants are awarded to topics unlikely to challenge the National Party Line. Federal funds have been denied to studies of illicit drugs which may confirm beneficial usage. This is hardly unusual in science. Try getting government money to study organic farming or pest control using fewer chemicals. You run up against powerful trans-national corporations who lobby against such funding. The Drug Industrial Complex does exactly the same with regard to research that could prove competitive.

This situation is analogous to, perhaps worse than, when the Freudian school ruled psychoanalysis. Freud spent his life studying very sick people, the ones confined to the darkest wards. His prognoses and theories about general humanity were based on these worst-case scenarios. After some initial skepticism, the scientific community flocked to Vienna. The result: the view of humanity reflected in psychoanalysis was for decades based upon those unfortunate sufferers. Sure, there were healthy people, but that was only because their defenses were strong enough to contain inner chaotic forces of libido and death. In a way, they were faking. Why bother with healthy people? Though there might have been some scientific truths to be discovered, there was no money in it. So the Freudians got the grants, got the big salaries, won the awards, and were invited on all the talk shows.

Not until psychologists like Abraham Maslow, Erich Fromm,

and other self-actualization advocates attacked Freud's basically pessimistic view of human nature did another relatively strong school emerge—the Human Potential Movement. Here, theories and therapies were based on the idea that lots of people were satisfactorily coping with life (the normal). Some even achieved mental health and happiness to the extent that they actualized creative and altruistic potentials within themselves. They reached a plateau of enlightenment. Maslow (who was my teacher) and his school of thought are today very acceptable, but forty years ago they were considered kooky and radical.

Here is probably the most famous example of the research system running on empty. In 1974 at Tulane University, a scientist demonstrated that dead brain cells in rhesus monkeys were "caused" by marijuana. Then California Governor Ronald Reagan, a scholar of reknown, cited this study when he told the Los Angeles *Times,* "The most reliable scientific sources say permanent brain damage is one of the inevitable results of the use of marijuana."

The methodology was veiled in secrecy, not subject to independent verification. The media did not question its conclusions. Potheads flocked to get brain scans as "chromosome damage" became a new and frightening trade-off. In 1980, using the Freedom of Information Act (since federal funds were involved), lawyers from NORML and the Playboy Foundation publicized the research procedures. The Rhesus monkeys had been strapped into a chair, and a gas mask was attached to their heads. Thirty joints were passed through the gas mask directly into the monkeys *in five minutes!* No smoke was lost; the monkeys inhaled it all. Not surprisingly, within ninety days, death occurred. Adjustments for body weight always have to be made in small-animal drug studies before leaping to conclusions about humans (as Reagan did). That would put daily human marijuana intake at well over one hundred average strength "reefers" a day. Carbon monoxide poisoning and oxygen deprivation were probably more to blame for the loss of brain cells than THC. Dr. Heath, who conducted the study, was later criticized for his conclusions and methodology. There were other serious errors, but the Tulane study survives as "fact" in many political arguments. An average pot smoker would take longer than a year to consume one hundred reefers, perhaps two or three.

An abuser or misuser would have to push their limits to manage that much inhalation in six months. Not even a Lower East Side regular I knew named "Chimney" Brown could have matched one of those little monkeys in a week. ("Chimney" is today a computer engineer who gave up pot ten years ago: "I got bored with it!")

Don't deduce from the debunking of this study that marijuana smoking is a harmless activity. Common sense would indicate that inhaling any hot smoke with contaminant particles presents *some* danger. Obviously moderation is a major element of responsible use.

Responsible drug education—education which recognizes drug use as a permanent fixture and tries to mitigate potential damage—is extremely controversial, a distant voice in today's scientific community. It wins no grants or status, and it doesn't help in research departments or funding $2,000-per-diem country-club treatment facilities or slum methadone-addiction dispensaries. When was the last time an advertisement suggested taking no medication for headache? In the seventies marijuana was officially cited as alleviating the side effects of glaucoma. Not today.

The Various Types

It's important to emphasize and re-emphasize that the overwhelming majority of drug users are "normal" people free from illness.

Drug *users* can be recognized by their ambivalence, a take it or leave it attitude. Common expressions they use are "I rarely buy," "It's a social experience," or "Drugs are fun on a Caribbean vacation." There is no compulsion, no frantic search for some misplaced roach or pill. They more often accept a drug than offer one. And they just say no when the occasion is wrong.

Drugs are seen as an unexpected source of pleasure, in the same league as good food, music, art, sex. Dangerous aspects of drug use are recognized and respected. Users differentiate between drugs (head drugs include pot, mushrooms, hallucinogens; body drugs are stimulants and depressants), and between good and bad highs.

Most important, the user cultivates a personal relationship with a drug. What to take, how much, how long the experience lasts, how to "ride out" or "bring down" a bad experience, or where to get help are all known quantities. And it *is* almost always a social experience with friends or lovers. Users feel no need to increase the dosage and frequency, certainly not to the point where they lose complete control.

Users are not prone to wrecking lives. Aware of the trade-offs, they enjoy the experience and don't present a burden to themselves or society. Within limits, their genetic, biochemical, or personality structure is such that it allows them to escape abuse.

We should briefly mention *misuse*—that is, the behavior of a user who *occasionally* exhibits the wrong relationship to a drug. The dosage is too high, the setting bad, the mood wrong. Perhaps you took a drug to forget about a bad experience only to find yourself focusing on it more intensely. If you drink to forget a heartbreak, you only become more miserable after the first ten rounds. Try not to be alone, try to be with someone you trust where you can talk about the experience. Some drugs facilitate dialogue, but no one has a dialogue *with* a drug.

Not surprisingly, users are the easiest to treat. If "addiction" were forced upon them, they could successfully treat both the physical and psychological symptoms of temporary body habituation. The record shows that users randomly pressured into heroin experimentation quit with comparative ease. Pregnant women, fearful about the effects of drugs on their fetus, can just stop. People treated with psychiatric medication and asked by their doctor to refrain because of unpredictable side effects can stop or certainly cut back. Anyone taking temporary medication should not be afraid to ask their doctors about the effects of recreational drugs, unless you mistrust the opinion. There are other doctors.

Moving along the continuum, we come to a drug-dependent class. Habituation, physical and psychological, is an easy trap to fall into. Marijuana, a drug considered not to be physically addicting, is nonetheless habit-forming, simply through psychological stimulus-response associations with pleasure, other emotions or circumstances. A traveling salesperson might find sleeping on the road difficult, use sleeping pills over a few weeks or months, and then find it hard to get to sleep without them. Breaking the need can be done by gradually reducing the dosage or going "cold turkey," ending the pill cycle. After two or three restless nights, sleep without pills (which is a healthier, deeper sleep) can resume. If self-discipline fails, therapists can help with support or with chemicals to speed up the termination of withdrawal symptoms.

Contrary to what you might think, symptom elimination is the easy part. Because of the drama, the physical intensity (tremors, fits), and the perceived power of the drug to "hook," withdrawal symptoms get more attention than they deserve. Perhaps this is why a famous athlete caught by a test or a snitch and ushered into a treatment program can walk away after being pronounced "cured." He probably never had an abuser illness to begin with. This works out very nicely for the fancy treatment facility (which can rake in $60,000 for one month's care), the team, the league, the player who is willing to parrot anything (who wouldn't, with a multi-million-dollar career on the line?), sports, the kids, the country, and, of course, the National Party Line. Nothing's wrong with it unless you care about privacy, civil liberties, truth, and honest medical practice.

Use is not abuse, and habituation is not addiction. Confusing one for the other leads to distortions and bad conclusions. In a way, the oft-repeated miracle cure is the opposite of "faith healing." In faith healing, there's lots of faith, but no healing, unless you consider temporary remission a cure. It's very easy to repent and have "faith" in NPL tactics when there was no addiction to cure in the first place.

In the middle of the continuum are two categories of user personalities often overlooked. The first is not only acceptable but necessary drug use. *Drug dependency* is a trade-off sometimes necessary to maintain one's ability to cope, or maintain life itself. Heart patients on digitalis, diabetics on insulin, epileptics on dilantin or phenobarbital, manic depressives on lithium—all use the currently preferred drug for their illness. Dependency in these treatment plans is a calculated risk. Side effects, including dangerous toxicity levels, are tolerated.

Even in the illicit or self-medicating drug field, it's possible for some people to have discovered a drug that treats anxiety, loss of temper, or insomnia. Although much self-prescription is self-deception, some users can manage even dependency without dangerous consequences.

What's also interesting here is that some patients who *should* be dependent (diabetics, heart-disease patients, etc.) distrust the pill-popping and injections. Rejection of life-prolonging dependency is common even when the patient seems intellectually to accept its necessity. A group of drug-dependents neglects, intentionally or otherwise, to take their medication, preferring the consequences of illness to "artificial" sustenance. By some estimates, 20 percent of all drug-dependents at one time refuse medication or treatment. These people, in my view, would not be abuser-personality candidates.

A second class of people rarely considered would be people with allergic reactions to commonly used illegal drugs. Obviously, if people can be allergic to ragweed pollen, aspirin, or penicillin, there certainly are people who can be allergic to marijuana or cocaine. I've seen cocaine users who love the stimulating rush but just can't understand why their elbows and knees swell up, or pot smokers who go into sneezing fits. Some allergic reactions can be fatal. Unnoticed by the press are 180 to 1,000 aspirin-related deaths a year. Allergy patch tests for illicit drugs, an easy scientific matter, should be developed. Again, a sensible way to relieve suffering, even save lives, is unavailable because of narrowmindedness.

Obviously the largest category of people who shouldn't use drugs are those on the abuser/addict side of the continuum. The term "addict" has an interesting medical history because it passes through phases of acceptability and nonacceptability, depending on one's allegiance to a particular school of treatment. The term was discouraged fifteen or twenty years ago because it tended to focus on the withdrawal symptoms and also because of the social-outcast connotations. It also was thought to retard treatment: "What can I do? I'm an addict, I'm hooked." Rehabilitation specialists who primarily use talk therapies today talk only of generic *substance abuse* and *abuser personalities*.

However, because of new research on genetics and brain chemistry, the healing world is returning more and more to the use of the term *addict*. Perhaps this is mincing words, but language defines the treatment. This time around there is a marked difference in linguistics. The preferred term is becoming *addictive disease*. Dr. Nathan Kline, a pioneer in antidepressants, demonstrated that alcoholics could be treated as if they were biochemical depressives and began similar studies on other types of chemical addiction. His work was inconclusive when he recently died, but the implication was that addiction itself is a symptom of deeper depression. (Most biochemically based theoreticians are content to see addiction disease as an entity unto itself.) The concept of addiction disease rests on a biochemical network inside some people's brains which goes haywire with any psychoactive drug—so haywire that a biological need for more stimulation or disruption is created.

Differences aside, science has no problem identifying a disease or abuser personality by its symptoms. The idea that we are finally talking about a *disease* is very recent. For decades, if drug-taking wasn't a sin, it was some other character weaknesses. The idea that addiction disease, once identified, applies to *all* mood-altering drugs is even more recent. Sufferers apparently cannot safely switch from one drug to another.

Now to the generalizations. Typical drug abusers are young, probably because they have not had time to develop any real knowledge about drugs or mechanisms to cope with abuse. (Although some evidence suggests the median age is increasing.) They often appear self-destructive, straining bonds of friendship and family. They have trouble functioning socially and economically, a behavior pattern that leads them into dangerous social situations and poor health. Theirs is a fatalistic view of life—few goals, fewer values.

Deception, lying, and stealing are part of the lifestyle as abusers manipulate people and the world to satisfy their illness. The illegal and expensive nature of the drugs is only partly responsible; rich addicts do the same. Their conversation, because of unconscious fantasy buildup, usually leads to drugs, the way a person who's hungry might shift the conversation to discuss good restaurants.

Clinicians of all schools examining abuse agree the common symptom is that more and more drugs are needed to fulfill a craving. "Getting high" has long been forgotten as a goal. Drugs are needed to maintain a plateau. Like moths flying closer to a flame,

the psychophysical symptoms worsen as the individual deteriorates.

It's not a steady decline. Some serious abusers are able to swear
off drugs for months, only to binge later. A keen observer can see
one coming on when the unconscious fantasy buildup starts to be
vocalized. Eating and sleeping patterns go completely out of control (one of the best early indicators of trouble). Behavior becomes
erratic.

Abusers can reach states where they cannot tell you what drug(s)
they are even on, how much they've taken, or even who they are
or where they live. They nod in and out of consciousness. You can
find them at times lying face down in the gutter or, if they're lucky,
in emergency wards. And sometimes they die, not as often as
popular mythology portrays it, but drug-induced toxicity and drug-
related deaths are in the cards. Opinions vary as to the inevitable
fatality of addiction disease if it is untreated. Certainly depression
and suicidal tendencies are common at this end of the continuum.

A Word of Advice to Parents

Drug abusers ruin lives—their own and others. They are a constant source of irritation: the drunk falling down at parties, the
coworker bending your ear about some new hotshot chemical, or
your kid coming home in a spacy, scary state, often in trouble at
school or with the law.

Abusers are not happy people. They have a need for treatment
and counseling that they themselves don't recognize, certainly not
in the beginning. The general deception central to drug abuse
includes self-deception. Like any serious illness, there is a strong
tendency to reject and deny reality.

To penetrate this denial, you must be a firm, responsible ally,
not one ready to label all use as abuse, not one ready to "blame
yourself" for bringing up a "junkie" when your kid might only be
experimenting with some substance and will soon stop.

I know this isn't easy, but it's also not impossible. I have three
kids of my own. All have experienced drugs at one time in their
lives. None are abusers, but there were moments of misuse—in
my own experience as well—which were just as frightening to
each kid as they are for us parents.

If your relationship is open, chances are good your kid will seek guidance on these points. *Be ready for the bad drug experience to broach the subject if other times seem awkward.* It works better if your kids bring up the subject, easing into it at their own pace.

Increased drug use and other patterns leading to misuse and/or abuse are in great part unconscious acts. They must be accepted and made conscious before they can be corrected. It takes a good deal of love and patience to break through the defenses of any abuser and reach a common reality. Often it means self-examination of the parents' behavior and a willingness to see the problem not in isolation but as part of a complex family social pattern.

Parents should not leap to conclusions just because a kid sleeps late, does poorly in some subjects, or spray-paints "Life's a bitch, then you die!" on the family dog. Don't follow the PTA approach to search your kid's hiding places for strange pills and roach clips. The privacy of citizens extends to kid citizens as well. When Meese successfully pushed the Supreme Court to exempt school lockers from warrantless searches, kids were denied their Fourth Amendment rights. Spying only increases suspicions and makes a difficult dialogue even more difficult.

Hypocrisy and information that comes from suspect sources or a false heart will not bridge the communication gap. Lay the groundwork by establishing trust. Hopefully, this book and others recommended can be used as props to begin the dialogue. If no dialogue exists, consider *that* problem more serious than drug use.

All my kids discuss drugs with their parents, but it would be the height of arrogance to declare flat out the formula for raising kids. One clue I've picked up because of my "unusual" lifestyle and because at colleges and high school speeches I've met so many young people: bringing up parents isn't all that easy for kids, either.

Good luck! Dear Abbie is with you!

6.

Aiming Toward Reality

"New prospects coming to Daytop are systematically besieged by recovering addicts, who call them names, humiliate them, and make them admit 'I'm a baby, I'm an addict.' To get help from Daytop one must beg for it. There is a chair called the Prospect Chair, and every new applicant must sit there for an indeterminate length of time, contemplating his commitment to treatment and recovery. The prospect is made to stand up on the chair and beg for help." [*Playboy*, 5/87]

These are the words of Monsignor William O'Brian, founder of Daytop Village in New York City, which, aside from the government's center in Lexington, Kentucky, is probably the oldest drug-abuse treatment facility in the country.

Like most programs founded in the fifties, Daytop relies on what is called "breakdown therapy." The idea is to shatter a drug abuser's defenses, rationalizations, and bad behavior patterns, and to create a clean slate upon which can be constructed new, healthy behavior. It's done under strict supervision and in reformatory-style living conditions. Infractions of house rules are punished with ostracism. A misbehaver might be ordered to sit in the Prospect Chair for a day and a half. Daytop, until recently, used other acts of humiliation, such as shaving heads or making resisters wear signs reading "I am an Addict."

The majority of American treatment centers continue to rely on breakdown therapy, especially the ones Nancy Reagan chooses to visit. For one thing, it's easy to break down addicts, since they

79

tend to have dependent personalities. All too often, they have suffered from child abuse. An abusive, authoritarian approach is easy discipline for young people lacking strongly developed inner-ego strengths. It's no surpise the Moonies use the same kind of breakdown treatment, and it's not so different from that popular fifties term "brainwashing" (which was mistakenly attributed to our enemy in Korea). Of course, Daytop and the others are not engaging in torture. There is no physical violence, only verbal. They are not creating Moonies or little Nazis, but if they wanted to, they could.

Once a "nobody" has been created, it's easy to graft on any personality. At the point of breakdown, Daytop "showers the subject with love." Love is not freely given; it is earned. It's no surprise that Daytop Village comes out of the Catholic church, because, to a non-Catholic anyway, it seems the notion of "original sin" is implied in their abuser treatment. Locate the origins of sin, exorcise the demon, and then shoot for redemption.

Phoenix House is another well-known program in the same vein. In Egyptian mythology, the phoenix is a bird that self-destructs in fire after a long life and is reborn from its own ashes. Death to rebirth and resurrection, discarding of worthless flesh (the ashes) and the freeing of the spirit. You're talking big- and small-time religion here.

This religious model is not just the property of institutionalized religion. In Freudian psychoanalysis, the id serves much the same purpose. The id is seen as something deep inside, our "real" self that constantly hungers to be self-destructive. In all these approaches, it's almost as if the individual who presents himself or herself to the world is irrelevant, a vessel to be filled with society's moral judgments. In addiction, the relationship is between drugs and some deep inner force.

This model does not fit my view of the world, my *weltanschauung*, the German word for something we live by that is stronger than a point of view but not as strong as ideology (religious or secular). Therefore, if any of *my* kids were in serious trouble with drugs, I would not send them to any program using the breakdown model. Like their parents, none of my kids are "born-againers." I personally think being born once was tough enough.

Why go through a second time with breakdown therapy? My kids concur; so does my mother. The key word here is "my." Pat Robertson, Phyllis Schlafly, or Nancy Reagan can send *their* kids and possibly achieve their goals. Robertson could choose one of many Evangelical treatment centers.

Although it's not my decision, I still have a problem with guilt-therapy. This is *the* Enforcer model of choice, and it rules the land. It gets the lion's share of government funding, and is prejudiced against programs based on very different philosophies. Let's not rule out class hypocrisy. Celebrity moral experts would not send their kids to Daytop Village any more than they would sleep at the Salvation Army. These programs are for poor people. They are programs to recommend for *other* people's kids. Their own kids would probably go to the next group of centers.

The two most famous treatment centers for the "rich and famous" are Fair Oaks Hospital in the East (New Jersey) and the Betty Ford Clinic in the West (California). These are treatment resorts—plush mansions, gardens, doctors, the works! The cost can run $60,000 or more a month, and although both centers do auxiliary *pro bono* work for some who are poor and not famous, the wealthy are their bread and butter.

These programs use individual and family therapies to attempt to fix something that has gone wrong deep inside the abuser. Rehabilitation relies heavily on biochemical models. Science has replaced religion. Chemicals such as clonidine for opiate addiction and bromocriptine for cocaine are used in the early stages of symptom treatment. These drugs are not to be confused with a drug like methadone. They do not replace one addictive drug with another. Withdrawal symptoms can be agonizingly painful. These medications only reduce the pain; they do not switch the addiction. All this is extremely new to modern pharmacology, but they are considered relatively benign substances. How they work is a matter of speculation. Their sponsors postulate they block the chemical haywire created by the addictive substance. Chemical messages are inhibited from transmitting harmful and confusing signals to endogenes or internal drugs.

Biochemists or geneticists will be the first to tell you that biochemical treatment can only modify; it is not a cure. Unfortunately, the media is again more simplistic, confusing a drug that effects symptom removal with a drug that permanently solves the basic condition. The media, in a strange way, is reflecting a desire as ancient as humanity, for the perfect elixir, the permanent one-time use/instant cure with no side effects. That's always been a great idea, but pharmacology has rarely achieved such miracles. No pain, no gain. No gain, no pain. Trade-offs predominate.

The first criticism of these treatment centers is rather obvious. Unless we used almost all the money from the defense budget, uniform treatment of this nature is beyond the country's economic capacity. The Daytop Villages cost about $35 or $50 a day per resident. An effective public program has to be in that range, certainly under $100 a day. This, incidentally, is half the per-capita daily cost of sending someone to prison, the place where most "apprehended" addicts in America reside. That cost, depending on which state and level of security is involved, is between $150 and $225 per inmate per day—three times the cost of one year at Harvard.

Actually, economics aside, there is much to recommend this biochemical model. It removes the onus of shame, putting addiction disease in the class of diabetes, heart illness, cancer, and other long-term illnesses that are not the individual's fault. Having a strong or weak character is also irrelevant, since you are not responsible for a chemical imbalance in the brain. Guilt is not completely removed. Victims of serious long-term illness inevitably feel "it's my fault." The brain, the mind, and the soul are not easy for mortals to distinguish.

Instant cure for addiction is not foreseen in the near or even distant future. If a chemical solution is discovered, it probably would be linked to long-term treatment, something one might have to take daily. Thus the individual still would have to take responsibility because a regimen of treatment (and medication taking) and abstinence would have to be established.

Genetic factors in addiction cannot be dismissed, given the scientific evidence. University of Colorado studies suggest that children of confirmed alcoholics have a higher potential for abusing any drugs than do children of nonalcoholics. Any chemical abuser or addict has a responsibility to inform their children that they are at greater risk than the general population—about four times as great.

Science may make it possible to screen for potential victims of addiction disease before abuser tendencies manifest themselves. Indeed, researchers at the University of California at San Diego believe they have such a screen. But, to use Reagan's pet phrase, "There you go again." Mass screening has the disadvantage of easily being misused by politicians and other ethicists to isolate or weed out the "weak" from the "strong." There is a second disadvantage to the genetic model. Dr. Darryl Inaba, director of the Drug De-Tox Project of the Haight-Ashbury Free Medical Clinic and assistant professor at the University of California, phrased it best in our interview: "You just can't say to a black teen from the ghetto, 'Your mama's to blame.' They might get up and punch you in the mouth." Dr. Inaba refers to the "Chinese menu" approach to treatment. One from column A, two from column B—whatever rehabilitation mix works best for the individual. Different strokes for different folks.

Before getting to models (sometimes in the trade these are termed "modules") I do like, let me mention one that's very prevalent that I do not approve of. Methadone, as far as I can tell, is simply heroin without any pleasure. That's all. It's substituting one substance which is addictive or habituating (take your pick) for another of exactly the same magnitude and risk. If your *weltanschauung* is not deeply rooted in sin (i.e. carnal pleasure is bad), then you should not distinguish between methadone and opiates. Naturally, as far as the Enforcers go, this is *the* treatment for heroin addiction. Worse. Listen to Dr. Inaba: "The government doesn't want to help addicts. It wants to control and keep them under a sort of 'chemical house arrest.' Other treatment modules are in a sense illegal."

Methadone did not come out of the fifties. Rather, it came into popular preferred use under Nixon. Methadone dispensaries just don't dish out drugs. There is lengthy probing and surveillance: sometimes polygraph tests, always urine testing, and almost always fingerprinting. It's the ultimate control-mechanism approach, and anyone who likes free choice should hate it with a passion. One of Karl Marx's most famous quotes is "Religion is the opiate of the masses." Opium (not heroin) is not as bad a drug as methadone.

It's religion without any good music, no interesting myths, no morality, no chance for a hint of liberation theology. Methadone is Big Brother's solution for the masses. It is *1984*, *Brave New World*, *We*, the movie *Brazil*. It saves neither lives nor souls and doesn't even pretend to. It's just control. This book goes on record as saying that no drug is inherently evil, but if I ever felt close to breaking that rule it would be with methadone. Incidentally, per-capita methadone treatment runs between $75 and $100 a day on an outpatient basis.

Now it's time to consider programs I *can* recommend. Unfortunately they are few and far between. Some general criteria:

Treatment must be client-oriented. The client's needs take precedent over the needs of all surrounding institutions, especially the institution of law enforcement. Sadly, no therapy program can forget that abusers are criminals in our society. This is what differentiates addiction disease from all other long-term illnesses. At various times in human history, mental disease and any illness that confused or frightened the majority got classified as criminal.

Some progress has been made since the Dark Ages. However, this hasn't been true of all addictions. Let's be more precise. Betty Ford, in confessing her biochemical dependence (the *New York Times* reviewed her latest book under the headline THE FIRST LADY WAS AN ADDICT), has done a lot to bring addiction out of the closet. Compared to Nancy Reagan, I'd almost call Betty Ford a saint! But recognizing that Betty Ford was an addict allows an easy out. Booze, Valium, barbiturates all become acceptable addictions while illegal substances are not. The distinction is between good and bad addicts, a situation unacceptable to anyone serious about healing illness. *A good treatment program does not pass such a moral judgment. Furthermore, it cannot be in conspiracy with the Enforcers. It must defend its clients, residents, or patients against the law*. It must embody the same sanctuary principles that exist in any physician-client relationship. Psychiatry simply could not function if its first allegiance was to the state.

There is a gray area here that I can illustrate with a personal dilemma which haunts me to this day. In 1960, while a graduate student in psychology at Berkeley, I was also a therapy counselor at a nearby junior high school. I had a fourteen-year-old client. I told this very tough kid that everything between us was secret. After a few talk sessions, he told me, "I have a gun in my locker." Did I freak! Inside my head, pages of textbooks kept flipping, but as hard as I tried, I couldn't find the right chapter. I did the best I could and told the kid to get the gun off school premises that day or I would tell the authorities. He jumped up, called me a liar, and burst out of the room. I was absolutely stunned. Intellectually I felt rather smug, concluding he was a "passive-aggressive personality." Classification can be very reassuring. But I felt terrible. I went and told the school authorities to search his locker. To this day I feel bad that I lied to that kid. I'm not sure there ever was a real gun, since my defense mechanisms have blocked out how this incident ended. I can rationalize my behavior even better than you can, but probably not in the same way. Anyway, it's the closest I can recall to ever being a squealer.

Every therapist today faces an even worse bind than I did. The addict who has no gun, without necessarily posing any violent intrusive behavior for the rest of society, is still an outlaw. This was ultimately why the Rockefeller Drug Laws (penalties that did not fit individual situations but made harsh sentences mandatory) got amended out of existence after six years. You just couldn't stuff nonviolent offenders in prison at the rate New York was doing. It was an economic decision.

So here are some criteria for success. Rehabilitation programs must defend the individual against the state, and they must be economically feasible. Next, I would rule out substituting one addictive drug for another. And lastly, I'm no fan of breakdown therapy. There are a few scattered, small-budget programs that I have heard are okay. I'm sure there are more I don't know about. I hope so. But they are on the fringes of the rehab industry. The majority are well connected to the Enforcers—hook, line, and sinker.

A word on therapists. Good healers can definitely work wonders in a program they don't even approve of if their personal commitment and love of humanity are strong. Sad to say, the staff turnover rate is high. Dedicated people quit, often in terrible states of disillusionment.

My list of favorite facilities boils down to two I know well. The rehab center I worked for while on the prison inmate release program is called Veritas (officially, the Veritas Therapeutic Community). I now sit on the board of the foundation that supports the project. It is an in-house, residential treatment center. The views expressed in this book are not the views of Veritas. Veritas has to survive in the real world. Ninety percent of its funding comes from New York State, the rest from private donations which I help to hustle. It fulfills all the criteria I mentioned above, but its approach is more diplomatic, a voice softer than mine. They could not exist if they publicly criticized other programs.

It's small, with an excellent staff-to-resident ratio (one to eight). Veritas maintains a drug-free environment. Residents (ranging in age from sixteen to thirty) are referred by other programs, their families, or they come on their own. Some are sent by the courts. All are detoxified or not on drugs when they arrive. It is an interracial, bilingual working community and is neither a slum nor for the rich. Five years ago, in smaller midtown Manhattan quarters, its residents came from all over, even suburbia; today it mostly serves the smaller community from its base on West 106th Street. A Veritas rural community has recently been opened in the Catskills. Both facilities serve only one hundred thirty-five residents in total. It is half black, a quarter hispanic and a quarter white. No matter whom it serves, its philosophy remains the same.

Treatment is based on an eighteen-month cycle. For the first thirty days, the resident gets adjusted to dormitory-like sleeping arrangements, the meal schedule, and house rules. Jim Little, executive director and a personal friend, explains that this period is critical: "There's a lot more hand-holding the first month; the staff and all the peers pay more attention to newcomers."

Residents then graduate to the second level of therapy, which lasts about a year. Each sees a counselor virtually every day, and group therapy is held three times each week. A job therapist is available for vocational training. Education is emphasized. The residential house has a permanent school teacher, two visiting instructors, and six volunteer tutors from nearby Columbia University. School lasts six hours daily and is geared toward a high school diploma.

The residents maintain the facility. They manage the kitchen, do most of the repairs, serve as receptionists, and arrange parties and lectures. First-aid materials or prescription drugs for a special medical condition are kept under lock and key. Medical cases are treated at nearby St. Luke's Hospital.

"We never see drugs as the issue," says Jim. "It is the handle that allows us to get funds to survive. We see *dependency* itself as a killer—we want the resident to become independent and self-sufficient. Veritas practices 'buildup' therapy, as opposed to 'breakdown.' Kids don't come here with a basket overflowing with faults. They also have real strengths. The kids are not rejects. *They are trailblazers, pioneers because they are trying to break out of a destructive cycle.*" The therapeutic community model supports and builds on those strengths. Simultaneously, individuals are taught to see themselves as part of a larger community. Today Veritas, tomorrow the world. Everything is put in a more positive way than at the typical rehab center.

In due course, the nuclear family gets involved in the community. Counseling techniques vary from confrontational to laid back, but all view the kids and their families as brave people trying to do the right thing. No blame is assigned, and the clinician searches for strengths to reinforce. Veritas, in a sense, protects the whole family from the "failure" image society has placed on it. There are punishments, naturally—weekend passes revoked, loss of privileges, demotion in the chain of responsibility. If anyone feels treated unfairly, they can bring it up on Complaint Day, every Wednesday, where you can say or yell anything, provided you don't leave your chair (interpreted as a loss of self-control, or a sign of aggression). Racist or sexist language is prohibited.

A central idea is that no one acts alone, that relationships with other people are the key to coping with drugs. "Addiction" and "addict" are words frowned upon, since they reinforce notions of dominance and submission which the program tries to move beyond. Responsibility for one's actions is consistently reinforced as each resident takes on more decisions and plays a greater role in managing the premises. As progress is made, the individual can trace back to experiences where they were in charge and gradually build up a memory bank of responsible decision making.

Residents, even those on probation, can withdraw from the program anytime they wish, but 65 percent choose to go at least a full year. After that, there is a six-month period where residents work or go to school, using Veritas only for room, board, and minimal counseling.

Since its founding, five hundred people have gone the distance. Veritas realizes the long-term volatility of the condition. Half of those who leave get into some kind of trouble. "We keep in touch, but we're not anxious to substitute as their new dependent authority. We encourage AA programs after that," says Jim. "They really have to make it on their own."

Veritas operates on $38 per resident per day, with both facilities at full capacity, which is always the case. "We are noninstitutional," according to Jim Little. "How could we do this with five hundred people and a staff of twenty? That's how it is at most places. Kids here have shopped around. They love Veritas because they don't get lost in the sauce."

Sadly, Veritas turns away fifty applicants a month it could help. I asked Jim to name other places doing a decent job with rehabilitation. He folded his hands behind his head, leaned back, and stared at the ceiling for a long, silent moment. "I like The Door down on Sixth Avenue in Chelsea, and Apple out in Hauppage, Long Island, and I guess that's it," he shrugged. There are an estimated 200,000 heroin addicts in New York City alone. Established programs, good or bad, can currently provide even minimal services for only 35,000 people. Being on a waiting list for over a year is not uncommon. Jim Little learned patience at the helm of a small ship sailing in what everyone admits is an ocean of misery.

The other program is in the West, in San Francisco's Haight-Ashbury. Where else? It's called the Free Medical Clinic, because that's what it is. Twenty years ago, Dr. David Smith asked, "Why don't we save some lives without telling lies?" The clinic grew out of the 1967 Summer of Love. Its roots are in the hippie era, the days when you wore a flower in your hair and headed for the Haight (renamed Love Street). Community organizers were called the Diggers, and they promoted the utopian Vision of Free. They lived by what we referred to in the sixties as the ideology of the deed. Free stores, free food in the parks, free music, art, and dope, too. In the sixties we probably had the opposite of hysteria in our attitude toward drugs. I don't know what the word is. More than tolerance. Indulgence. Part naïveté, part experimentation, part romanticism, part revolution. Part right and part wrong. You can read my sixties books (if you can find them); it's all there.

(I love my books as much as I do my kids. And like my kids, they often call collect. You can't hang up or disown them either, not in my religion.)

In twenty years, I can't say that I've changed that much either. I don't have flowers in my hair. The hair itself gets thinner as I write. My body's still in the Big Apple, but my heart's in San Francisco.

We, meaning those who organized, symbolized, and led the counterculture, did not champion unlimited or undifferentiated drug use. To the contrary, we had very sharp distinctions between head (psychedelics) and body drugs (stimulants and depressants). Cocaine, by the way, was almost unknown in the sixties. Amphetamines were the choice of those who went nuts over the "up" rush. In terms of popularity, they were latecomers. There may be an economic rule that, like money, bad drugs drive out good drugs.

The big clash was between pot and booze, each symbolic of the generation gap. Pot was what made us, in the Jefferson Airplane's words, "all outlaws in the eyes of Amerika," even though we were "Volunteers of America" (the name of the album). If we were wrong about drugs, we were not *precise* enough. Of course, we tried as volunteers to care for the wounded users. LBJ and Nixon certainly didn't.

No apologies or regrets for the sixties.

The Free Clinic is all that remains of what was noble and utopian of that era and Haight-Ashbury. It's part Robin Hood, Florence Nightingale, Emma Goldman, and Don Quixote. In a rational system, David Smith would be making national policy, not fighting it. The fact that the City of San Francisco funds 90 percent of the project is to its credit and glory. The fact that the Free Clinic has to battle each year for funding to stay alive is similar to the problem Veritas faces.

The Free Clinic is not a small residential program like Veritas, but it is an equally valid model. It is outpatient treatment for whoever wants it, under whatever conditions the individual sets—

all for free. It's a sprawling complex of big, old-fashioned houses (some the old Digger crash pads), storefront offices, a research center, publishing house, consultation rooms. The switchboard handles referrals for every health problem imaginable, and provides information for any number of satellite programs. It services 10,000 people a year ($20 to $35 per capita per day). Ninety percent come on their own.

They treat every addiction you can imagine, from heroin and methadone (55 percent), to booze (20 percent), to coke, Crystal, uppers (15 percent), to Valium, Librium, and the other downers (6 percent), to pot, Ecstasy, and other hallucinogens (1–3 percent). Nicotine, sugar, caffeine, and substance addictions that have no defined category are also treated. One client is a fourteen-year-old kid still badly shaken by a trip on Adam, another a sixty-five-year-old man who can't kick Darvon. Any case mentioned in this book could be treated at the Free Clinic.

Best of all, they are totally nonjudgmental and nonpunitive. You are not required to give your real name to get treated. In fact, some people are encouraged to use pseudonyms, in case the Enforcers try to turn the place into a big snitch factory, and get curious about patient data.

"Our goal," says Dr. Inaba, director of the De-tox Clinic, "is to free the individual of dependency. We serve the individual. We believe you have to protect addicts *from* society, not vice-versa." If individuals wish to control habits or quit forever, the Clinic will adjust its treatment plan accordingly. They are superconscious of civil rights, use no controlling drugs, and consider urine tests "just crazy, good for nothing."

Dr. Inaba is typical of the staff. Low-paid. Crusading. Activist. Overworked. And a twenty-year veteran of the Clinic. Astonishingly, many of the founders are still working there, giving new meaning to the word dedication. Dr. Inaba is a Japanese-American born in a concentration camp (forced relocation center) in Colorado during World War II. All the staff have interesting backgrounds.

The Free Clinic uses drugs for symptom removal—for example, clonidine, an anti–high blood pressure drug which seems to lock out stimuli to the locus cerelius, the section of the brain responsible for withdrawal symptoms. Since they are a full medical service, they also use drugs to treat side effects, like nausea, and insomnia. But they use "substances with credibility." Benadryl for insomnia. Quanadine for pain. No Seconals or Darvon with these two symptoms. Methadone is forbidden.

Therapy of every possible description is the backbone of treatment. Everything from one-on-one psychotherapy to group therapy, outpatient groups, Alcoholics Anonymous, Addicts Anonymous, Artist and Writers Support Groups. Family therapy is difficult, given the itinerant street clientele.

Many patients are runaways. Many are homeless. The waiting rooms flow into the stoops and streets. A visit is a personal trip back in time and consciousness. You'd swear every strung-out hippie, every casualty back from Nam was right there, just as they were on June 9, 1967, when the place was founded.

The Clinic hasn't changed its ideals, but there's been increased acceptance by the national treatment community. *The Journal of Psychoactive Drugs*, which it publishes, is considered full of important data by serious researchers and clinicians of all persuasions because of the vast numbers treated, also because whatever new drug problem exists hits the Clinic first. When cocaine and subsequently crack hit the streets of America, the Clinic gained a respectable niche because they had helped the first victims. They recently reported an increase in the median age of users. In the sixties, most users were in their late teens. In 1987, it's thirty-year-olds. This augurs an aging addict population that will occur nationwide shortly. Even Reagan once paid a compliment to the Free Clinic because it fit the supply-side notion of not sending the federal government the bill. But worry not, Nancy will never pay a visit there.

Inside, it's hard to tell amateurs from professionals, paid staff from volunteers. Sometimes glassy-eyed staffers are confused with glassy-eyed clients. They hire ex-addicts, like almost every rehab center, but they are more aware of this being a tricky and complex issue. "Ex-addicts can be very good, or they can often be too arrogant or too sympathetic," says Dr. Inaba. "Since we admit the long-term nature of the illness, they often go back to drugs." There is no such thing as a cure. Success is measured by how many "bond" to a recovery process. Forty percent bond to some form of treatment, while the majority limit use of drug intake by developing slightly longer coping periods.

Sadly, the only thing wrong with the Free Clinic is that it can't handle the load. Five hundred people per month are turned away. "People literally die to get in here," says the Good Doctor. "Our figures show 15 percent attempt suicide [about seventy a week] because we can't provide the facilities." There is just the right proportion of anger, compassion, and cold-blooded warrior in his eye.

Welcome to the real War on Drugs.

PART II

Urine Testing

7.

Courting Disaster
with the Constitution

On May 26, 1986, Memorial Day, the city of Plainfield, New Jersey, inspired by the War on Drugs, launched a dawn attack on its own fire department.

At 6:30 A.M., the Plainfield fire chief, the director of public affairs, and a small battalion of Bladder Cops burst into the city firehouse, bolted all exits, woke everyone up, and announced, "Rise and shine!" A surprise urine test was about to begin.

One by one, each worker present was led into the fire chief's office and ordered to submit a urine sample under the direct observation of hired voyeurs. Some protested. Months later, fireman Fulton Allen, on PBS's public-affairs program "Currents," recalled, "When I went to take my urinalysis, they had a guy in there with me. I never saw this guy before, and I couldn't urinate with somebody watching. So he said, 'I'll turn my back.' I said, 'No, what are you, gay?' This is how I felt!" Allen threw his hands up in a combination of despair and disbelief.

Objections by the firefighters were overruled on the spot, and the city extracted what it wanted. Each urine sample was carefully labeled, sealed, and shipped off for drug evaluation.

Flush with victory, the city decided to strike again. Twice more, on May 28 and June 12, urine troopers raided the same station, on different shifts, until virtually all 103 workers had been trapped and tested. Those who refused were threatened. "I felt that my rights were being violated," said Cecil Allen, another firefighter. "I didn't see any reason why I had to give this urine test. But according to the city, I either had to give the urine test or be suspended . . . I felt totally violated."

While both city officials and firefighters awaited the next strike, the atmosphere at the station house grew tense. No one was sure exactly what or who was going to go down. And then, as mysteriously as they had begun, the raids stopped. A few weeks passed, the fire fighters thought the issue was dead, and no one was any the worse. They were happy to join with millions of their fellow Americans in celebrating Liberty Week. The firefighters offered silent thanks to the great Statue Goddess in the harbor that their bladders hadn't turned them in. "Thank you, great Lady of the Light," they murmured, as the sky above their heads exploded with 3 million dollars' worth of fireworks.

Suddenly, the light went out. Between July 10 and July 14, sixteen workers were notified that their urine had tested positive for "controlled dangerous substances." They were summarily terminated. No severance pay. No appeal. No confirmation testing. Nothing. They were simply out of their jobs and on the street. Laboratory results and the substances found in their urine were, as far as the Firehouse 16 were concerned, classified information.

As if losing their jobs wasn't enough, ten days later they were charged with "commission of a criminal act," and informed that legal action against them was pending. Miller Time this was not.

Striking back, the Firehouse 16 sued (Ben Capua et al. vs. City of Plainfield). U.S. District Judge H. Lee Sarokin was impressed enough with the complaint to issue a temporary restraining order. He ordered a halt to all drug testing (the city had already started in on the police department), and reinstated those who had been fired.

Harold Gibson, Director of Public Safety for Plainfield, claimed responsibility for the whole operation. "The firefighters were not the enemy," he explained to the PBS audience. "I'd be the first to admit that. However, in determining who the enemy was in this particular set of circumstances, it was necessary to put everybody through the metal detector, so to speak. And that's what we did.

"We, as administrators, should be allowed to impinge on those

Constitutional rights in order to accomplish the objective of determining whether they're drug abusers or not," he finished.

At the subsequent trial, Judge Sarokin held that the discharged workers' expectations of privacy were severely compromised by random compulsory urinalysis:

> The sweeping manner which the [officials] set about to accomplish their goals violated the firefighters' individual liberties. The search was unreasonable because defendants [the city] lacked any suspicion as to that [individual] firefighter. . . . The indivious effect of such mass, round-up urinalysis is that it casually sweeps up the innocent with the guilty and willingly sacrifices each individual's Fourth Amendment right in the name of some larger public interest. The City of Plainfield essentially presumed the guilt of each person tested.

The Court ruled for the discharged firefighters. They were permanently reinstated, with back pay. The Judge's rebuke was a strong legal blow to urine testing. He did not mince words:

> We would be appalled at the specter of the police spying on employees during their free time and then reporting their activities to their employers. Drug testing is a form of surveillance, albeit a technological one. Nonetheless it reports on a person's off-duty activities just as surely as if someone had been present and watching. It is George Orwell's 'Big Brother' Society come to life.

Judge Sarokin added:

> If we choose to violate the rights of the innocent in order to discover and act against the guilty, then we have transformed our country into a police state and abandoned one of the fundamental tenets of our free society. In order to win the war against drugs, we must not sacrifice the life of the Constitution in the battle.

The city of Plainfield grudgingly reinstated the workers and did not appeal the decision. As strong as Judge Sarokin's ruling was, it should be noted that it attacked only the *circumstances* surrounding urine testing. It did not rule that the procedure in and of itself is unconstitutional. The Court of Appeals was not asked to review judgment. The District Court's findings are narrowly limited to this single incident, and possibly to others involving random, compulsory screening in the judge's district.

Others have not been deterred. The Tennessee Valley Authority, for one, currently sanctions dawn raids on the homes of suspect workers, demanding that they accompany agents to a place suitable for collecting urine samples. Regarding mass surveillance without adequate suspicion, the case most under discussion and probably the first to go before the Supreme Court (possibly within one year) is the *National Treasury Employees Union, Chapter 168 vs. U.S. Customs Service*. In November 1986, the union sought an injunction against a U.S. Customs Service drug-testing program. All workers seeking promotion had to submit to a urine test. Employees who tested positive were denied promotion and subject to disciplinary action. The injunction, which would have been applicable throughout the Customs Service, was filed in the U.S. District for the Eastern District of Louisiana. The District Court judge agreed with the plaintiffs and ordered a halt to all testing. The Justice Department appealed, and on April 22, 1987, the Fifth Circuit Court of Appeals in a two-to-one decision overturned the lower court. The Customs Service was permitted to reinstate its program. Judge Alvin Rubin, writing for the majority, declared:

> Compulsory urine testing by the government constitutes a search for purposes of the Fourth Amendment. . . . Because of the strong governmental interest in employing individuals for key positions in drug enforcement who themselves are not drug users and the limited intrusiveness of this particular program, it is reasonable, and therefore it is not unconstitutional.

Two factors—a search's reasonability and public safety concerns—have been the focus of additional appellate court decisions.

McDonell et al. vs. Hunter, in the Eighth Circuit Court of Appeals, concerns prison guards in Iowa who brought suit to invalidate what they considered persecution, that is, urine testing precipitated by an unsubstantiated letter accusing several guards of keeping "improper" company. The U.S. District Court judge found for the plantiffs; the procedure was an unreasonable search under the Fourth Amendment, lacking probable cause, standards, and specificity. Civil libertarians breathed again.

But on January 12, 1987, the Federal Appeals Court for Iowa reversed *McDonell,* declaring "the need to maintain prison discipline and security justifies urinalysis. . . . Reasonable suspicion to test any employee exists within prison property by virtue of the criminal atmosphere." Public safety is placed above the guards' reasonable expectation to privacy.

Similar logic had been applied in New York State *(Storms et al. vs. Coughlin),* the significant difference being this action involved prisoners instead of guards. The court ruled: "Because of their debt to society and the enhanced need for security, prisoners have severely limited rights." State officials have the power to ensure internal prison safety by applying mass drug-testing techniques as they see fit.

Another group in our society also faces limitations of their rights as compared to the rest of the population. In 1983, a U.S. Military Court of Appeals case, *Murray vs. Haldeman,* affirmed the government's contention that Department of Defense personnel, by virtue of their pledge to service, should have comparatively limited expectations of privacy than their civilian counterparts. This factor, coupled with a proven high incidence of drug abuse among recruits (i.e. reasonable suspicion), earned the Pentagon the right to screen *all* its troops under any conditions. Since 1981, the Pentagon has made full use of the ruling and tests all troops. In general, confined societies, whether enforcing the law or being punished by it, have truncated rights.

Often cited by testing proponents, *Shoemaker et al. vs. Handel* was a landmark decision. This case, advocates claim, established reasonable search without justifiable suspicion directed at any particular individual. Willie Shoemaker and four celebrated jockeys brought suit in fall 1985 challenging the New Jersey Racing Commission's regulations requiring mandatory breathalyzer and urine tests at state racetracks. U.S. District Judge Brotman dismissed their action: "Warrantless [biochemical tests] were reasonable in light of the regulated nature of horse racing and the government's interest in maintaining the integrity of the industry and safety of the sport." The decision was upheld on review by the Third Circuit Court of Appeals. The District Court judge made it clear that he was ruling not for compulsory testing, but only for integrity in this particular gaming sport. He also reasoned that jockeys had already come to expect limits on their privacy by previous regulation: "The public has a special interest in the strict regulation of horse racing. This industry has always been pervasively regulated in order to minimize the criminal influence to which it was so prone."

While the ruling did not appear to support unrestricted applications, it has since been used as a precedent in disparate cases. Judge H. Lee Sarokin thought that a narrow interpretation of *Shoemaker* would be in the national interest. In *Capua vs. Plainfield* he explained his reluctance: "Widespread application of *Shoemaker* would violate that court's apparent intention." Nonetheless, appellate courts in Iowa and Louisiana both cited *Shoemaker* as a precedent for their findings against prison guards and customs workers.

While the above case histories appear pretty damaging to urine testing opposition, the future is not without hope. *Capua et al. vs. City of Plainfield* is not the only case that has invalidated a urine-testing program. Challenges have struck down testing involving high school teachers and students, police officers, school bus aides, and municipal workers. However, Attorney General Meese is confident that most will be overturned on appeal. Success in Louisiana and Iowa testify to his determination.

The judicial history of biochemical testing is fairly new, dating back to 1966. It was then that the Supreme Court first applied the Fourth and Fifth Amendments to medical surveillance technology, specifically blood tests. The case, *Schmerber vs. California*, was a landmark decision that established precedent for two decades.

The facts were straightforward enough. The defendant was a driver involved in a serious auto accident. The policeman at the scene smelled alcohol on his breath. This observation, coupled with outward familiar signs of intoxication, led to Schmerber's arrest. A blood sample was taken, without court order and over the objection of the defendant. Chemical analysis revealed a blood alcohol level sufficient to imply impairment. The blood test was accepted as evidence in trial and Schmerber was convicted.

On appeal, the defense claimed that involuntary withdrawal of the defendant's blood violated the Fifth Amendment right against self-incrimination. It also argued that Fourth Amendment rights were ignored and that the blood test was an unreasonable search and seizure.

The Supreme Court's ruling, as is generally the case with groundbreaking decisions, was decided along narrow lines. "The Fifth Amendment privilege protects an accused from being compelled to testify against himself, or otherwise provide the State with *evidence of a testimonial or communicative nature.*" (Emphasis added.) The Court decided that the blood sample constituted *physical evidence*, not testimony. Further, physical evidence, since it is silent, does not incriminate a witness against oneself. The upshot: the Fifth Amendment did not protect Schmerber, and it does not today apply in any urine-testing cases.

The second argument concerning unreasonable search and seizure was more analogous to modern-day screening. The Court found that a blood test *did* fall under the definition of a search, as defined by the Fourth Amendment. However, the Court felt the search was reasonable since the arresting officer made an *objective* inference regarding Schmerber's intoxication. The warrantless blood sample was necessary to obtain evidence before metabolism diluted the alcohol. Further, the blood was extracted *in due process* since it was done by a trained medical authority. Without the objective inference, the search would have been unreasonable and the evidence invalid.

Schmerber set two precedents which have since been mentioned in all drug-testing trials: 1) Physical evidence—blood, hair, breath, or urine—taken directly from a witness does not come under protection against self-incrimination; 2) Any medical test is a Fourth Amendment search, subject to Constitutional limitations.

Although the Court ruled against Schmerber, the majority opinion narrowed testing's legal applications. Justice William Brennan cautioned: "That we today hold that the Constitution does not forbid minor intrusions into an individual's body under stringently limited conditions in no way indicates that it permits more substantial intrusions, or intrusions under other conditions." In 1966, no one could predict mass drug screening, but the Earl Warren Court had enough prescience to caution against potential abuses.

The *Schmerber* doctrine was updated in 1985, when blood samples became passé and urine became the "in" specimen. The case was *Division 241 Amalgamated Transit Union vs. Suscy*. A labor union representing bus drivers brought action against the Chicago Transit Authority. At issue was the constitutionality of a work rule requiring *all* drivers to submit urine samples following a serious accident, or when suspected by superiors of impairment by alcohol or drugs. The Federal District Court noted that the Transit Authority, as a public operator, had an overwhelming interest in protecting the public from injury. To achieve this, it tried to ensure that its drivers were fit to work. *The court concluded that the drivers' expectations of privacy could legally be compromised when an issue of public safety is involved*. The conditions for imposing a drug test were limited by the "serious accident" or suspected impairment work rules. These built-in restraints, if adhered to, made any drug test given by the Transit Authority valid under the Constitution.

Suscy declared that a government agency can place reasonable restrictions on public employment. It went beyond the Supreme Court's decision in *Schmerber*, creating a balancing test for drug screening: "The Fourth Amendment protects an individual's reasonable expectation of privacy from unreasonable intrusion by the State. Whether the individual has a reasonable expectation of privacy and whether the intrusion is reasonable are determined by balancing the claims of the public against the interest of the individual." Today, the applicable standard is that drug tests are a suitable means for detecting impairment when *just cause* for their use can be determined. This decision has been upheld by the appellate court. Subsequent cases, notably *Allen vs. City of Marietta*, reaffirm the principle of balance.

"Public safety," "just cause," and "reasonable suspicion" are phrases common to most drug-testing decisions. They are also the vaguest, most subjective part of each decision, and definitions vary from case to case. At present, no guidelines exist telling an employer or police officer when testing is or isn't absolutely permitted. Tests have been judged appropriate and reasonable in strangely divergent situations, allowed when a supervisor smells alcohol on a worker's breath, an employee displays erratic and unusual behavior, or a manager has "on good authority" an indication of drug use. In *McDonell*, a simple unconfirmed letter tipping off association with "improper" company was sufficient.

On June 9, 1987, in the most encouraging decision to date, the New York State Court of Appeals ruled unanimously to limit drug testing of public school teachers without reasonable suspicion. Chief Judge Sol Wachtler held that individuals subjected to urine tests fall under protection of federal and state constitutional provisions against unreasonable searches and seizures. A dozen different state courts have been asked to rule on cases identical to *Patchogue-Medford Congress of Teachers vs. Patchogue Board of Education*.

Yet other courts have invalidated drug testing programs for apparently similar reasons. *Patchogue-Medford Congress of Teachers vs. Patchogue Board of Education* struck down compulsory testing where the Board of Education "failed to show an objective, factual basis for inferring that any one of the subject teachers uses or has used illegal drugs."

Although state courts are independent of other state judiciaries and the federal system, the New York State court system is highly respected across the country. Ultimately, *Patchogue* could lead to two distinct bodies of law, where the states limit testing and the federal courts allow random, mass applications. Such a standoff only hastens Supreme Court action.

The New York City Police Department's Organized Crime Control Bureau was forced to abandon its program when the New York Supreme Court found no "reasonable belief" of suspicion to invoke testing (*Caruso vs. Ward*). Yet at the same time regular police officers in New York City are required to submit to drug tests three times during their probationary period and the Department has proposed random tests for all officers. The random program is presently being challenged in court. The Superior Court of New

Jersey invalidated a Bergen County requirement that high school students be tested when no individualized suspicion existed (*Odenheim vs. Carlstradt-East Rutherford Region School District*). There are several other examples.

With respect to "public safety," the broadest range of occupations seems to be accepted. Just think for a minute about the variety of occupations that relate to your own "public safety." Construction workers, elevator operators, electricians, drivers, sports fans, pharmacists, rock bands that show up three hours late for concerts, hospital personnel, hang gliders. You get the idea. An argument could be made for just about any occupation.

Not all matters in the court system are determined by formal suit ending in final adjudication. If a party facing litigation decides not to contest the charge, a consent decree may be issued by the court, binding both parties to a mutually acceptable resolution. A few federal agencies appear so uncertain of their right to test workers that they've settled actions out of court, rather than risk judicial censure. Other agencies have accepted consent decrees. In Philadelphia on February 28, 1986, a class action was filed against the U.S. Postal Service. The plaintiffs, a group of job applicants, were required to submit to urinalysis drug screening as part of the hiring process. They claimed their rejections based on positive test results were discriminatory and unconstitutional. Instead of going to trial, the U.S. Justice Department approved a consent decree requiring the Philadelphia Post Office "terminate its present policy and practice of requiring all applicants for employment to submit to urinalysis drug testing." The Post Office also promised never to test again in Philadelphia unless mandated by the Postmaster General. $5,000, priority employment, and legal fees were awarded each of the plaintiffs as partial settlement.

Consent decrees have limited value to persons beyond the immediate case, since no precedent is established and no guilt is assumed. The Justice Department in the Philadelphia case feared the plaintiffs had some legitimacy to their argument. A consent decree was an expedient way of avoiding a direct hit to the Presidential Executive Order mandating a drug-free federal workplace.

Unreported by the press, a substantial number of actions have been settled out of court by urine-testing proponents, who prefer a discreet ending to unfavorable judgment or prolonged litigation. From February 1983 through March 1986, hundreds of individual, small group, and class action suits were weaving through the federal court maze. And although no court flatly ruled against urine testing per se, the clear trend was to see things from the plaintiffs' (i.e. the aggrieved) point of view. Thirteen of seventeen key District Court decisions, a worthy majority, limited testing procedures.

The tide turned quickly, however. In spring 1987, appellate courts reversed several decisions and affirmed others where the federal agency or municipality was initially judged to have committed no wrong. The Louisiana treasury employees decision was an especially cruel blow since Meese had earlier decided not to pursue a reversal. Once optimistic, civil liberties attorneys in May 1987 sounded a more pessimistic note. Paul Samuels, executive vice president of the Legal Action Center (NYC), expressed his chagrin in a *New York Times* interview: "Before [the Louisiana customs workers reversal], we had virtual unanimity against drug testing. The only fair statement to say right now is that we're in a new ballgame, and we don't know what the rules are going to be." (*New York Times* 5/18/87) Many lawyers, according to the *Times*, considered urine testing *the* privacy issue of the decade: "The legal problem posed by unannounced random testing is that it may permit arbitrary 'searches' which courts have long rejected." The problem is compounded when you consider that such searches are not only unlawful, but that hysteria itself may be defining legality.

Every case discussed above concerns federal, state, or municipal employees, the military, prisoners with forfeited privacy rights, and high school students—the whole public sector. In short, the courts have traditionally held that custodial power resides with a supervising agency. But these cases represent scarcely 20 percent of the entire labor pool. Despite talk of big government and bloated bureaucracy, at least 80 percent of our labor pool works in the private sector. Moreover, assumptions or findings made about these cases are not applicable to the overwhelming majority who do work in government.

Workers in private industry have always had comparatively fewer protections than their public-sector counterparts. Devised as a pact between citizens and their government, the Constitution protects citizens from intrusive government activity only. Regarding employment, the Constitution controls only the public workplace. It was never intended to monitor citizens' economic relationships. (After all, slavery was condoned for seventy-five years.) On this matter, states were left to their own devices. Extension of fundamental rights was up to the localities themselves. When regular workers are protected, it comes from state constitutions, human-rights and privacy legislation. These differ across the nation; in fact, most states lack any real protection from overbearing employers.

Varying protections have meant a weaker workforce. Unless specifically proscribed by legislation, a private employer can impose virtually any standard he wants. Over 100 years ago, federal courts determined that employers could dismiss their workers for good cause, for no cause, or even for cause morally wrong, without running afoul of the law. The principle remains unchanged today. Ira Glasser, executive director of the American Civil Liberties Union, commented, "The absence of statute or union agreement gives an employer virtual free rein."

Free rein is not an absolute. Over the years, limits have been applied where safety or dignity is jeopardized. Minimum wage laws, occupational safety and health requirements, child labor laws, civil and vocational rights acts are testimony to American industry's insensitivity when left unregulated. Without restraint, business has often put itself above human dignity for the sake of profit or domination; employers have the upper hand when it comes to employment. Still, challenges to hiring and firing practices are generally brought against contractors doing business with the federal government. The recent Simpson-Mazzolli Illegal Alien Act is one example of government deciding whom private business can and cannot employ. In practice, these laws are often ignored, and a labor force less than 20 percent unionized has little power to press grievances.

Even in the face of disintegrating power, collective bargaining agreements remain one area where unions can effectively enjoin drug testing. Both the District Court of Oregon and the National Labor Relations Board (NLRB) declared that drug testing is a required collective bargaining issue, included among mandatory negotiating subjects (i.e. wages, hours, and working conditions). An employer who refuses to negotiate in good faith or violates a contract is subject to punishment by the NLRB *(Association of Western Pulp and Paper Workers vs. Boise Cascade Corp.)*. This is one reason why compulsory drug testing has so far not come to professional sports. Players' associations, stronger than industrial unions, have refused to accept such procedures without negotiation.

Some state constitutions (nine, to be exact) have individual privacy codes stronger than the federal Constitution. But except in relatively minor matters (i.e. an employer cannot discharge a worker for serving on a jury), state courts back off from the issue of disrupting employer controls over workers. Only in California have courts actively sought to use the state constitution to protect those in the private sector.

The disparity between public and private employees is frightening. It seems like a worker is being penalized for his or her selection of workplace. Rules which prevent excessive intrusion have not kept pace with corporate growth. A company security guard faces far fewer constraints than a real policemen or federal agents with respect to privacy. While underground, I once had a job in a large hotel restaurant. Every night upon leaving, each and every worker was patted down by security guards in an effort to prevent illegal steak exportation. Police, under Forth Amendment constraints, do not have this right to pat down indiscriminately.

As companies have expanded, they have tended to assume more and more control over their workers. The Reagan battle cry of "less government" has ostensibly encouraged employer domination. When government is not anxious to control, Corporate America is only to happy to step in. If companies want to weed out undesirables with urine tests, the Reagan Administration stands ready to hold the cup.

Despite limited protections, a handful of suits have been filed in the private sector. All are based on violations of state privacy laws. The cost of litigation is prohibitive to most workers. Legal organizations (such as those recommended in the appendix) recruit victimized employees, in the hopes of establishing precedent cases that may ultimately protect others. Often, litigation is the only chance a penalized worker has to gain reinstatement and/or restitution. As of this writing, no final decisions in private sector cases have been given. Challenges are too recent. However, a few pending actions are worth noting for the promise they hold.

• *Jennings et al. vs. Minco Technology Labs.* Brenda Jennings, a gutsy Texan, brought a class action suit challenging the legality of Minco Labs' mandatory, mass urinalysis. She contends they are issued randomly, and without just cause. This violates the State of Texas Right to Privacy; the Texas right to be free from unlawful search and seizure; and due process. Among other complaints is the degrading way the tests are administered. Workers are placed under close physical surveillance while urinating, to prevent sample tampering. There's a fine line between watching someone urinate and sexual harassment. The confidential information contained in the urine "gives rise to the spectre of pretextual use for illegal job discrimination and unjust employment deprivation." Jennings contends that urine screens give the boss access to information long considered private. Ms. Jennings is seeking injunctive relief, damages, and a halt to drug screening of all Minco workers.

Similar charges were brought in a federal case discussed earlier, *Ben Capua vs. City of Plainfield.* Judge Sarokin ruled against the testers: forcing an employee to urinate in front of another person violated all standards of human dignity and was particularly distasteful to the court. Is it any less distasteful in the private sector?

• *David Sutton vs. Olympia Forest Products.* Several employees were discharged after a single unconfirmed EMIT test (taken as part of a physical exam) proved positive for marijuana. The workers denied ever reporting to work impaired by any drug. Members of the suit contend Olympia had no probable cause to suspect employees and issue such a test. The urinalysis and subsequent firings, they argue, go against Washington State public policy—that an individual shall be free from invasion of private affairs without authority of law (Constitution of State of Washington, Article 1,

Section 7). Also, the Washington labor code prohibits the basing of employment decisions on tests which are unconfirmed and have a propensity for error. The plaintiffs have filed for permanent injunction against Olympia's testing programs, and compensation.

While these cases are pending, more encouraging news has come by way of temporary restraining orders. Randy Price and four colleagues had been urine-terminated by the Pacific Refining Company, and have sued (*Price et al. vs. Pacific Refining*). Their allegations are similar to other cases. The plaintiffs hold that Pacific's policy violates the freedom from unreasonable invasion of privacy, as detailed by the California State Constitution; that the confidential information in the urine sample violated the California Civil Code, which grants citizens the right to maintain confidentiality of medical information; that Pacific's labor screening policies were unlawful business practices under California Business and Profession Code, and the California Labor Code.

Judge Edward L. Merrill of the California Superior Court was so impressed with the complaint and its implications for the remaining Pacific workforce that he issued a temporary restraining order prior to hearing the actual case. The judge required immediate reinstatement of the fired workers and suspension of all drug testing until trial, which is expected to begin late this year.

To the ACLU of Northern California, which represents the dismissed workers, *Price vs. Pacific* has the makings of a major victory for opponents of drug testing. Remarked ACLU lawyer Loren Siegel, "Companies which have implemented universal or random drug-testing programs are on thin ice and can expect to be challenged in the future."

Even greater optimism is building over Montana, Vermont, and Iowa recently (spring 1987) signing into law bills limiting the circumstances of urine testing. This trend, along with a growing propensity for state judges to become more activist on the issue, leads anti-testing authorities to view state legislatures as a more productive battleground. Says Loren Siegel, "Given the political climate in the federal system, state courts probably offer the better chances." The New York Appeals Court decision against mandatory testing of teachers lends weight to this strategy. At the risk of restating the obvious, the more states that have enacted limits on drug testing the better. The Supreme Court gives serious consideration to the states' legislative right.

Predicting the future of drug testing in the courts is about as easy as picking the NCAA Basketball champion. No court has yet ruled out urine tests, and the cases involving the public sector have generally not met with success at the appeals level, where it really counts. "I think it's going to be very difficult now to overturn the Executive Order," commented Kenneth Feinberg, Professor of Law at Georgetown University Law Center (*New York Times* 3/18/87).

The status of arbitrary mass surveillance is still unclear. Permitted for Louisiana customs employees, similar tests were not judged legal for the Plainfield firefighters. However, when the circumstances hinge on "reasonable suspicion," "public safety," or where a measure of privacy has been signed away, urine testing appears to have the upper hand. Also, the testing of new job applicants presently appears acceptable since this segment of society lives virtually in no-rights-land. In order to avoid potential lawsuits, standard company policy is not to disclose why a job applicant has been rejected. Millions of people fall into each allowable exemption. Besides, in our mobile society, the vast majority of workers will at one time or another find themselves "new job applicants." If random, unannounced tests are ultimately approved by the Supreme Court as well, a dark cloud will descend upon the civil liberties of all Americans. The paranoids in this case could be right.

The Supreme Court, which will eventually decide the urine-testing issues, has not been as isolated from the rest of the government or the clamor of the mob as high school civics books would teach.

Political fashion often sways the interpretation of legality. When slavery was in existence, the court approved the Dred Scott decision, leaving Missouri a half-free, half-slave state. After the sit-ins and freedom rides of the late fifties, the Court reversed its stand on segregation (read: apartheid) and that triggered Congress into passing a series of Civil and Voting Rights Acts. In 1972, it outlawed capital punishment as being cruel and unusual. Later it changed its mind and left the life-and-death decision to the individual states. Obscenity rulings bend with the crowd noise. Public sentiment may—in theory—be a secondary factor in determining civil liberties, but given enough pressure, politically expedient decisions are common. Washington D.C. is the place one learns to rise above principle. All branches of government live by that premise.

With two more Reagan appointments, the Supreme Court could be ready to reverse *Roe vs. Wade* and women would lose the right to choose what goes on in their own bodies. Issues of morality, like drugs, are influenced by the prejudices of the Justices themselves. As one of our greatest Chief Justices, Charles Evans Hughes, remarked, "The Constitution is what the judges say it is."

This is clearly a Reagan Court. Chief Justice Rehnquist and Associate Justices Scalia and O'Connor are his contribution to judicial conservatism. Retirement of Justice Powell, considered an unpredictable swing vote, allows the appointment of another solid Reagan ideologist. Already he is responsible for half the appointments to the federal bench, and the bulk of decisions supporting testing have the blessing of Reagan appointees. Supreme Court Justices Brennan and Marshall, guardians of civil rights, are in their late 70's and reportedly in poor health. What marks Reagan's candidates are their strong, similar political convictions and comparative youth by federal judgeship standards.

In closing, let me mention one of the most flagrant misuses of mass drug screening imaginable. About four years ago, the Washington D.C. Superior Court's prison system began a urine-testing program which is so outrageous several other jail systems are, naturally, beginning to copy it. All arrestees facing *any* criminal charge and held overnight must submit to a urine test. Using EMIT screens, inmates are tested for five controlled substances—amphetamines, cocaine, opiates, methadone, and PCP. About 300 people arrested are tested every morning between 6 and 9 A.M. (the first urine of the day is the most concentrated, and therefore the most potentially damaging). The results, which take about 20 minutes to process, are used in establishing conditions of release. A positive result can affect amount of bail, conditions of bail, release on personal cognizance, and the like. *Everyone is tested,* whether the alleged crime is drug-related, murder, or civil disobedience.

The Pre-trial Services Division of the Superior Court runs the program. "There is virtually one hundred percent compliance," noted Supervisor John Carver. What happens if you refuse? "If the judge wants to, you can be held in contempt of court," he said. "If you refuse to be tested," says Washington attorney Nina Kraut, "you get no appearance before a judge. Which means no release conditions are set."

Someone has to defy the program successfully, or it will soon become common practice. Mayor Koch has recommended a similar system for New York City's Rikers Island. Anyone in jail is naturally very anxious to get out and get out quickly. Giving up Constitutional rights along with some urine seems minor compared to the horror of a crowded, violent jail. My last experience in the D.C. jail was memorable. I was arrested for wearing a shirt that resembled the American flag, while protesting being hauled before the House Un-American Activities Committee. The news, without telling of the details, claimed it was "desecration of the flag." The guards assumed that I had burned Old Glory. In jail, refusing to give a blood sample, they pinned me to the floor and jabbed in the needle. Eight weeks to the day, I came down with serum hepatitis. It was a type transmitted only through infected needles, with a two-month incubation period. I was convinced the guards had infected me on purpose. A subsequent lawsuit proved unsuccessful, but did reveal an extraordinarily high rate of serum hepatitis in that rotten D.C. jail. Someone—maybe me if arrested protesting government policy in a demonstration—has to just say no to the D.C. jailer. Lawyers cannot go to court without clients.

Fighting urine tests is lonely work, carried out in dark places. But someone's got to do it!

8.

Washroom Politics in the Age of Hysteria

In the Washington Heights section of Manhattan, one of the most original examples of Enforcer guerrilla theater took place on July 10, 1986.

The scene: early evening, a tenement block. Run-DMC competes with Public Enemy on the ghetto blasters, skateboard freaks cartwheel, double-dutch jump rope teams strut their acrobatics. People in undershirts lean out of brownstone windows, fanning themselves with the *Amsterdam News*. Three-card Monte gets hustled on the corner while folks play chess on the stoops or read the *Daily Racing Form*. Prostitutes congregate by the all-night deli, spandex fantasies for the bridge and tunnel crowd. Young entrepreneurs in friendly competition hawk their products to sidewalk and street traffic. Smoke, 'ludes, crystal, and the "Live at Five" hit of the week—crack.

The street teems with apartment dwellers, free of their sun-baked cubicles for a few hours. What looks like chaos to tourists appears perfectly normal to the relative up from Atlanta or Chicago, or even the brother from another planet. Virtually everyone is black. Just a normal summer night in the Heights.

Enter a plainclothes mobile Enforcer team on special assignment. The mission: seek out and purchase $1,000 worth of crack while maintaining absolute secrecy about the members' identities. Difficult, given the presence of an unmarked van with a protruding twelve-foot TV antenna.

Three of the team members nervously break away, looking for

the big score. Passersby watch in confusion. Even in this area of displaced persons they are strangely out of place. This is no run-of-the-mill Mod Squad.

The paunchy, aging UPS deliveryman is none other than U.S. Senator Alfonse ("Big Al") D'Amato, minus the trademark horn-rims. The tall Hell's Angel sporting a fifty-dollar custom razor cut (but without the Harley) is U.S. Attorney and nightly TV news actor Rudolph Giuliani. Benjamin Baer, chairman of the U.S. Parole Commission, incognito, pulls up at the rear.

Their quest isn't as tough as finding gold in the Klondike, and is accomplished with all deliberate speed. They are well briefed, these bureaucrats; they know all the lingo, the gestures. "Crack?" "Yeah, two hits." "A Jackson?" The hands mesh, the "wool" (money) is passed, the vial palmed. Taxpayer dollars quickly exchanged for a ten-minute rush. The same exchange is repeated several times so the van can film the best angles and cutaways.

One chess player looks up, recognizes the white faces and ill-fitting disguises. He jokes that election time must be near and goes back to the game.

That night, millions of TV viewers witness the most famous drug purchase/campaign stunt in history. The Washington Heights crack dealers also watch the news, with an extra dose of paranoia. When no police arrive the next day, they are confused. Then, as paranoia and confusion ebb, they assume that selling crack to senators must be legal. Close curtain.

The headlines came and went. Big Al easily won re-election in November and Giuliani soon moved on to bigger news dramas on Wall Street. The crack dealers relocated to Washington. Whether D'Amato's crack was any good, where it went, whether the three were fronting for a dangerous ring, we'll never know. There are 8 million stories in the Naked City; there are still 8 million tonight.

For a nation so inclined to monitor the smallest details, the absence of legislation regulating biochemical testing is surprising. In contrast, penalties for *drug abuse* have flourished. Certainly, time has something to do with it. Abuse has been a problem for centuries. Drug testing is only a few decades old. Nonetheless, testing has led to misuses which should have been addressed earlier.

Blame for the imbalance can be placed at the top. For the last seven years, the Reagan administration has hammered the evils of addiction into the public consciousness. Intensive lobbying efforts have led to severe criminal penalties for smugglers, manufacturers, users, and paraphernalia distributers. Glass pipes, cigarette papers, scales, fancy little spoons, razor blades, even common plumbing supplies have been legally confiscated by police. From the age of five, schoolchildren are indoctrinated with the First Lady's mantra, "Just say no." With these impressive tactics, it's little wonder that suspect Enforcer traps for "catching" drug users are unrestricted.

Other than the stated moral imperative, the political foundation of the hysteria is clear. Soviet military superiority and foreign subversion—two favorite obsessions—threaten a society allegedly swarming with junkies. "Drug pushers and users are as dangerous to our national security as any terrorist or foreign dictatorship," claimed the President. In other words, getting rid of drug users reduces spiritual weakness and restores the will to resist a Communist takeover. Hey, you saw ABK-TV's "Amerikaka." Who wants to be forced to watch ballet instead of "Wheel of Fortune"?

Before the 1986 elections, before everything boomIRANged in the President's face, a pro–drug-testing bill, given his and the issue's popularity, would have probably gained strong bipartisan support. That the President didn't pursue this route is suspicious. There are two possible explanations. The first is that random drug testing was still too new and error-ridden to be proposed to Congress. Not that the programs were *illegal*, according to the President, but the overtones might not be supported by the media, and 1984 was too ominous a year to impose Big Brother tactics. At least, that's what the liberal media would say. In time, legislators, the media, just about everybody would grow used to the idea of biochemical surveillance.

The second and more plausible explanation: the Administration, aware of the possible unconstitutionality of random screening, suspected its bill, introduced by Senator Robert Dole, could expose ill-concealed flaws. On the other hand, an executive order mandating the testing of federal workers was a convenient way of circumventing Congress. Up to two million civilian employees would undergo drug testing as a condition of federal employment without Congressional interference. This would be a *fait accompli*. Before the first doubts could be voiced, it already would be a working program.

The legislative history of drug testing actually begins in 1791, when the Bill of Rights demarked government boundaries. While the Founders couldn't predict the dilemma of drug abuse in the twentieth century, they were familiar enough with abuses of power. Two hundred years have passed, and despite great social transformations those same ten amendments (with minimal revision) continue to protect us from similar government intrusions. One amendment above all others guarantees citizens protection from random drug testing:

> Article IV. The right of the people to be secure in their **persons,** houses, papers, and effects against unreasonable searches and seizures, shall not be violated; and no warrants shall issue, but upon probable cause, supported by oath or affirmation, and particularly describing the place to be searched and the persons or things to be seized. [Boldface added.]

Clearly, a horde of cops busting down your front door without adequate suspicion (or a warrant) is still a violation. But politicians consistently ignore the Bill of Rights when they sanction drug screening, exactly the excessive intervention the colonists were anxious to avoid. "There is no doubt about it," commented U.S. Circuit Judge Harold Vietor on a recent drug-testing case, "searches and seizures can yield a wealth of information useful to the searcher. [That is why King George III's men so frequently searched the colonists.] That potential, however, does not make a governmental employer's search of an employee a constitutionally reasonable one." Every citizen is unreasonably made suspect: the born-again worker and the junkie shooting up at lunch will both be required to fill the specimen cup if they want to work. So far that's been okay with our elected officials.

Webster's defines legislation as "the exercise of the power and function of making rules that have the force of authority by virtue of their promulgation by the state." Under democracy, authority rests with the general public, which elects officials to administer its needs. Officials are expected to legislate the people's will. In theory, a representative votes not for his or her own interests, but those of the community represented. But that's civics class.

Reality is another story. Popular sentiment is often ignored when politicians pursue what they judge our best interest. Typically this is explained to them by high-priced lobbyists, the overwhelming majority of whom work for corporate interests. For example, Exxon's lobbying staff is larger than the staffs of all the senators combined. This risks the Preamble becoming not "We, the People . . ." but "You are the people we say you are." But polls repeatedly show that the Bill of Rights, when not identified as such, is too anarchistic for the majority.

True, the public may not always be sympathetic to what the Constitution *actually* says, but our system assumes the public knows its own will better than Washington. And without fail, whenever individual morality has been forced on the populace, the results have been disastrous. Prohibition reflected the anxiety of a few well-connected special interests. Their morality was dictated to the nation: the government ordered a national ban on alcohol. The public responded by quickly and defiantly circumventing the ban. Organized crime, smuggling, and bootlegging flourished. More damage was done in the fourteen years of Prohibition than boozing could have matched. Repeal required a constitutional amendment. Just ask anyone championing the ERA, this is not an easy thing to do. It was even more difficult to admit that a serious mistake had been made.

Prominent among liberties sacrificed in the Crusade Against Drugs are due process, protection against self-incrimination, and the presumption of innocence. But these losses are trivial compared to what may lie ahead. Attorney General Edwin Meese, long a staunch opponent of due legal process, continues to trumpet the Administration's intentions to rewrite the lawbooks. He takes Reagan's Enforcerism beyond government workers, recommending that all employers survey their employees "wherever possible,

in the locker room, the parking lot, and even nearby taverns."
More recently, he has sworn to overturn the Miranda decision,
which simply requires that the police inform suspects of their
constitutional rights. His justice department recently convinced
the Court that suspects "presumed dangerous to society" could
arbitrarily be held without bail until trial. (In some cases this could
mean two years of purgatory.) Meese has stated that the Supreme
Court is not the highest law in the land—implying, I guess, that
his good buddies are. Greater public ignorance would give him
more freedom to apply what he intriguingly refers to as "new
standards." The *New York Times* noted, "It is hard to take Mr.
Meese seriously as a legal strategist, much less a constitutional
scholar."

President Reagan was certainly not the first to push for harsher
drug laws. Richard Nixon increased the federal penalties, as did
Gerald Ford. Applying mass-surveillance techniques to presumed
innocent citizens is Reagan's unique contribution to the problem.

Let me offer an example of harsh drug laws that proved to be
disastrous: Nelson Rockefeller spent the summer of 1972 trying to
win the good graces of conservatives. In 1973, he finally hit upon
drugs as his road to glory. He would show everyone that he was
tougher than anyone on drugs. This would balance his image as a
"bleeding heart liberal."

Rocky came to this decision on the advice of political consultants
and public relations experts looking for an opening to the right.
He did not turn to scientists, doctors, or educators. He was the
first major Enforcer to call for the death penalty for selling drugs.
The New York state legislature couldn't tell him to go to hell (or
Malaysia, where they do such ridiculous things), because legislators
know enough about the National Party Line that hinting at such a
thing could cost them their jobs.

Enacted by September 1973, the eventual compromises added
up to the strictest, most inhumane drug laws in America. Within
a few years, though, the Enforcers threw in the towel and admitted
that the Rockefeller laws had not exactly produced the intended
results. Drugs had apparently quadrupled on the streets of New
York. Also, the children of some well-to-do parents were getting
fifteen-years-to-life mandatory sentences. At least some legislators

had enough sense to repeal and modify the laws out of existence.

Remember, Rocky had been appalled by Woodstock. Enraged, he called it a disgusting nightmare and declared the greatest cultural event of the century a state of emergency. He lambasted the casual sex and drugs. But later, he died in the arms of a woman one third his age, whom no member of his family met until the quiet settlement.

Like Reagan, Rockefeller thought that putting drug users in jail would get them away from the stuff. (Possession of an ounce of cocaine was enough for the maximum penalty.) Let me add a personal observation here: drugs are easier to get inside prison than outside. I know this from having been in several jails and prisons throughout America. The price of drugs in prison is cheaper, the supply greater, and the practice is more tolerated than on the outside.

Political analysts, politicians, and drug experts admit the Rockefeller laws were a dismal failure—virtually everyone except the Enforcers, who say the laws were right in theory, but wrong in practice, since there were not enough judges, cops, or jails. But they're wrong. The real failure was a reluctance to look beyond the National Party Line and examine the true drug world.

Occasionally, sanity rears its head. After years of legislating increasingly severe penalties, Congress in 1973 recognized that there were victims of drug abuse who had some rights worth protecting. The Vocational Rehabilitation Act of 1973 was designed to protect all handicapped persons from discrimination on the job. The definition of "handicapped persons" was expanded to include former alcoholics and drug users. The key cop-out word is *former*. As interpreted by the courts, the act did *not* protect any individual whose current use of prescribed chemical substances (i.e. methadone) does not impair job performance. Congress refused to protect people under medical treatment or rehabilitation. That's to say, it turned its back on people trying to get well. But this act, though timid as a church mouse, was the first to show a trace of humanity.

Like Title VII of the Civil Rights Act of 1964, which protects minorities from discrimination, the Vocational Rehabilitation Act was designed to remedy past wrongs to the handicapped. Courts have used it to prevent newer violations, enjoining employers from discriminating against employees or applicants solely on the basis of prior abuse. All antidiscrimination laws have one goal: *that workers should be judged by performance alone and not any ancillary factor*.

In accordance with the Constitution, the Rehabilitation Act covers federal employers, contractors, and recipients of federal grants. Private-sector employers remain free to impose any labor standards they wish, as long as they are clearly not *illegal* or prohibited by state statute. With an attorney general like Ed Meese and a chairman of the Civil Rights Commission like Clarence Pendleton, this leaves plenty of room for tacit discrimination on the basis of race, sex, and physical handicap, never mind former drug abuse.

A few states have tried to go beyond federal laws, binding employers outside the government's jurisdiction to similar restrictions. For example, the California Administrative Code protects individuals *currently* in treatment programs from employment discrimination by private employers.

Naturally, Reagan's Prohibitionists are against applying the Rehabilitation Act to *any* abuser, reformed or otherwise. The President's drug-testing legislation, would, if passed, change the judicial interpretation of "handicapped." An individual would not be so classified under the act merely because of an earlier substance addiction. "This change is needed," said Assistant Attorney General Richard K. Willard, "because of the propensity of some courts to adopt an overly broad reading of the act, requiring repeated offers of rehabilitation before allowing the government to take action against the drug addict." No one ever accused Reagan of being soft on the downtrodden.

What about federal workers with no history of drug abuse? Their privacy is dependent on each agency's discretion. Some form of chemical testing has been a Department of Transportation fixture for twenty years. The Federal Aviation Authority (FAA) probably has the strictest standards in the nation. Not only are crew members prohibited from flying under the influence of alcohol or any impairing drug (prescribed or not), they're not allowed to drink for eight hours before takeoff. Blood tests for pilots and air traffic controllers are required during physical exams. Of the FAA's workforce of 47,000, over half must pass a biannual test. But for some even this is not enough. New legislation sponsored by Senators Ernest Hollings and John Danforth would make the standards harsher, requiring that personnel submit to random urine tests before flights and shift changes without any cause of suspicion. That bill left the Senate Commerce Committee on a twelve-to-one vote in March 1987.

The difficulty is not with the *FAA's intent*—improved safety—but its singling out of pilots for no valid reason. American Civil Liberties Union (ACLU) lawyer Loren Siegel asked for proof that drug tests would prevent air disasters: "Are airplanes falling out of the sky because of stoned pilots? Is this a national problem? The FAA already has sufficient regulations that monitor pilots for substance abuse. My sense is that pilots are not risking their own lives and the lives of their passengers. There is no cause shown which would lead us to testing as a preventive measure. What you have is false justification for a program. A routine neurological exam would reveal more about an employee's fitness than an error-prone drug test, which doesn't reveal impairment." The Pilots Union agrees and has filed suit protesting the regulation. The data overwhelmingly substantiates their objection. According to FAA statistics, U.S. air-safety standards were the highest ever in 1983, 1984, and 1986. This was achieved without urine testing. Further, there is absolutely no indication of drug abuse among airline pilots. Urine tests would be superfluous and intrusive. However, the successful 1985 strike by the Airline Pilots Association is probably one reason for the increased surveillance and harassment.

In addition to filling potholes and rebuilding collapsed bridges, the Federal Highway Administration (FHA) busies itself with interstate trucking. As with pilots, it is a federal offense for truckers to operate under the influence of anything other than coffee and cigarettes. Further, licensed interstate drivers cannot have a recent history of drug abuse. (How recent depends on the FHA.) But unlike their skybound colleagues, truck drivers are difficult to pin down. Long-haul drivers have been ordered by their companies to violate regulations and take amphetamines to ensure they didn't fall asleep behind the wheel. "Without uppers, I couldn't make my deadlines," commented one Teamster trucker. "Which is worse, popping a pill or risking an accident?" Or not getting the rig in port on schedule, he could have added.

Senator John Danforth, with one eye on re-election and the other on the road, drafted legislation in 1984 to curb highway violations, drunk driving, and especially drug abuse. The Commercial Motor Vehicle Safety bill would, if enacted, give states the authority to conduct random drug tests of truck and bus drivers, regardless of adequate cause.

Not to be left out, the Federal Railroad Administration (FRA) requires that all conductors and engineers submit to urine tests at management's discretion or after a serious accident. The January 4, 1987, Amtrak-Conrail collision, which left sixteen people dead, renewed talk of mandatory predeparture drug testing when drug use was suspected.

Train wrecks make a strong case for *impairment testing,* but not for drug testing. Secretary of Transportation Elizabeth Dole has ordered pre-employment screening and has taken steps to make it mandatory across the industry. In the summer of 1985, the FRA planned a comprehensive testing program of 100,000 railroad workers. Unlike airlines, rail workers have a history of drug dependency (especially alcoholism). Many accidents could have been avoided, she argues, if the crew were tested. Opposition from the Association of Railroads will not brake the Dole testing express. Or Dole's "two for one" drive for the '88 presidency.

The legislative mood is clearly in favor of more testing for more people, Constitution or no Constitution. We are made to feel that protecting civil liberties can lead to serious public catastrophe, that only through the vigilance of drug testing can disaster be avoided. And who's to define "public safety"? A congressman who was badgered on a C-Span interview included gas-station attendants as workers in the public-safety sector. Ed Meese says teachers are. Already, police are randomly stopping private cars in hopes of finding anyone who is intoxicated. Drunk driving is terrible, but the tactics used to eradicate it should not infringe on the right of free travel.

Facts are often fudged when it helps the NPL. The FAA's forensic toxicology research unit, which examines urine and blood samples following an air or rail accident, announced in April the "temporary reassignment" of Dr. Delbert J. Lacefield, Supervisor for the FAA's Forensic Toxicology Unit, following allegations of irregularities in the Amtrak-Conrail investigation. Dr. Lacefield claimed to find THC in the blood of two crew members, which rallied drug-testing proponents and made national headlines. Later, Dr. Lacefield's associates said they could find no documentation supporting the THC conclusion. The prosecutors in the trial of the conductors never mentioned drugs. On May 26, 1987, Dr. Lacefield pleaded guilty in connection with falsified blood-analysis reports from 1986 train wrecks. Officials at the Federal Railroad Association, which had contracted for Dr. Lacefield's services, said, "he was unable or unwilling to do the tedious and complicated job of preparing blood plasma extracts for analysis. As a result, he routinely reported that any drug use had occurred more than six hours before an accident when no testing had been done to confirm that." Prosecutors claimed that Dr. Lacefield was familiar with urinalysis, but lacked equipment and the knowledge to test blood plasma for drugs. Dr. Lacefield faces up to 15 years in prison and a $30,000 fine.

The initial reports on all three train wrecks involved in this case made national headlines because drugs were "involved." The false testing reports have not to date been mentioned by any TV network news show. Routinely on talk shows I am asked to "explain the drug use" in the Conrail-Amtrak tragedy. No host has been aware of this entire sordid history you have just read. And the mass media's instant verdict of "drugs are to blame" has not been severely altered.

So far I've done three radio talk shows on the subject of urine testing. Within the first minutes, each host brought up this train disaster as having been caused by drugs. None was aware of Dr. Lacefield's confession. In the upcoming tour to promote this book, I doubt that anything will have changed. It's the rare host that will even read this.

A public unaware of what the tests do and do not prove would accept, even demand, the screening process. Same here. But get your mind off the six o'clock news plane crash and get it back to where it belongs—on the tests!

The scope and quality of the scrutiny are seriously flawed. *Current drug tests, even if 100 percent accurate, indicate only the presence of drugs. Nothing about the amount, nothing about how or when that presence got there. And no one has yet correlated urine test results with job performance.* A Breathalyzer, at least, shows a level of alcohol in the bloodstream that is statistically related to impairment; the scientific correlation is well established.

Drug tests, which occasionally get tossed out of a trial as inconclusive evidence, are continually used to end careers. The drug test does little more than enforce the morality of the tester. It says: "Drugs are illegal. If you show the presence of drugs, you are a danger to the public—no matter that your fifteen-year record is unblemished."

Keep remembering that a positive test on a pilot for marijuana could mean the presence of at least a half dozen other nonpsychoactive, nonprescription medications. It could mean that the pilot passively inhaled pot smoke two weeks before the test (some say even longer). It very well could be the result of human error. Meanwhile, there is no scientific correlation between that "positive" test result and job impairment, although the press has presented this assumption as fact. On top of this, actual lab tests purporting to establish a definite relation between pot smoking and motor-response or memory-skill deficiencies are often flawed by inconclusive data, biased experimenters, or faulty methodology. Sure, a lab rat who has just consumed half his body weight in marijuana or been forced to smoke the human equivalent of one hundred joints might indeed mess up on certain stimulus/response tests. I wouldn't want any of those rats flying me to Houston tonight either. But these "garbage" studies prove absolutely nothing about a particular crew which is about to board. The only sure thing they do is increase our fear of flying and intensify paranoia in general.

Are we as a society going bananas or what? I fly 100,000 miles a year. I love pilots. They've done a lot more for me and my public safety than doctors and the government. Furthermore, I suspect a pilot who is brave enough to resist such a stupid intrusion into his privacy would perform better in a crisis situation, would actually care more for the passengers than some empty-headed wimp who buckled under to Big Government's whim. What do you think Chuck Yeager would have done?

The mania has gone way beyond conventional definitions of safety-related jobs. Federal employees, grouped into so-called "sensitive" positions, are expected to comply merely because of their potential for misusing confidential information. Desk-bound bureaucrats, customs workers, postal inspectors—no one is free from Uncle Sam's sweeping specimen bottle. Do you think giving convicted spy John Walker a urinalysis would have shown him to be a security threat and prevented him from selling secrets? As current affairs concerning guard duty at the U.S. Embassy in Moscow show, testing marines for excessive libido might definitely improve national security.

If the public feels job performance related to public safety is lax, industrial psychologists would have no problem designing job skills and performance tests. NASA psychologists already use a battery of sophisticated dexterity, hand/eye-coordination, and stimulus-reaction tests on would-be astronauts.

The federal workplace has been hard hit by ignorant laws, and worse, by executive orders, but the private sector still holds even more potential for abuse. As noted, often no standards exist for screening. A lack of legal protection makes workers ready game for management's arbitrary power. Peter Ueberroth, commissioner of baseball and self-appointed drug czar, has pushed hard for urine testing. Sounding more like a politician than a sports administrator, Ueberroth represents the private sector at its most intrusive. His "modest" proposals include mandatory screening, enforcement, education, and the defoliation of foreign coca and marijuana crops. With his political sensibility, Ueberroth has the ear of both the President and the mass media, and the savvy to recognize drugs as a low-risk crusade that can keep him in the spotlight.

The rapid expansion of drug testing has taken even its advocates by surprise, making many reconsider their own vulnerability. Across America, civic groups are protesting this denial of their rights by sponsoring legislation and court challenges that would give concrete assurance to unwritten principles. And political hopefuls are caught in the middle. They don't want their organized constituents to be forced to urinate, but they do want to appear tough on drugs.

Privacy, to be protected, has to be converted into law. Again, drug testing is too new an issue to have made significant inroads on the lawbooks, since law is much more reactive than active. There is a time lag. But things are not hopeless; there has been some resistance.

Polygraphy, which preceded the drug hysteria as the ultimate mind probe, is today illegal in half the states. For some strange reason, the same politicians who have been spooked by the unreliability of lie detectors swear by urine tests.

In 1985, San Francisco became the first municipality to adopt anti-drug-testing legislation. The expansion of unrestricted drug testing in local industry frightened city legislators, as did stories of victimization. In December, the Municipal Code was amended to correct two wrongs—first, to prohibit employer interference with worker relationships and extra-office activities, and second, to regulate drug testing of employees.

The legislation made no bones about its intent.

> It is the public policy of the city and county of San Francisco that all citizens enjoy the full benefit of the right to privacy in the workplace guaranteed to them by . . . the California Constitution. It is the purpose of the Article to protect employees from unreasonable inquiry and investigation into off-the-job conduct, associations, and activities not directly related to the actual performance of job responsibilities.

The bill championed personal rights and privacy. Highlights included:

- Sec. 3300a.3 EMPLOYER INTERFERENCE IN PERSONAL RELATIONSHIPS OF EMPLOYEES PROHIBITED. No employer may make, adopt, or enforce any rule or policy forbidding or preventing employees from engaging or participating in personal relationships, organizations, acitvities, or otherwise restricting their freedom of association, unless said relationships . . . have

a direct and actual impact on the employees' ability to perform
their assigned responsibilities.

- Sec. 3300a.5 EMPLOYER PROHIBITED FROM TESTING OF EM-
PLOYEES. No employer may demand, require, or request employees to submit to, to take, or to undergo any blood, urine,
or encephalographic test in the body as a condition of continued employment.

A big however. The San Francisco City Council did not wish to
proscribe *all* drug testing. (As with court rulings, no legislation
has attempted to stop all testing.) When an employer feels he has
objective evidence and just cause that would hold up to the same
standards as any court-issued search warrant, testing is valid:

> Nothing herein shall prohibit an employer from requiring
> a specific employee to submit to blood or urine testing
> if: (a.) the employer has reasonable grounds to believe
> that an employee's facilities are impaired on the job; and
> (b.) the employee is in a position where such impairment
> presents a clear and present danger to the physical safety
> of the employee, another employee, or to a member of
> the public; and (c.) the employer provides the employee,
> at the employer's expense, the opportunity to have the
> sample tested or evaluated by a State-licensed inde-
> pendent laboratory/testing facility and provides the em-
> ployee with a reasonable opportunity to rebut or explain
> the results.

In any case, the burden rests with the employer. He must first
prove an employee's associations are deleterious if he wants them
enjoined, and that the employee is clearly impaired, not just suspected of abusing some substance. Even if the suspicion was well-
founded, the drug test used must only reveal chemicals which
affect work performance. San Francisco recognized that the information contained in bodily fluid is confidential and took measures
to limit access to medical surveillance:

> In conducting those tests designed to identify the pres-
> ence of chemical substances in the body, . . . the em-

ployer shall ensure to the extent feasible that the test only measures and that its records only show or make use of information regarding chemical substances in the body which are likely to affect the ability of the employee to perform safely his or her duties while on the job.

Employers can't test for epilepsy, pregnancy, or prescribed drugs. The legislation also took a crack at the keystone of Reagan's War on Drugs: "Under no circumstances may employers request, require, or conduct *random* or *company-wide* blood, urine, or encephalographic testing."

Compromises were required to get the legislation through. Certain workers were excluded from coverage. These included employees in safety- or security-related areas: police, firefighters, police dispatchers, and emergency service-vehicle operators. (Mayor Diane Feinstein, with national political ambitions, refused to sign the bill, but it was passed by override.) Nonetheless, it served as a catalyst for other anti-drug–testing legislation. Ira Glasser, executive director of the ACLU, said, "The law strikes the delicate balance between an employee's fundamental right to privacy and the legitimate business needs of the employer."

In April 1987, Montana became the first state to restrict biochemical testing. Governor Ted Schwinden signed into law a bill which curtailed blood and urine testing by employers in both private and public sectors. The law expressed outrage over screening abuses, and required that tests be given only when based on objective fact. Random and mass screening are illegal. Further, when it is suitable, at least two confirmation tests are required.

The Montana law is tighter in its exclusions than San Francisco's, and its coverage is wider. Current and prospective employees, as well as job applicants are covered. So if things get really uptight in your home state, move to Montana. Fresh air, open spaces, cheap living, great steaks, and an enlightened populist government (at least on this issue).

Others have tried bringing enlightenment to their hometowns. A local scandal in which Suffolk County (N.Y.) police were discovered using seized contraband for their own pleasure precipitated countywide urine testing. Steven Levy, a county legislator, introduced a bill in March 1986 that would have barred municipal and private employers from imposing drug tests on applicants and employees, in the spirit of the San Francisco code.

The resolution was passed by the Suffolk County legislature in August 1986 but was vetoed by the county executive. Drug testing became a political hot potato, then quickly died. As Legislator Levy explains, "The bill didn't have enough private sector support to win the majority required to override a veto."

But from acorns of challenge grow oaks of resistance. In May 1987, Vermont Governor Madeline Kunin approved a bill similar to the Montana statute. Two months later, Iowa became the third state to restrict biochemical testing. New resolutions are springing up throughout the country.

But for every allemande right, we take one allemande left. Utah passed legislation granting private employers the right to test anyone—job applicants or tenured employees—for any reason, at any time. The only restriction is that the employee must be forewarned in writing (which will make it a lot easier for folks to beat the test). Especially frightening, Utah permits testing for every substance in any pharmacopoeia or formulary, an unusually broad range of potions, including aspirin, hair restorers, and acne medications, as well as "naughty" drugs.

Remember those three presidential drug panels in the seventies discussed in earlier chapters? Well, Reagan and his staff were determined to stifle such official permissiveness in a big way. No namby-pamby talk about illness and treatment. No use/abuse confusion. These top guns wanted to talk tough and get tough.

In the summer of 1983, President Reagan pulled together a Commission on Organized Crime (COC). Eighteen "experts" from a gamut of conservative occupations were appointed to study all aspects of mob-related activities—its sources of revenue, membership, violence, and so on. Included were a *Reader's Digest* editor (the magazine runs at least one anti-drug story in every issue and regularly sponsors full-page newspaper ads condemning drug usage) and a lot of law enforcers and criminologists. Judge Irving Kaufman, who became famous for ordering the execution of the Rosenbergs and censoring Lenny Bruce, was named chairman. Don't expect Timothy Leary at any of their parties.

A massive undertaking by anyone's standards, the Commission was also charged with making "recommendations concerning appropriate administrative and legislative improvements and improvements in the administration of justice." Its real goal was to undo the drug-defiant sixties and the drug-permissive seventies.

No objections were raised to the members' narrow sensibilities. Sending this panel to study drug abuse was tantamount to Klan members drafting civil rights legislation. They went in with extreme bias and only took notice of facts that reinforced their prejudices. Make no mistake, although it was labeled a "Crime Commission," its job was to set the stage for the War on Drugs.

The Commission worked hard. By March 31, 1986, it had heard hundreds of hours of testimony and released thousands of pages. No Timothy Leary here, either. There was nothing shocking or new revealed. To no one's surprise, the Commission substantiated what Reagan claimed as divine inspiration.

The one conclusion prominent among the drivel was that illegal drug trade is the single, most dangerous component of organized crime. Rodney Smith, deputy executive director of the Commission, summarized the findings at a House of Representatives hearing. "[Drug trafficking] stands alone among criminal enterprises in its impact on our citizens, our families, our communities, and our national life." Unless something was done quickly to stop the drug menace, America would find itself caught in an epidemic of plague proportions.

Where the three previous White House panels soothed fears, this one fueled the flames of hysteria. Fear was mainlined into America's heart.

Unleashing its horses, the COC rode full stride. Recommended was nothing less than a complete overhaul of policy:

> The ultimate goal of the Nation's drug policy is the effective suppression of drug abuse in the United States. While efforts to reduce the supply of drugs in this country, such as interdiction and source-country crop controls, indirectly advance this goal, efforts to reduce the demand for drugs can make a more direct contribution. For this

reason, the Nation's drug policy must emphasize more strongly efforts to reduce the demand for drugs.

This council, so removed from social theory (to quote Jimmy Cliff, Jamaican reggae philosopher, "You can get it if you really want it . . ."), found tenable a drug policy that baffled experts for decades. Included were some traditional recommendations that would do nothing to increase our understanding of drugs. *Basically*, the report implies, *if you eliminate the laws of supply and demand, you eliminate the problem*. Typical Reagan-in-Disneyland logic.

The Commission urged the federal government "to provide the example of the unacceptability of drugs. "The President should direct the heads of all federal agencies to formulate clear policy statements, with implementing guidelines, *including suitable drug-testing programs*, expressing the utter unacceptability of drug abuse by federal employees." The Commission continued, "State and local governments and leaders in the private sector should support unequivocally a similar policy that any and all drug use is unacceptable." Financial persuasion would be the best way of getting the ball rolling: "Government contracts should not be awarded to companies that fail to implement drug programs." There are very few big companies not doing business with the government. Interesting phrase, "financial persuasion." "Blackmail" would have been more honest. But then, sin was about to be driven out of River City.

In his enthusiasm, Judge Kaufman, the chairman, seemed to share Edwin Meese's obtrusiveness toward civil liberties. The judge reasoned that drug tests are no more an invasion of privacy than airport metal detectors. California Representative Don Edwards rebutted:

> Drug tests are considerably more intrusive than metal detectors. But Judge Kaufman's comment says more against his proposal than he could have realized. If metal detectors at airports are a precedent for urinalysis in the work place, then what will urinalysis serve as a precedent for? The judge's comment illustrates how one little erosion of

our civil liberties leads to another. Every little intrusion lowers society's "expectation of privacy." If liberties can be lost by increments, then surely this latest challenge must be resisted.

Flying on airplanes is optional, working a necessity. The metal detector analogy is frivolous. Edwards was one of a distinct minority. Liberals, fearful of Reagan's anticipated power at the polls just seven months away, ran for cover. In fact, most Democrats praised the Commission's work and began the contest to see who could scream louder about this DAMN EVIL SCOURGE!

These must have been great times around the White House in the spring of 1986. Criticism was sidestepped; the President was at the peak of his popularity. Bitburg was a distant memory. The President had totally avoided any compromise on Star Wars. The ever-increasing deficit was something only red-faced Democrats talked about. Tax reform was winning bipartisan support. In April, he gave a national speech on Central America. The *Nation* counted over forty errors of fact, but no one seemed to care. Even his social issues were being taken seriously by the public. Only a few bleeding hearts, like Ted Kennedy, still rattled on about the poor. At North Carolina State, Reagan sang the praises of the Empire and free enterprise, making Rachel's Cookies (a new Southern chain) the yuppie version of Horatio Alger. A giant spectacle, Hands Across America, had been very reassuring. Though Reagan had cut eighteen billion dollars in anti-poverty programs, his participation was welcomed by the Hollywood sponsors. The pride was back. Bruce Springsteen's instant classic, "Born in the U.S.A.," was being misused as false jingoism.

Reagan was being compared to Franklin Roosevelt (by Pat Buchanan). Barbara Walters asked Reagan what he thought was wrong with the presidency. Of all the possible answers, he responded by criticizing the wisdom of the Twenty-second Amendment. "If the American people decide they like someone, why shouldn't a President be allowed more than two terms?" I actually expected someone to walk on camera and put a crown on the man's head. For it was springtime in America for Reagan. Kick! Kick!

Congressional Republicans were doing all they could to latch onto the President's coattails. Drug testing seemed a good rallying point. No one could appear *for* drug abuse, and advocating any program to eradicate it would surely be a vote-getter. Democrats didn't argue. Several bills were proposed in the House of Representatives, putting the COC's recommendations to use. The harsher the legislation, the better. One bill (H.R.4636), for example, required heads of federal agencies and congressional offices to institute screening procedures for all workers who had access to classified information. By rough estimate, there are 4.2 million employees (excluding the military) who have confidential, secret, or top-secret clearances. They include congressmen, the Capitol architect (who knows the secret passageways), Washington Botanical Garden workers, and Capitol guides. In our Northampton "Trial of the CIA," defense witness Daniel Ellsberg mentioned that there were eleven levels of secrecy higher than "top secret."

But despite unrestrained enthusiasm from the White House and a willing Congress, the bill never made it out of committee. Too many agency heads resented the expense and suspected its unconstitutionality. Just to be sure, the House Subcommittee on Civil Service in February 1986 asked seventy-six federal agencies about their policy on drug testing. *A solid majority (75 percent) didn't require urinalysis testing and saw no need for it in the future.* Charles A. Bowsher, comptroller general, issued an especially thoughtful reply:

> Although the decision to establish these programs is a matter of policy for the Congress to decide, we cannot support enactment of the proposed legislation. The bill raises a constitutional problem and is vague in numerous respects. In addition the potential benefits are unmeasurable while the estimated costs are significant. . . . The bill does not assign responsibility for oversight, [nor] provide for due process protection for individuals adversely affected by actions taken by agencies.

Bad attitude for a Reagan team player.

Congress adjourned for summer recess without establishing a national drug policy. All bills were mired in committee, with little chance of any passing. Not to be outdone by a slow-moving bureaucracy, the President pushed hard for mandatory drug screening. With Congress away in August, the President played with the media, setting an example to the nation. **He took a urine test.** The chief executive's vital fluid was tested for marijuana, PCP, cocaine, amphetamines, barbiturates, and heroin. The results were never made public. Speculation as to why hints that several other prescription drugs tested positive. Publicizing the results would have alerted the public to the all-spying nature of the tests. Some say the tests might have revealed he was heavily into Iranian food. Then again maybe his aim was bad.

This act of humility was aimed at critics. If I can do it, why not you? What have you got to hide?

It was a busy summer. Reagan strapped on the armor and announced his Crusade Against Drugs—a social plan in the tradition of the Great Society. At its heart were six points that together formed a panacea for drug abuse:

1. Drug-free workplace for all
2. Drug-free schools
3. Public health protection
4. International cooperation
5. Stronger enforcement
6. Expanded public awareness.

It was great public relations. Who could support drug-infested schools? The implications, on the other hand, were devastating. The phrase "drug-free" in the Reagan thesaurus is interchangeable with "drug testing." Always. Public health protection was touted as a centerpiece of the Crusade. But federal public-health funding actually declined from $404 million in 1981 to $279 million by 1986. International cooperation meant joint ventures between America and its satellite drug suppliers. There was great talk about how pressure had been put on Turkey to eliminate or reduce opium production. (Opium production simply shifted from Turkey to Mexico. In a few years, the clandestine farming in Turkey will again be public. It's been this way for over 2,000 years.) Operation Blast Furnace tried to eradicate Bolivian drug fields and marked the beginning of counter-insurgency tactics. Even the innocuous expanded public awareness was filled with distortions. It warned only of illicit drug abuse. Oversaturation from the legal drug industry was never mentioned.

At some point you have to step back and consider what was actually going on. In the fall of 1986, the War on Drugs had transformed an illness into a plague, with urine testing the panacea. The public believed the sky was falling. People who objected could do nothing but watch in horror and await the next attack on civil liberties in the name of health. Mass testing of AIDS-virus carriers was obviously the next campaign. That would mean identifying over two million people who would then, logically, have to be isolated. Would San Francisco become perhaps the first walled city in America?

On September 15, 1986, the bombshell landed. President Reagan issued Executive Order #12564, otherwise known as the *Drug-Free Workplace*. Reagan summarized his War on Drugs in the preface. The federal government, an altruistic body, is concerned with both the well-being of its employees and the need to maintain productivity. "Federal employees who use illegal drugs on or off duty," the President cautioned, "tend to be less productive, less reliable, and prone to greater absenteeism than their fellow employees who do not use illegal drugs." Workers were then ordered to stop using drugs, as if they had been excluded from the drug laws that apply to the rest of us. The meat of the order: All federal agency heads were told to come up with plans for drug testing.

The Order contains what the President considered lenient treatment of offenders. Anyone who voluntarily identifies himself as an abuser, obtains counseling, and afterward refrains from drug use cannot be subjected to discipline. That same worker, however, can't remain in his job unless given a clean bill of health by medical and supervisory authorities. All others caught in the dragnet were subject to termination and criminal prosecution. However, "Preliminary test results may not be used [against an employee] . . . unless they are confirmed by a second analysis of the same sample." This was seen as so fair that junkies by the hundreds of thousands flocked to Washington, threw their syringes on the White House lawn, and personally thanked their new benefactor.

Drug tests weren't the only way the feds could now conclude an employee is an illegal user. The Order sanctioned other detection procedures: direct observation, criminal records, or administrative inquiry (read: witch hunt) can result in termination.

The Justice Department, acting as adviser to the President, contended that the order was completely constitutional. Meese said that Fourth Amendment provisions aren't violated, since the government has the right to ensure that its workers are functionally unimpaired. (Meese is on to something here—government rights.) Further, the reasonability standard of searches and seizures is met, since workers, by virtue of their continued labor, consent to drug testing as a condition of employment. The sophistry overwhelms: drug screens must be reasonable, according to Meese, if no one quits.

Constance Horner, director of the Office of Personnel Management (OPM), was made responsible for enforcing the Order. Her interpretation was more severe than even Reagan had intended. Not satisfied with the already high unemployment rate, she ruled that employees may be terminated for refusing a test or for one positive (and unsubstantiated) result. Even Reagan in August 1986 was not so cold-blooded. "I would rather see a voluntary [drug testing] program in which we can say they won't lose [their jobs], there won't be punishment. What there would be is an offer of help to tell people, if this is your problem, let us help you cure yourself of addiction," said President Reagan. Yet the President didn't mitigate Horner's OPM standards. He just signed the Order and left for the ranch. Appropriately, while working on the 1980 Reagan campaign, Constance Horner was offered her first job while in the bathroom of the transition team.

What followed was unusually chaotic, even for the government. Members of Congress either loved or hated the Order; there was no middle ground. There couldn't be. You either had to back civil liberties and the Constitution, or hold that eradication of drug abuse was paramount to human dignity. Midterm election campaigns revolved around the issue. "Reagan timed the order perfectly," remarked one legislative analyst. "He knew elections were coming up, and the issue might split the Republicans. The congressmen who were depending on Reagan's endorsement had no choice but to okay drug testing, whether or not they personally supported it."

But when elections came, Democrats regained control of the Senate. Iranamok broke, and major proponents of mass, mandatory urine testing (i.e. Danforth, Hollings, et al.) retreated to a low profile.

Working from the outside, labor unions, civil rights organizations, and lobbyists have promised lawsuits at every opportunity, challenging both the constitutionality of the order and the President's right to impose it in the first place.

The House of Representatives has been more vocal than the Senate in opposing the Reagan plan. This is only partly attributable to party lines. Charles Schumer (D-N.Y.) was the first to propose anti–drug-testing legislation. His bill (H.R. 5530) restricts the situations in which drug tests can be applied. It recognized the limited constitutional protections afforded the private sector and holds that drug testing without cause is an invasion of privacy for all citizens, regardless of workplace. And like the San Francisco code, H.R. 5530 narrows the occupations and situations under which drug testing is permitted.

Schumer also requires confirmation of a positive test result before action can be initiated, and recommends a review and appellate procedure for anyone who feels victimized by a test.

Like legislation on local levels, his House bill falls short on the exemptions. An employer may require a drug test if there is reasonable suspicion of drug abuse, if the employee is engaged in a drug-sensitive occupation, or has been contractually obligated to submit under a labor contract. ACLU lawyers stress that the "drug-sensitive" condition is the downfall of the entire bill. Just as President Reagan broadly defines "sensitive" to include most members of the civil service, so private-sector employers can argue that they too need protecting. Any half-baked prosecutor could make a case that "drug-sensitive" applies to anyone from top management to a dishwasher. That broad exemption takes you right back to the original problem: unreasonable testing, where none but the boldest tread, and ever so lightly.

Schumer admits the exceptions are broad, but claims there was no other way of making the bill appealing enough to stand any chance of passing the House. Another New Yorker, Representative Gary Ackerman, has proposed legislation designed to curtail the sweeping exemptions in Schumer's bill. "I am not yet convinced," claimed the congressman, "that the President's definition of 'sensitive' is sufficiently restrictive." Ackerman's responsible drug-testing programs would be limited to employees in occupations involving health, safety, or national security.

Loopholes in both bills are wide enough to allow the testing of millions of Americans. And these are the *only* bills designed to place minimal curbs on the practice. *There is no movement at all in Congress to block urine testing.* To the contrary, congressional attitudes range from "wait and see" to downright enthusiasm. Maybe it's time we started sending some wet letters down to Washington.

The greatest threat to Reagan's initiative might actually be the Gipper himself. The intensified focus on drug abuse and detection would require increased federal expenditures. But six months after the President announced his War on Drugs, he proposed *cuts* in drug enforcement. The 1988 proposed budget eliminated $225 million to state and local governments for enforcement, reduced education funds by another $250 million, and recommended no money for treatment. Enforcer-Representative Charles B. Rangel, chairman of the House Select Committee on Narcotics Abuse and Control, said, "The reduction in funds seriously calls into question the depth of their commitment to an effective drug abuse strategy." Members of Congress and the public were appalled by the apparent hypocrisy.

The President was keeping in character. Real spending for prevention and treatment *declined* 5 percent in the seven years since Reagan first took office. It should have surprised no one that nothing was added to the 1987 budget to bolster the Crusade. Of the remaining appropriation, law enforcement receives the largest chunk—nearly 85 percent. Compare that to 1 percent of funds earmarked for public education. However, Reagan has control over additional discretionary funds, which he swears will be used to cover the costs of urinalysis of federal workers.

Representative Patricia Schroeder expressed dismay: "Giving every federal worker a urine test once a year would cost about $100 million for the tests alone. For this sum, we could hire about four thousand new FBI agents with $25,000-a-year salaries." But Pat, who needs more FBI? Instead of testing federal employees that year, we could fund fifty treatment centers across the country. Incidentally, her $100 million figure is unusually low. Supporters and critics agree that a minimum of two tests per employee each year would be needed. Plus, there are lab fees and lost work hours to consider—$300 million annually is a more appropriate estimate for testing civil servants, excluding the military.

There is no executive privilege I know of allowing Ronnie to spend that kind of money without congressional approval. Then again, Ron didn't think he needed congressional approval to sell arms to Iran, or to skirt Congress and funnel cash to the Contras. And we all know how well that worked out. Reagan generally treats Congress as he would tend mushrooms: he keeps them in the dark and feeds them lots of manure. (Ex-CIA agent Ralph Magehee says this is an old CIA joke about handling congressional oversight committees.)

Only a handful of congresspeople have questioned the President's authority to mandate a drug-free workplace. Congressional opposition to urine testing is a drip in the proverbial toilet bowl. Don't look to the Hill for courage, truth, or relief.

9.

Fear and Loathing in the Workplace

Philosophers have been debating the concept of labor ever since the ancient Egyptians decided that the pyramids would get done a lot faster and cheaper with slaves. Today, only 3,500 years later, academic journals are saturated with studies of work place psychology. Everything from shift length to caffeine to wall color has been cited as affecting worker motivation. The experiments and research dollars all confirm what a sixteen-year-old discovers on the first summer job: that work is essentially repetitive, alienating, and only marginally productive. In the argot of the people, work is just another dirty four-letter word.

Labor—especially for someone else's profit—is not a source of comfort and security, but more often a source of anxiety, boredom, and depression. From the Enforcers we hear the cry, "Jobs, jobs, and more jobs." Slavery knocks out unemployment quicker than any other solution, so there has to be more to this labor question than simple sloganeering. Obviously, we want "jobs with dignity," jobs that don't make people feel like worthless crap. Johnny Paycheck's "Take This Job and Shove It" was more accurate about workers' real feelings than anything you heard during that five-day commercial called "Liberty Week."

Exceptions exist, but rewarding careers, *Lifestyles of the Rich and Undeserving*, can be claimed by only a fraction of those qualified. There would be no one left to envy—or *People* magazine to feature—if everyone had an interesting job. The majority are relegated to pure drudgery. One factotum of forty years in and out of the Help Wanted pages remarked, "I've been a cook, a soldier, a toll-booth collector, and a construction worker. Believe me, there's no such thing as a good job." The poet Charles Bukowski wrote of one job he had mopping up blood off the slaughterhouse floor. "You've never had it so good," said the foreman, with an encouraging slap on the back. "You'll have this job for fifteen years; you've never had it so good." He quit after two days.

Such frankness is rarely heard in public. But recognizing the limits of the American career path could save the bright-eyed job-hunter a lot of frustration later on. The Age of the Service Economy, the "fast track," doesn't particularly require ambition or devotion, as did, say, the craft guilds of the Middle Ages. Modern job-hopping seems to be the method of choice for corporate ladder climbing. The ones who don't or can't hop grow lame. Contemporary Social Darwinism means the survival of the best résumés. Networking implies "it's not who you are, but who you know that counts." Every firm has a stagnant pool of employees spinning their Rolodexes, going nowhere, but performing their jobs diligently. Like the mutt who's kicked around but returns to his master's door, these are the true believers in the benevolence of the great Shop God.

Now to prevent mass revolution, as well as sand in the carburetors on the assembly line, the bosses use a variety of tactics. Throughout this century, for example, we have always had a pool of unemployed homeless and people living below the poverty level. In the best of times, that last measurement has ranged from a low of 10 percent in the early seventies (even with Great Society programs, plus, of course, the Vietnam War) to a high of 28 percent during the Depression. Today, under Reagan's supply-side economics, about 16 percent—34 million—are living in poverty as defined by the Bureau of Census. This reality is easily transmitted and understood by workers. "If I don't do exactly as they order me to do, I could be out on the street."

This is a spoken and unspoken threat. But mythologies of all sorts are also used to control the workforce. Repeated examples of successful workers and entrepreneurs are displayed not just as role models, but as proof that the system actually works. The rags-to-riches story is told and retold as often as religious parables.

Indeed, a Gallup/London Weekend poll of several industrial nations showed that Americans lead everyone else in believing that most people become rich through hard work. Not even the Japanese believed that to nearly the same degree. To the question "How do people get rich?" 43 percent of Americans answered "through hard work"; only 12 percent of the Japanese chose that reason. Closer to truth, 51 percent of the Japanese surveyed believed inheritance was the primary road to wealth, while only 20 percent of Americans saw it that way. We think of ourselves as a nation of self-made winners.

I call this the "lottery effect." Who has ever seen a photo in a newspaper of a lottery loser? Despite the ridiculous odds, we all take a shot at winning; even I do. Our concept of material success is overloaded with winners. Everyone wins instantly in commercials, crises are always resolved in sit-coms, heroes triumph in adventures and dramas. The nightly news ends on upbeat "human items" or happy talk. In major sports, even the losers go home millionaires. Losing is symbolic of opportunity later on. Watching "Hands Across America," you got the feeling that if we really had poor people in America, by golly, they were the luckiest poor people in the world!

Mythology is often stronger than reality, certainly more appealing than cold statistics and surveys. But the real story on wealth in America would shock most workers. In 1983, the Federal Reserve Board (not your typical commie front!) published a study on accumulated wealth in America. (Accumulated wealth is what you have beyond your clothes, car, house, etc. It's basically real estate you don't live on, stocks and bonds.) *Only 840,000 families (the country's wealthiest 1 percent) own half of all accumulated wealth, currently estimated at 10.3 trillion dollars. The top 10 percent own 84 percent, while the bottom 90 percent own next to nothing.* A mere 1 percent tax on accumulated wealth could generate $100 billion annually, with more than half this tax being paid by the first 840,000 super-rich households. As to the mythology of hard work promoted every day in our culture, the study found that only one third of all capital was accumulated through hard work, individual ingenuity, and savings. Fully two thirds was inherited. Enough said about the yuppie marching songs.

I could, by the way, show you charts of who owns the land we live on—America the Beautiful. The figures are not too different from those on accumulated wealth. Few economists expect the trend toward oligarchy to do anything but increase over the next decade. The rich will get richer, and the poor will get whatever trickles down. "Trickle-down" was a more than accurate depiction of Reaganomics.

Americans are famous for ignoring truth. That's why advertising is such a big, hip business. We talk about career fulfillment when we just want to make it through another eight hours with as little damage as possible. Popular culture echoes the frustration: C'mon guys, hang on long enough to make it to Miller time; get away to Club Med; prepare *now* for retirement at Happy Oaks. The Industrial Age has given way to the Age of Anomie. Modern technology has made physical labor less strenuous, but at the cost of the pride that accompanied it.

Two divergent theories about work life are worth noting, if not for what they reveal about workers, then about how industrial psychologists think. The first, Theory X (honestly, its academic name), holds that most people are essentially industrious and honest. They derive great satisfaction from *labor*, not just the paycheck. Employers should encourage devotion with challenging and self-actualizing jobs. The worker should never be a mere link in the chain, but an active participant in decision making. The surrounding environment should be stimulating, conducive to thought and relaxation.

The second, Theory Y, is less sanguine. People are inherently lazy, unambitious, and deceptive. They will try to get away with as little as possible. The employer must be coercive, demanding, and stubborn, simply to get an honest day's work out of the sly ungrateful bastards. The working environment should emphasize *labor*—that is, stress. Relaxation happens in the home.

Which theory does *your* boss side with? Check your personnel manual, or if that fails, the look on his or her face when you arrive at the office five minutes late. Speaking from personal experience, I'd say people have a proclivity toward the deceptive. This is bound to increase as work becomes more detached from the final product, and more unrewarding in any creative sense. And more nerve-racking as job jumping, community abandonments, and practices such as urine testing increase.

While on the subject, I'd like to present my own labor theory. The human animal is reluctant to work because it is inherently untamable. Education stresses individuality and personal achievement. Kids rarely learn about collective efforts, or organizing. American heroes are the great loners, the Ayn Rand egoists— Thomas Edison, Henry Ford, Albert Einstein; or today Ted Turner, Lee Iacocca—people with tremendous ambition and intelligence to match. A "career" is for the individual. There is little encouragement for the idea that workers share a communality of conditions. In fact, relying on the group for strength is pictured as a weakness by the individual. In this sense, unions are for losers. It is no wonder we are the least-unionized industrial society in the world.

When we're put in a cubicle or on the assembly line, our bonds to other workers are broken. The anonymity goes against the basic need for attention. No wonder people resent being fettered behind a desk or welding mask—it threatens self-esteem. Minimum wages, job insecurity, and unsafe working conditions shatter ambition. Most of all, workers resent being given orders that they don't respect.

Everything in my seven-year fugitive life confirmed this. For the most part, my running mate and I held menial jobs. Low pay, unsafe conditions, and job security that depended less on one's ability than on how one got along with the immediate supervisor. I was once fired as an assistant cook because the hotel manager needed a place for this neat-looking cowgirl who had just drifted down from Denver. This was not, I can assure you, affirmative action taking place. And in this world of gypsy labor, sexual harassment was more common than not. Not getting paid or being docked for fabricated reasons was also common, since management assumed correctly that workers had no way to redress grievances.

Most of these years, the three children I left behind lived on welfare. No one who's been underground recommends the life by a long shot, but I was forced to learn truths that class privilege, education, and later fame had removed from my vision. In the sixties, a variety of factors were used to organize—age, sex, race, counterculture, and later, sexual preference. What would strike any student of protest movements as unusual was the absence of class. You use what you can; it was a time of relative affluence. The AFL-CIO was a strong supporter of Vietnam, many unions fought against affirmative-action programs, some were used by Nixon to attack anti-war demonstrators.

Jimmy Hoffa, with all his corruption acknowledged, was the last labor leader who had the power and potential to even threaten a general strike. That must have been thirty years ago. If the economy takes a nose dive over the next five years, with the farm belt, the oil patch states, and areas based on heavy industry all hard hit, don't be surprised to see more militant workers. Don't be surprised to see people talking more about class differences. Already our attitude of praise for the yuppie lifestyle is contributing to that polarization, since workers are seen as so many "dumb poor slobs" with one lucky job elevating them above the homeless bums in the streets.

If workers are perceived as lazy or unambitious, it's probably because the jobs they take are not those which they would voluntarily choose. No one starts out wanting to be a men's room attendant (although with increased urine testing, the prestige and power—not to mention bribes—might affect this position). People fall into careers more often than they make conscious decisions to pursue a defined path. We work because we must, because of mortgages, children, Visa bills, and because we're hooked on some form of over-consumption, from the Home Shopping Network to the Neiman-Marcus Christmas Catalogue. Honestly, most of us would rather be sleeping, eating, having sex, and listening to rock and roll. Some, like myself, would find enjoyment in challenging the powers that be. Others would find themselves in various art forms. (Although most writers will tell you that writing is hard, painful work). Charles Kingsley, a nineteenth-century poet, summed up the frustration: "Men must work and women must weep / For there's little to earn and many to keep." Today both work and both weep.

The old standards which demand that people must work are as much to blame for bad attitudes as a basic dislike for work. Ultimately the employer who recognizes the reasons for the staff's ambivalence is going to survive longer than the one who ignores it.

There are as many solutions to the workplace crisis as reasons for its origin. Two personal favorites would first encourage, through government loans and tax breaks, that American industry follow the worker participation model used in Scandinavia. There employees are made wholly *responsible* for a manufacturing process from start to finish. The scope of the job is greater than screwing one bolt endlessly.

The second insists that business must be made more accountable to the community than it is now. Actually, this is Gore Vidal's idea. If transnationals insist on bankrupting communities by pulling out because the workers want better conditions, or the community complains about pollution, they should pay a price. They were given all sorts of goodies to lure them to town (tax deferments, zoning changes, etc.). So it's fair to penalize them when they turn their backs on the community and callously leave: "So long, we can do it cheaper in Korea!" There is no way now that the local community can retaliate. The federal government should penalize huge corporations for destroying our productive capacity and increasing our lust for consumer toys. Those products should be taxed accordingly when they re-enter the country. Since executives are mobile enough to glide from one location to another, from the industrial to the information age, the workers should also have that same right. The taxes could be used to retrain workers and preserve local communities. This is called economic democracy. We are not yet free to vote on such issues in elections. Only a wave of serious recession met by a rising tide of grassroots populism could possibly put economic democracy on the agenda. Ultimately, programs to ease tension between workers and management must be built on justice and honesty.

Of course, hating work may not come naturally. Like any habit, it can be cultivated. Some companies have a knack for bringing out the worst in their employees. In 1956 I had to sign a loyalty oath to get a summer job in a local metalworks plant. It was misery, in a way a lot like prison. I worked the swing shift, which meant rotating the eight-hour shift each week. This practice not only made off-hour relaxation impossible, it also seriously destroyed sleep patterns. At seven A.M., half groggy, I was given a heavy, whirling wheel grinder and blistered my hands on newly fabricated metals for endless hours. Sparks flew, oil sprayed in the air, the heat was impossible, and tiny shards of aluminum penetrated my skin. I was one of the lucky ones. Older men, twice my age, let me know how much they resented and envied me. I appreciated their captivity. I was only there for a couple of weeks more and then back to college. They had twenty years in, and another ten to serve before they could get out, rarely with their lungs and limbs intact. Imagine having to go through all this hardship and face the humiliating act of signing a paper to prove you were a loyal American.

Four years later, as a graduate student at Berkeley, I heard one of the country's most esteemed psychologists, Dr. Walter Tolman, talk about the battle to abolish the oaths in California. As I listened to him speak about the courageous people who walked away from careers on matters of principle, I wondered why so many Americans, myself included, had allowed ourselves to be bullied by overbearing bosses and adherence to phony rituals. The answer remains the same more than thirty years later. *We give in to intimidation because the alternative is fear.* Unemployment, even if based on lofty principles, is a stigma. It has a stink to it. Employers wield this unvocalized threat to hold workers in subjugation.

Sadly, the way things look now, a New Order may well spring from the pages of L. L. Bean sooner than from *Das Kapital.* The 1980s have sharply redefined the goals of the middle class beyond the reach of middle-class people. Sending three kids to college can cost up to $200,000; average medical insurance, which runs about $1,200 a year, has more and more fine print excluding a host of new diseases; proliferation of computerized databases has made it impossible to escape credit hunters and the IRS.

The Protestant work ethic, out of favor in the sixties, has had a rebirth. More and more, men and women are sacrificing their personal time—"quality time"—for twelve hours at the office. Helping handicapped kids or fighting a toxic dump project only takes time away from career goals. Time *is* money. Lunch is no longer a period to eat but an opportunity to make a deal. Reality is now pronounced realty.

In a *Newsweek* cover story on the newly affluent ("The Year of the Yuppie"), one woman prototype remarked, "I can make it on $200,000 a year if I don't have kids and limit myself to one new outfit a week." By the way, some people think $200,000 a year is middle class.

Census bureau statistics show that of 76 million persons born between 1945 and 1961 (generally considered to be the "baby boomers"), only 3.6 million earn $35,000 plus annually, while 23 million earn $10,000 a year or less. That means for every possible yuppie dashing around in a financed Porsche, about eight single mothers with kids are sucking the glue off food stamps. The Rutgers Center for Urban Policy Research, in an exhaustive study of baby boomers concluded, "They [the majority] are dramatically worse off than people their age were 20 years ago and are falling steadily further behind." Persons now aged twenty-five to thirty-four are facing the greatest economic difficulties. "Most," says the Rutgers research, "cannot afford the kinds of homes their parents, and even their predecessors in the baby boom were able to buy." Notice how sharply this reality collides with what's considered "average" in the lifestyle section of your local newspaper.

There are hidden problems with the "new" work ethic. The dual family income is more a sign that two people can't make it on one check than of the liberated new lifestyle. Remarked one investment banker, aged thirty-two, "You work hard, you're supposed to play hard. But who can afford to play?"

Play? No one's sure this constantly upward activity is even *work*. Real productivity has not increased over the past five years. Yuppies spend like crazy but save little. There are signs of economic breakdown everywhere—from the individual overdrawing on his or her credit card to the government's deficit spending, from E. F. Hutton check-kiting to insider trading. From acquisitions and mergers to leveraged buyouts. Because interest rates and inflation remain low (due in no small part to OPEC falling apart) and the stock market sets record levels daily, what looks like prosperity might actually be a lot of fancy paper shuffling, refinancing already borrowed money. A floating prosperity at best, nothing solid here.

In such a state of anxiety—where violent mood swings lash the economy—it's not just the working class that gets edgy. Every time you read about a merger or acquisition, you don't read about the jobs cut out in the process. Welcome to the leaner, meaner corporate world of the eighties. Heads are rolling, left and right. No wonder some Wall Street investment brokers have resorted to making money the old-fashioned way—by selling drugs. And no wonder cocaine is the drug of choice. You lose appetite (weight), you stay up all night, you become, as Malcolm X described it, "Superman of the moment." Our economy, our society is now on a moment-to-moment relationship with reality. Doomsday financiers in fancy three-piece suits get huge fees for telling investment conferences the bubble could burst any moment. Few call them crazy.

The rules of the labor game keep changing. That shouldn't be surprising; America thrives on transition—occasionally at the loss of our national identity. The demise of small business in the sixties marked the end of personal work relationships. The Employer is now an abstraction, perhaps not even an American. It is not the harried supervisor yelling at you over a cubicle partition, but the anonymous entity at the top of the organization chart. It's hard to feel loyalty to a multi-national with its headquarters in tax-free Monaco, its ships registered in tax-free Panama, its mines in Chile, its factories in Taiwan, its lawyers on Wall Street, and maybe a final assembly plant in Texas. That is, after the basic assembly has been done across the border in Mexico by fourteen-year-old kids earning two bucks a day.

The faceless board of directors has the power of God over its subjects. Merge and acquire, engulf and devour. Concentrated economic power has made it possible for the Company to act out any fantasy in the workplace, prohibited or not.

Want some examples? "What's good for General Motors is good for America." Unless you're trying to get around Los Angeles without a car. General Motors was charged with hindering the development of urban mass transit and national passenger rail systems in the fifties, so the nation would be dependent on the automobile and ensure GM a captive market for aeons hence. That one company had enough political and economic clout to obstruct a national priority tells you a lot about government policy. Lately Dow Chemical has been selling itself as the hope of the emerging world. "Gosh, Dad," ejaculates one commercial, "I'm going to take the job with Dow and work on new ways of increasing the food supply." Never mind that twenty years ago Dow came up with wonderful ways of defoliating the developing world with napalm. Along with its fellow industrial contaminators, it still unloads chemicals judged unsafe for the domestic market on poor countries too desperate to read the fine print on the labels. After all, what do long-term hazardous effects mean if the average lifespan is only forty-nine?

To have insensitive, autonomous, all-powerful directors at the top, one must also have disorganized, compliant sheep at the bottom. Above all else, selfishness rules America.

We deliberatively avoid a global economic vision as well as a social awareness of reality, forcing ourselves to look out for number one. The problem is, fewer and fewer number ones can make it. The walls are closing in.

10.

Enforcers at Work: All You Can Lose Is Your Job

Anarchy and mayhem, a certain amount anyway, can go on, is even encouraged in the streets. But on the shop floor, things are strictly business—order, control, and the laws of profit prevail.

The company has always tried getting the most for the least. Labor is classified as raw material. The best raw material, as far as management is concerned, is one which doesn't pay attention to the economic realities already described. Companies seek workers who accept the myths, especially about hard work and honesty paying off.

The notion of employee testing—ensuring that workers meet the standards established by the company—is centuries old. Every civilization fashions on its own ways of establishing virtue. Most involve trial by fire. In tribal Africa, suspected criminals had to thrust their hands into boiling water. If unscalded, the victims were honest. In Arabia, Bedouins forced legal witnesses to lick a red-hot iron bar. If the tongue was burned, the witness was lying, and was marked for more torture. If the tongue wasn't cooked, testimony was accepted. Three centuries ago in Salem, if suspected witches who were dunked in water drowned, they were innocent. If they survived, they were burned as witches.

The difference between modern America and ancient Arabia is not in the *idea* of testing; rather it is the *type* of test that has changed. *Sophisticated technology makes the superstitious and irrational seem reasonable.* Good P.R.—good for progress, good for business. And high-tech is ever so fashionable.

In the 1800s, sheer brawn was the sole requirement for most factory jobs. Prospective applicants, mostly immigrants, lined up outside the foreman's door. (Younger readers may be surprised to learn there were no résumés or headhunters involved.) Likely candidates were ordered to lift boulders, pull laden carts, or even beat the hell out of each other—all to pass the test. Those who survived got to put in ten hours of the same, only this time for cash. The rejects? Back to the pushcarts.

As science improved, so did tests of fitness. Medical examinations and psychological tests were given to make sure the company was hiring undamaged goods. God forbid that someone with asthma should be brought in undetected! Oaths of loyalty, to God, the boss, and America (not necessarily in that order) were all popular for a while.

And then came the lie detector. Where a smile and words could deceive, the brain could not lie. When a psychology student, I studied sensory deprivation and self-hypnosis with polygraph responses. My teacher was Dr. Martin Orin, Brandeis Visiting Professor from Massachusetts General Hospital in Boston. He is today considered the world's leading authority on polygraphs (and how to beat them).

In 250 B.C., the Greek physician Erasistratus observed an increase in the pulse rate when someone was lying. The ancient Greeks, a philosophical people, thought better of using the phenomenon and let it rest. Americans are more suspicious. A mere twenty centuries later, in the 1940s, John E. Reid came up with the first "practical" polygraph machine to measure distortion in several fundamental human responses—breathing, pulse, muscle contraction, emotional tension. The underlying theory holds that "lying produces intervening emotional states which reveal themselves in recordings of physiological activity" (Skolnick, "Scientific Theory and Scientific Evidence: An Analysis of Lie Detection," 70 *Yale Law Journal* 696, 696–700 (1961).)

It seemed a great idea at the time, a machine that did away with the charred tongues and gave investigators a voyeur's thrill by peeking into the psyche. Not until the 1960s, though, were lie detectors added to the prescreening arsenal. This was the first overt use of technology to indicate distrust was built into the business relationship—on the employer side. (However, in South African diamond mines, workers leaving after six months of confined labor were routinely X-rayed for gems.) As with today's urine test, prospective workers had to prove their virtue psychologically before they could be hired. It wasn't limited to high-security fields, either. Everyone from Radio Shack to the CIA gave them. My underground running mate was required to take a polygraph before she could become a cocktail waitress in Miami. She was told testing would take place every three months, and one of the questions she found particularly annoying required her to snitch on theft and drug use among other workers. Angels never lie, but they also never submit to polygraphs.

The modern polygraph is designed to recognize changes in physiological-electrical impulses emanating from reaction to external stimuli. In plainspeak, it senses shock waves when you lie. There are several variations, but this is the basic principle. Probing, occasionally unfair questions about honesty, family history, and substance abuse provide the stimuli. The applicant, technically known as the victim, is strapped into a reclining chair and ordered to relax, in much the same way a death-row convict is told to take it easy. Electrode sensors are taped to the temple, chest, and several fingers of each hand. The fingertips, experts claim, give the best results. A conductive jelly and electrode measure levels of electrical resistance termed the *galvanic skin response*.

The victim is first requested to lie *intentionally*, so the technician is aware the machine is working properly. In the trade this is called digging your own grave. Then the real questioning starts. Every fifteen seconds, the interrogator randomly poses questions. The victim is expected to answer "yes" or "no." "No comment" is unacceptable. Unlike court, there are no rules prohibiting self-incrimination in the workplace. Responses are graphed automatically.

When the battery of questions is finished, a technician compares the printout to a standard reference. Any obvious lie and the victim is rewired, confirming or qualifying the alleged deception. Eventually a decision is made.

The polygraph is badly flawed. False positives are rampant. Anxiety, heartburn, and headache are known to distort the results.

And the subjective interpretation of the interrogator adds the chance of human error. The legal and scientific communities look down on it. In 1983, the Office of Technology Assessment (OTA) found that there was very limited scientific evidence validating polygraphy. The American Medical Association (AMA), in September 1986, went the OTA one better and found a high risk of error in lie detection. The AMA vehemently discouraged the use of polygraphy in industry, adding that the potential savings in employee fraud and theft were negligible. Half the states have outlawed polygraphy. The military, to no one's surprise, relies upon it heavily.

Like any subjective, unsubstantiated test, it's possible to beat the polygraph. A couple of tranquilizers, a shot or two of bourbon, a pinprick in a place unseen by the questioner (physical stimuli to counteract or dull the probing questions), or simply biting the tongue could distort a natural response—and, more importantly, turn a lie into truth. An irritating stone in your shoe will produce a constant low level of pain that will make all answers react similarly, throwing off the test. The basic idea is to give your brain something else to deal with than fully concentrating on the questions and answers.

Initially more frightening than polygraph technology were the social implications. Employers were getting deep into Orwellian territory, and the public was confused and alarmed. Was there no privacy left?! A dangerous tool was marketed as a way of promoting honesty. Yet the basis for the test is ridiculous: even a perfect electronic indication of the past is no way of predicting the future. If an employee proves s/he hasn't stolen, is that a guarantee s/he never will?

Similar arguments voiced now about urine testing were raised twenty years ago but didn't slow its use. But there is a big difference in how the public reacted. Polygraphs were never hailed as a way of exorcising the devil. Honesty never became the focus of a national crusade. Lying and hypocrisy from Presidents to evangelist preachers is not seen as a threat to "the fabric of our society."

Once, however, in a rage over cabinet "leaks," Reagan in 1983 threatened to wire 100,000 civil servants to lie detectors. Secretary of State George Shultz and others publicly refused, and the plan was quickly shelved.

The courts don't exactly see it as a faulty test—not consistently, anyway. Polygraphy results are occasionally admitted as evidence. But as with sodium pentathol (truth serum), the debate revolves more around the morality of administration than accuracy. Let he who is without sin take the first lie-detector test.

The polygraph fad lasted about ten years—long enough for its advocates to make a very nice piece of change. It gradually faded but is still used residually. One unfortunate and permanent result: it gave companies a sense of control they had lacked earlier and instilled fear in workers. Here at last was insight into the employees' *minds*.

Technology is a function of two forces: present demand and anticipated demand. The former is the degree that consumers' desires are being satisfied by current products. Anticipated demand represents a manufacturer's hope that a new product can escalate consumer desires. For example, the lie detector satisfied a company's quest for information about an employee that was previously unavailable. The inventors of urine screens recognized the same need plus the brewing national drug hysteria. To cash in, they developed a more advanced product they believed would fulfill the company's need to identify previously hidden information. Identification is always the first step toward control in any science.

Urine tests were initially a supplement for, and later the heir to, the lie detector. By the late 1970s, urine kits became generally available, assuaging national fears about the drug monkey on the GNP's back. The private sector was at first unimpressed. The expense and error rate were prohibitive and the privacy issue unclear.

However, to the federal government, cost and reliability are no obstacle. The Department of Defense (with its $750 toilet seats and $2,000 hammers) became the first and largest customer—and chief promoter.

In the middle seventies, military brass wanted to identify Vietnam troops addicted to heroin and get them into treatment programs (or behind bars). The immunoassay urine screen seemed a good way of starting. Unfortunately it opened up a silo of worms. By 1981 the military discovered that almost 20 percent of the troops were using some controlled substance regularly. Marijuana was the most popular, but cocaine and heroin were also in the top ten. Each branch of the service was ordered to begin mass testing. Since 1981 the armed forces combined have given troops over one million urine tests each year—at twenty to thirty dollars a leak.

The Navy was the first to devise a punitive program. According to its rulebook, all recruits get screened before basic training. If marijuana is detected in the urine, the swab is given a warning and is marked for future random testing. If any other illegal drug is detected, the seaman automatically gets a dishonorable discharge. Actually, it's more discretionary than that. The commanding officer can discharge the person for any *single positive test*. Without appeal. And they mean business. In 1985 alone, 6,000 enlisted recruits and 30 officers were tossed out.

With the military and the President going wild, the private sector started thinking. In 1982, several major corporations made the first, tentative step toward massive testing. Product reliability hadn't really improved, and the privacy issue was still vague, but that no longer seemed to matter.

Urine testing spread like herpes. *By 1984, 20 percent of the Fortune 500 corporations used it. By 1985, the level reached 25 percent. In 1987, nearly half of all major industries have some form of drug testing.* In a three-year burst, a once unheard of procedure has become routine practice.

"The formula for a high-paying job today is six or seven interviews and a drug test," according to a recent Dartmouth College graduate. A highly regarded survey of hiring trends, the Northwestern Endicott-Lindquist Report, claims, "By the end of 1987, 52 percent of the nation's largest companies will be requiring drug tests. Two-thirds will test only new job applicants." Jay Miller, executive director of the Illinois ACLU, believes that anyone who flunks a first test will be passed over, since a confirmation test also confirms that drugs are the reason for the refusal to hire. "If the Number 1 candidate fails a drug test, they'll just choose Number 2 or Number 3 and not bother to tell Number 1 why he or she didn't get the job. Why set themselves [the companies] up for lawsuits," he remarked. Al A. Wolf, manager of news and information at the Dow Chemical Company, expressed a common corporate view: "The applicant doesn't have to be tested—we just break off negotiations." There doesn't seem to be much concern about a shortage in the labor pool at any level of occupation.

Testing isn't limited to reactionary corporations by a long shot. The *New York Times*, vaunted defender of civil liberties, requires all job applicants, from editor to typist, squeeze their bladders. The people who set personnel policy apparently don't bother reading the editorial pages. William Safire and Tom Wicker have consistently taken shots at compulsory screening. The *Times* last fall conveniently left itself off a list of leading corporations which test employees. Capital Cities/ABC tossed around the idea of dragging marijuana-sniffing dogs though the city room at its *Kansas City Star*—that is, until the public heard about it. Capital Cities/ABC in early July, 1987, mandated that candidates for full-time employment must be screened for drug use. Street talk has it that *Rolling Stone*, the last bastion of gonzo journalism, screens its staff. This astounded me. I called the New York editorial office and asked if the rumor was true. "I'm sorry, but I'm not allowed to discuss that," hedged Refused-to-Give-a-Name. "Oh, come on, do you or don't you? It's not that difficult?" "Sorry, I can't say," her voice implying "yes." The *Los Angeles Weekly* reported that the L.A. *Times* is regularly testing all staffers. It offered a $1,000 reward to any reporter who refused and told his or her story. There are at least fifty major news sources which regularly use or are about to start urine screening. How objective can they be with their heads at the computer terminals and their genitals in the jar?

In the early eighties, prompted by the War on Drugs, think tanks investigated the "true costs" of *all* substance abuse. The Research Triangle Institute, a Washington-based think tank, came up with six areas of drain: lost productivity; medical expenses; disability claims; employee theft; poor decision making; and wasted supplies. Less tangible costs result from "bad morale." And a great newspeak phrase, "on-the-job absenteeism," was born—meaning that the employee is physically present but the mind is out to lunch. The cost to the economy was estimated as $100 billion in 1983 and more than $108 billion in 1985. A quarter of this loss was attributed to illegal drug use.

Not to be outdone in the numbers game, Croft Consultants projected nearly 4 million workers abusing drugs at an average cost of $4,200 each—an expense of nearly $17 billion. (Spending over $4,000 a year on drugs could be considered one criterion of abuse!) The Employee Assistance Society estimates the cost at $39 billion. Peter Bensinger, formerly of NIDA and now one of the chief proponents of urine testing, estimates drug abuse costs us $65 billion. Bensinger fed the hysteria: "With 22 million marijuana users, 8 million cocaine users, and over 10 million Americans using prescription drugs without appropriate medical supervision, the work place is literally riddled with substance abusers." These numbers are pulled out of the same hat the Defense Department uses to justify Star Wars. You can do it too.

Drug abuse is only one part of a perceived illness in the workplace. Alcoholism is the truly serious affliction. There are 300,000 narcotics addicts in the U.S. Compare that to 5 million alcoholics, and you know right off that companies are not screening for the right substance. Corporate alcoholism costs between $15 billion and $30 billion, according to the Industrial Alcoholism Institute. The Cornell University School of Industrial Labor Relations estimated that 4 percent of an average workforce will be deviant drinkers.

Hypocrisy is built into all corporate testing procedures that exclude potentially more hazardous substances simply to nail drugs. Nicotine, alcohol, and caffeine all are potentially addictive but are excluded because they happen to be legal—and are enjoyed by CEO's, VP's, and legislators. And subsidized. And reinforced actually as business ritual—the coffee break, the three-martini lunch, smoke-filled rooms, cigars for the worker's new baby, the wild Christmas party.

The National Institute for Drug Abuse acknowledges a serious problem in the workplace but disagrees over its severity: *Less than 10 percent of workers under the age of thirty use marijuana on the job; 3 percent use cocaine, and half of 1 percent use heroin.*

It would be naive to think that drug tests are implanted solely to catch 2 percent of drug abusers while they are at work.

If the true cost and pervasiveness of on-site drug abuse isn't as high as employers make it out to be, why the hysteria? The answer is complex. If the workplace were perfect, job performance would be the only way of evaluating employees. Things like skin color, sex, sexual preferences, or off-duty activities would be disregarded. But employers are subject to the same prejudices as you and me. Possibly more so. Their immense economic power leads to delusions of grandeur and the accompanying paranoia. *All workers are suspect.* One grocer remarked of his staff, "They are outsiders who trespass on private property, my property, work a little, and get paid."

I suspect that the real appeal of the urine test lies in its control over a workforce that had become dangerously suspicious and potentially powerful. Pulling workers' pants down lets 'em know who's boss. It threatens their jobs and dignity.

The boss is under no obligation to fire anyone who has a positive test result. The implied threat in the urinalysis is sufficient control. The EMIT results could be tossed out or pocketed for a more auspicious occasion—as when the worker becomes a troublemaker, is beyond his productive years, or a merger simply requires some staff reduction.

Manipulation goes hand in hand with control. This isn't necessarily restricted to drug use, but may include all employee extracurricular activities. The U.S. Gypsum Corporation, in Wisconsin, is the first to prohibit its workers from smoking cigarettes at any time, *on and off the job.* One employee commented, "I'm not a smoker, but where will this end? Will the company tell me who I'm permitted to marry, where I should live, where I send my kids to school?"

Other controls are more reminiscent of Stalinism than what passes for democracy. It's not unusual for spies to be planted on the shop floor, digging up anything on the workers. Attorney General Edwin Meese promoted these tactics. He suggested, "Employers watch over workers in the lunchroom, the locker room, the bathroom, and even in nearby taverns."

The urine test makes a convenient weapon of discrimination. The *Philadelphia Inquirer* reported that one local union president was screened five times in three months, probably more because he was unpopular with management than a legitimate suspect. No surprise that OSHA found that company guilty of harassing its employees. The disproportionately high scrutiny of minorities is another problem echoed across the country. "If the company doesn't like blacks, the test is a convenient excuse to get rid of them," said one union representative.

Corporate lawyers argue that such restrictions are imposed to protect employers. They want and have the right to demand a drug-free workplace. Judges agree, ruling that an employer acts *in loco parentis*—that is, assumes responsibility for a worker while on the job. One employee who was visibly drunk was ordered to leave the plant. On his way home, the worker, drunk and driving, was involved in a serious collision. The court held the company responsible for the accident by sending him home impaired and unescorted (*Otis Engineering vs. Clark*, 1983). A urine test, they claim, will reduce the risk (and costs) of injury.

It doesn't take an OSHA bureaucrat to see hundreds of ways to safeguard the workplace without presuming guilt or resorting to unreasonable tactics. But the very unreasonableness of the urine test—its powerful deterrent effect—makes it so attractive. Virtually every company reports 100 percent compliance. Workers who know they are liable for a surprise drug test and who are equally aware the result could jeopardize employment, will lay off drugs.

Or find a way around them. If the urine test is a disincentive to drugs, isn't it an incentive to another high? "I gave up dope when they started testing," said one metal worker. "But I needed something, so I drank scotch, bourbon, gin, you name it. I never got hung over from dope."

One of the tenets of capitalism is that no one does something for nothing. I suspected testing would have some immediate financial incentive for the company. I was wrong. "No tax break or insurance discount for screening," say the underwriters. They're certainly doing the insurance companies a favor: drug testing allegedly removes one of the highest risk groups from the staff. (Consistent drug users have up to three times the average medical claims.) Both Metropolitan Life and Aetna insist drug screening is too new to warrant premium breaks that companies with non-smoking policies get.

There is a war raging in the workplace. The adversaries are natural enemies—management and labor. But one of the greatest threats to workers comes from their own ranks. Worker ambivalence to drug testing has allowed management to violate privacy rights without protest. The attitudes "Sure, why not test, I have nothing to hide," or "I think it's great that management will get rid of drug users," display a lack of concern among the rank and file toward civil liberties and solidarity. If more and greater intrusions are allowed, eventually there will be no liberties left to protect.

A March 1986 *USA Today* poll showed that nearly 80 percent of Americans did not oppose drug testing. These are your neighbors, co-workers, bosses. Strangely, the more education and training the respondent had, the more likely s/he was to come out in favor of drug testing. Doctors, lawyers, people who are familiar with margins of error and civil liberties were all apparently swept away by the tornado of hysteria. There are few people rushing to defend victims.

Allen Pettigrew, a Southern Pacific employee, was wrongly accused of abusing cocaine after a single EMIT false-positive result. In spite of a confirmation test proving negative, Pettigrew was ordered to attend a rehabilitation clinic for five days of evaluation and treatment. Southern Pacific, despite recommendations from medical authorities to the contrary, then shipped Pettigrew off to a twenty-eight-day program. They also demoted him and cut his salary by $11,000. The emotional toll and defamation forced him to file suit, charging fraud, malpractice, deceit, and battery. "Drug testing has made my life pure hell," he says. No co-workers offered support.

Allen Pettigrew's experience is not an isolated event. Hundreds of loyal employees, who have never been within a hundred yards of a drug sale, still wear the scarlet "A" for "Abuser." Many more are likely to join them. If a drug test has an admitted error rate of 5 percent and twenty people are tested, at least one person is always going to be wrongly accused. Multiply that by a workforce of 100, or 10,000 or 100 million and the magnitude of the injustice escalates. It's not merely isolated random victims, but legions. (In Chapter Twelve, "Deep Inside Urine Testing," you will see the margins of error are much larger.)

What about the worker who uses drugs on weekends or vacations? As long as his or her performance is unimpaired and the job gets done safely, the company should have no valid grounds for complaint. Confessed drug users in professions ranging from busboy to college registrar performed their jobs admirably and even earned promotions, while unsuspected by colleagues and supervisors. Psychiatrists have argued that occasional moderate drug use enhances performance.

Ultimately, the urine test is not used to secure a drug-free workplace, but a drug-free workforce. The difference is extreme. A drug-free workplace is a responsible goal, promoting better job performance and safety. A drug-free workforce, however, means imposing moral values unrelated to performance. This is the deception practiced from day one. All the costs and wasted effort are not as important as the risk to the company's reputation. The distinction is important. The employer is afraid of the stigma attached to drug users on the staff. Urine testing is used to regulate behavior *away* from the workplace.

Corporate policy concerning substance abuse treatment has lately been about 20 percent action and 80 percent rhetoric. At least, that's the breakdown between companies who test for drugs *and* have sponsored a rehabilitation program, and those who just test. When screening programs are hawked to prospective clients, the altruistic benefits are pushed: "Help your employees get the treatment they deserve," advertised one laboratory. To get treated, though, they first have to be ferreted out.

So if only one company in five has compassion, what of the others? The bottom line is that drug tests mostly result in demotion or termination without explanation. For example, Federal Express drug policy can be summed in one word: NO! Reasonable suspicion results in termination. No treatment, no second chance, no appeals. Most companies just go right out and hire another worker to replace the "defective" one.

Some companies can't afford the twenty dollars per worker for drug testing, but still want to play Sherlock Holmes. A Philadelphia computer software company had a policy which gave managers the right to fire workers they *thought* were "associated" with drugs or drug users. One chart highlighted the "warning signs of drug abuse": sudden weight loss, hair loss, anxiety, bloodshot eyes, excessive sweating, bumping into furniture, falling asleep at the desk, sloppy dress, frequent trips to the bathroom. Anyone fitting the description "should be referred for observation and consultation." These charts closely resemble similar ones posted in defense plants during World War II to uncover potential traitors.

Substance abuse is only one small area affecting job performance. Employers may just as well forbid all emotional entanglements— sex, love, hate, grief—since they can mess up the head just as surely as the joint copped at a party on the weekend. I've been through it all and can tell you that divorce, illness, being broke, and family trauma have screwed me up more than any drug you can name.

I think the employer really wants an emotionless automaton. Perhaps that's why robotics technology is displacing human sweat, forcing employees toward superhuman perfection—through the thinly veiled threat in every specimen jar. But the Japanese haven't come up with the perfect robot yet, and companies still have to take what they can get—imperfect human beings. There's lots of drugs in Japan, Germany, and elsewhere. With the exception of our subsidiary Canada, no other country in the world has a urine test policy.

As noted by Dr. Carlton Turner, Reagan's former drug policy adviser, "Every major corporation in the U.S. within the next three to five years—I'll say within three years—will have a pre-employment screen." Evidently, Dr. Turner took his own prediction seriously. He left Ronnie to pursue the big money as a testing consultant. (Dr. Turner, by the way, believes there is a link between marijuana and AIDS. Pot, he reasons, leads to hard drugs, which leads to sharing needles, which leads to AIDS. This guy sort of is the James Watt of the drug world.)

Others are skeptical, believing the mania for testing will cool down. John Zalusky, an economist for the AFL-CIO, thinks the issue has been blown out of proportion by the White House and the press. "What we're seeing now is the initial overreaction," he said. "The tests presume guilt and abuse lots of innocent people. Eventually, it's going to catch up with them." Zalusky was careful to distinguish between individual bias and the objective requirements of the workplace. "I personally feel drug use is wrong, in or out of work, even if there's no impairment. After all, it's illegal. But the employer is not a moral judge. He should be concerned only with performance. The employer is not a law enforcer, and he shouldn't be."

Labor unions, which in the past have brought strength to workers, are today in turmoil. A changing economy has reduced their power, and the Reagan administration has not exactly fostered a harmonious labor policy. (Remember the striking 1982 air-traffic controllers—fired even though they supported Reagan in the 1980 election?) Nonetheless, much of organized labor has taken a stand on drug testing. The National Treasury Employees Union has called it "disgraceful" in its suit against the U.S. Customs Service. The International Brotherhood of Teamsters in 1984 tried standardizing drug testing, requiring that tests be given only for reasonable cause, objective suspicion, after accidents, or during a physical exam, with the urine only being screened for specific drugs. Rigid appeal and confirmation procedures must be followed.) AFL-CIO locals had by 1987 curtailed or modified random drug-testing applications in a majority of collective bargaining agreements. But labor is limited in its economic power, and drug testing is not an issue it can afford to strike over.

The workplace has been stymied and confused.

Enter the National Institute for Drug Abuse (NIDA), which practically invented urine testing. In March 1986, NIDA hosted a forum discussing rampant abuses. Participants included major corporations, unions, and medical authorities. The participants established guidelines for biochemical testing in nonmedical applications. The recommendations included:

- No surprise or random testing.
- Potential testees must be given advance notice.
- Impairment or other "just cause" is required.
- Unconfirmed suspicion is an unacceptable basis for a test.
- Results are confidential.
- Treatment, not punishment, is the goal.

NIDA's suggestions were far from perfect. But all sides agreed that restraint must be used with such an intrusive measurement. Not that this had anything to do with actual corporate response. Industry continues to ignore guidelines suggested at the forum.

The best solutions to the substance abuse problem are those that labor and management have worked out together. As drugs and alcohol became issues of public concern in the sixties, companies and unions redefined employees' needs. Abuse, in the progressive sector, was considered an illness, not a crime. Cooperative management-labor treatment programs, called Employee Assistance Programs (EAPs), were devised as nonpunitive rehabilitation programs for gradual treatment. Typically, an EAP offers confidential psychiatric and medical counseling, and the opportunity to return to work. Most large corporations, over half of the Fortune 500, sponsor one. There are about 10,000 active. Still less than 20 percent of the workforce has access to any company-sponsored program, and though EAPs are founded on sound and sincere principles, many are just auxiliary cheering camps for the company and the National Party Line. The worker with a drug problem is not their primary concern.

The concept makes sense. One EAP director profiled in the *New York Times* estimated that for every dollar invested in the EAP, the company got back seven dollars in reduced benefits usage and absenteeism. It's a mutually satisfactory relationship: the employee keeps his job, gets treatment, and the company raises productivity.

But every cloud has a dark lining. Drug testing has invaded the EAPs. They have been used to discover which employees may require help. A positive EMIT results in an ultimatum: join the EAP or lose your job. In too many corporations, EAP's drum up their own business, detecting abusers and counseling them. They take on the roll of the company stoolies, the "good guy" Enforcers.

Paul Samuels, executive vice president of the Legal Action Center, testified before the House Select Committee. He stressed rehabilitation over persecution:

> The best way to eliminate drug abuse is to establish a good EAP. Employers should train supervisors to identify and refer troubled employees. The EAP should include appropriate diagnosis, referral, treatment, and aftercare . . . Employers should retain those employees who overcome drug abuse; they need not continue to employ substance-abusing employees unable to perform the job.

Remember, in no other case of a serious medical illness is a single laboratory test used to diagnose and assign a prescribed treatment program. If drug testing *must* be imposed, there are model programs. General Motors Corporation, which spends over $5 million each month on worker treatment and rehabilitation, expects to screen any of its 400,000 hourly workers "for cause"— that is, for suspected substance abuse. GM, though, will not expel the worker *if s/he enrolls in the EAP*. Compare that to Phillips Industries, which tests all job applicants and permanent employees. A positive test means immediate suspension for one month. A second positive test means the pink slip.

Employees victimized by urine testing must resort to legal action if they seek redress. As drug testing has expanded, so have the number of lawsuits. "We're seeing a lot of litigation on this issue, hundreds in the past year alone," said Paul Samuels. "It's not going to subside."

Only a handful—the real tearjerkers—have been publicized enough to make people think twice about the new Yellow Peril. One of the most celebrated suits was initiated by Barbara Luck, a computer programmer for the Southern Pacific Railroad (yes, the same SP that burned Allen Pettigrew). Ms. Luck refused to take a surprise urine test and was summarily dismissed. Her refusal was reasonable: she was not in a safety-related area, her work was acceptable (by the company's admission, she was a model employee), and there was no reason to suspect her of abuse. Nonetheless, SP booted her for "failing to comply with instruction of proper authority." Barbara sued Southern Pacific for wrongful termination and invasion of privacy under the California Constitution. "The case will try to define what an employer can do and under what conditions," said her attorney.

As it turned out, Luck was reluctant to be tested because she was three months pregnant. Urinalysis could have revealed such personal information to her employer, and, she argues, have had a profound effect on her career.

This intrusion bothers even "clean" employees. Aside from snitching on illegal drug use, testing discloses health conditions or treatment which have no impact on performance, which employers would not be entitled to know through customary confidential medical policies. As Barbara Luck feared, involuntary disclosure could result in discrimination. A range of psychotropic drugs, illnesses, or pregnancy can be revealed from a single sample. Employers can review any of a hundred psychotropic drugs or health conditions without the workers' knowledge.

Richard Pollack, a writer and spokesman for the Epilepsy Foundation, noted one of the soundest arguments against random testing.

> The Epilepsy Foundation continues to receive calls from persons with stories of employers who found out they had epilepsy and who either fired them, or changed their responsibilities in such a way that the individual felt he or she was being pushed out of the job. Many individuals suffering from a variety of chronic but nonincapacitating illnesses are fearful that participating in such testing will force disclosure and possibly cause them to be subject to employment discrimination as well as a violation of their personal privacy.

These fears are well founded. One company fired a long-term worker after a urine test turned up asthma. Epileptics have been terminated. Others have been fired for psychiatric treatment when EMIT diagnosed Valium or prescribed barbituates.

Some companies are famous for the deviousness of their drug-detection programs. Physical exams—"for your health"—have been a pretext for getting urine and blood samples. Misdirection abounds. A blood drive in Memphis turned into a witch hunt when the samples were used as evidence of drug abuse.

The brand "abuser" may not be that easy to remove. Like a dishonorable discharge or prison rap, the past haunts the present. A computerized blacklist has been created, bearing the names and social security numbers of thousands whose only crime was to fail a faulty test.

Substance screening runs the gamut of occupations. Basic industry—steel, automobile manufacturing, mining—has cottoned to the idea as a way of improving safety. (Not that coal-mine disasters have been tied to stoned employees.) Other sectors, including computer service and entertainment, are refreshingly free of any drug policy. (How would it look if Hollywood, known for budgeting recreational drugs in their film costs, would screen actors? There'd be no one left to work!)

Generally, the white-collar market has been slow in accepting the hysteria. "The businesses come in clumps," said Margaret Brooks of the New York Legal Action Center. "You'll have no screening going on in an industry, and then almost overnight *everyone* will have some detection program. It's a domino effect; all it takes is one to begin, and the others get nervous, afraid they'll be missing something if they don't start soon."

Wall Street brokerage firms are infamous for their work ethic (or lack thereof) and salaries. Salomon Brothers Inc. is typical of the "in" yuppie houses. As one headhunter put it, "Salomon is where the financial world is happening. People are breaking down doors to get hired." And no wonder. Junior analysts *start* at about $35,000 a year, and are immediately eligible for a 30 percent bonus. Not to mention the perks, the suits, and the glory.

With incentives like these, most people shrug off exhaustive character probes, questionnaires, and urinalysis as the hazing rites to the sacred investment fraternity. To quote one such applicant, "As far as my rights, I'm not really bothered. If you really feel violated, you can become a priest and you won't have to take it [the test]." Before an applicant can rake in the dough, he or she must dole out personal data that would be called self-incriminating in the courts. But the employer is not an impartial judge, and any and all relationships with convicted felons, or with people under indictment or investigation, are suspect and could be checked. And don't think they won't!

The Salomon "Start Packet Forms," a one-inch-thick binder that all new hirees are obliged to fill out on day one, contains:

- Confidential medical history
- Fingerprint card
- Outside business connections sheet
- Security and Exchange Commission questionnaire
- Reference forms
- List of obligations regarding insider trading

After you get through that, "You will visit the Company's Medical Department for a brief interview, and for eyesight, hearing, blood pressure, and urinalysis examination." If your pee-pee isn't pristine, out you go. No ifs, ands, or buts about it. After wasting all that time confessing. What happens to the extensive confidential information you have provided is anyone's guess; you are not given the binder to keep or destroy.

Refusing to take a urine test—"just saying no"—is a welcome display of integrity in a world where principles are compromised daily. Julie Baer is one young woman whose strong feelings of justice made her leave an otherwise suitable job and share her story with us.

After working for Salomon as a temporary computer programmer, Julie was offered a permanent spot on a shift that accommodated her private business (she is the co-owner and producer of Club Soda Music). "It was the kind of job which I had been looking for over a year—flexible hours and excellent pay." She accepted the offer and worked one week when she was told she had to take a urinalysis. "I explained that I don't take drugs, that I had already been hired, and that I was not in favor of any of these tests," she said. "The personnel department answered that I had no choice, that it was an across-the-boards policy, and looked at me with what I interpreted as a specific kind of suspicion."

Julie appealed to her supervisor, and was informed the test was an inviolable condition of employment. "The sad thing is, they never mentioned employment conditioned on a drug test. If anyone had said *anything* in the original interview, I wouldn't have accepted the position. I then asked about other employment scenarios—free-lance, independent contractor—so I would not have to submit to the same requirements as a payroll-type position. The response was 'But how would it look, now that you refused to take the test?' " Essentially, Salomon was labeling her "guilty" until she proved otherwise.

"One person asked outright what drugs I was doing, and several people intimated that the reason I refused was because I must be taking drugs," she said. "No one listened when I argued the tests aren't job-related and don't measure performance. All they prove is that you can urinate on demand!"

Ultimately, Julie's refusal changed her employment status from "hired" to "not hired" (Salomon Brothers' discreet way of terminating someone). She left the job, earned some publicity for her resolve ("Computer Whiz Sacked—Refused Test for Drugs" and "Julie Baer's Dilemma," spouted the *New York Post*), and got in touch with Paul Samuels and the New York Legal Action Center. She testified before the New York State Hearings on Drug and Alcohol Testing, effectively describing her moral outrage at massive, random drug testing:

"The invasion of a potential employee's privacy, and his or her supposed guilt until being proved innocent are, I feel, significant civil liberties questions which must be considered. The simple fact that a policy is 'legal' is not justification for a policy that is *wrong*."

It's disappointing that Wall Street emphasizes urine testing and drug use while insider trading scandals really jeopardize the integrity of the financial markets. Unfortunately, there's no quick, cheap test for greed that the government will support. Little did I realize when we threw money onto the trading floor of the New York Stock Exchange back in '67 that the brokers who were scrambling on their hands and knees for a few lousy bills were prime candidates for bilking the public of billions in the years to come.

Urine testing on Wall Street, Main Street, or Mill Street is a distraction meant to take our minds off a crumbling economy, a shrinking workforce, and a citizenry being cowered into giving up its rights along with its urine.

Because of people like Julie, there might be a chance of beating the bladder cops. But the vast majority grin and bare it. Then they do it in the cup, just like Reagan and Meese want.

Where the hell are the folks who hate Big Government when you really need them the most?!

11.

The Short, Sordid History of Urine Screening

We've explored the world of drugs, enforcement, treatment strategies, and the ill effects on intelligent discourse created by hysteria. The Drug Industrial Complex is perfectly content to focus on these aspects as long as the argument gets limited to the evils of "the drug menace" in our society. Using garbage statistics (sloppy data in, faulty conclusions out), Enforcers appear to win most debates because the public is genuinely concerned, misinformed, and at the same time scared. The symptom becomes the cause, and the real problem gets forgotten.

Two years ago missing children was a hot topic. Talk shows, newspaper articles, TV public service scares—"It's ten o'clock; do you know where your children are?"—even milk cartons reinforced the spectre of perverts running off with our kids. In truth, such cases were fairly rare. The overwhelming majority had run away from bad family situations or had been taken by a concerned divorced parent. A Massachusetts survey, for example, found that in 1983 of all 1600 missing-children cases reported that year, not a single one fit the kidnapping hysteriotype. But, as with drugs, it's much easier emotionally placing the blame "out there" on slimy creeps, corrupting and perverting our youth than reflecting on the origins of the problem.

How the spotlight gets focused is critical in recognizing the ways deception avoids the real issue, how people can be manipulated into an emotional trap from which it can be very difficult to pull back and deal with reality. The Drug Industrial Complex has a public relations strategy that tries at every turn to reinforce people's worst fears about drugs in order to keep the spotlight off the procedure of urine testing.

Probing questions of accuracy, procedure, and constitutional rights will be treated with respect, but they will also be respectfully deferred. Facing this stonewall, I tried luring Drug Industrial shills into an off-the-record, philosophical debate: "Come on, guys, what are the real implications of your urine tests?" They looked reflective, spouted a platitude, and refocused on the drug menace.

What you are about to read in the next few chapters is the most important section of the book. Science relies on specificity, mass media on generalized images. This section attempts to nail things down.

If you'd take its advocates seriously, you'd believe that drug tests were intended solely for diagnostic, health-related reasons—and not for persecuting substance users or intimidating workers. Nothing surprising here. Favorable public perception is important to the Drug Industrial Complex and its advertising agencies, even if it means doctoring the truth. To workers caught with their pants down or skirts up, the manufacturer's intent is academic. Who cares *why* the damn thing was invented when you still have to fill the cup?

Urine screening is detection in its rawest form. Guilt before innocence, chemical finger-pointing, surveillance—all associations the Reagan Enforcers are eager to avoid. Diagnosis, on the other hand, sounds therapeutic. Brochures and trade advertisements of the late seventies turned the privacy violation into an almost altruistic gesture, completely in line with modern medical procedures. "More than thirty EMIT assays are available to measure levels of therapeutic drugs . . . such as those used to treat heart conditions, asthma, and epilepsy, to aid [physicians] in adjusting drug dosages for safe and effective treatment," reads a typical brochure put out by the Syva division of Syntex, a manufacturer of high-tech lab equipment. Ultimately, brochures get around to mentioning detection of drug abuse but always in the language of clinical diagnosis, not surveillance. This is tantamount to saying a urine test is good for you.

Testing consultants, the hundred-dollar-an-hour types, loved this angle. They first marketed their services to rehabilitation clinics as a means of ensuring that patients stay drug-free. "Establishing the diagnosis of chronic heroin addiction involves consideration of the patient's history, physical examination, and results of the urine test . . . . The earlier the problem is recognized, the easier it is to reverse," recommended one study. No mention was ever made of test results being used for other than medical reasons, by the police or employers.

As the drug phobia intensified, test developers got bolder. They took less trouble disguising the real uses of the urine test, and eventually dropped all pretense: "Immediate reliable drug detection has never been this easy," now boasts Syva. Meaning that within minutes you'd know whom to fire. Or bust. Or ship off to a rehabilitation program, needed or not.

The strategy paid off. The employers hungered to know, and the urine experts were more than ready to answer the call of nature. Almost overnight, hundreds of chemical companies and laboratories blossomed across America, some equipped with little more than a two-thousand-dollar machine, minimum-wage specimen handlers, and a Yellow Pages ad. A billion-dollar industry was born.

In contrast to the flamboyant and violent history of drug empires, the history of the urine test is hardly Hollywood material. Despite little bloodshed, though, there are just as many power struggles and politics. Ultimately the plot reveals the havoc government and private enterprise can wreak when they work too closely together.

Chemical detection has long been an intrinsic component of science. In the days of the Roman Empire, physicians and oracles scanned, sniffed, and tasted human by-products on their way to diagnosis and fortune-telling. Leonardo DaVinci was one of many alchemists who studied compounds and excretions in the hope of turning them into gold. It's been human nature to torture molecules, forcing them to confess their secrets of creation. Gradually the process became somewhat standardized.

As we might have expected, the breakthroughs leading to modern biochemical screening came not from academic curiosity, but military necessity. When the U. S. Government wanted a devastating new bomb in the forties, basic physics and chemistry became important business. Research funds led to particle accelerators, spectrum analysis, gas chromatography, and radiation identification, all methods of zeroing in on the basic component of the molecule—the atom. Along the way, scientists became good at positively identifying specific molecules as components of mysterious chemical soups.

At first the War Department (as it was more honestly named) didn't consider applying this new science on people. During World War II the emphasis was on destruction, not detection. Only a small group of physicians saw its potential, first for forensic applications and later diagnostic needs. But the equipment was expensive, the domain of specialized hospitals and research facilities. For a long time, the technology lay dormant.

Drug testing of *healthy* individuals arrived comparatively late. In the sixties America became aware of "recreational" drug use. It began with a counterculture and emerged as a social explosion. Conservative elements, alarmed over losing Vietnam and possibly a generation, banded together in an attempt to control "unacceptable social behavior." One outgrowth was the National Institute of Drug Abuse (NIDA), a Washington money pit responsible for analysis—clinical and social—of the drug scene. NIDA was the institutional force which put the fear of widespread addiction into the public consciousness.

Paranoia seems inextricably linked to bureaucracy. The Defense Department was afraid that wide-scale heroin use among troops in Vietnam would take root in the States when the "grunts" came home. Behavior tolerated ten thousand miles away simply could not be allowed the same latitude stateside. Something had to be done. The solution lay in finding methods of screening GIs for heroin addiction. NIDA, which wanted nothing more than the chance to develop a drug test, found eager allies at the Pentagon. When NIDA applied for research money, the alliance conjured the nightmare of hordes of heroin addicts—bitter, trained to kill, and, of course, black—returning to our peaceful shores as an epidemic. Red tape was cut and grant money guaranteed.

As usual the public knew little of this. The Pentagon minimized the high level of addiction among returning veterans, so funding and research were removed from scrutiny, and always downplayed.

The urine test is as much a product of human persistence as technology. One of the industry pioneers, the Einstein of urine testing, is Dr. Robert L. DuPont, Jr. In 1971 DuPont started a seven-year stewardship as the first head of NIDA, and later as Director of the Special Action Office for Drug Abuse Prevention. Right off he began a crusade to elevate drug abuse to the top echelon of governmental concern. In the mid-seventies, he emphasized honest drug education. NIDA even sponsored research into beneficial usages of illicit substances. With Carter as President, the nation developed a more relaxed, albeit cautious, attitude toward drugs. DuPont adapted to this style, even conferring with NORML about the possibility of marijuana decriminalization. The nation's real drug problems, he said publicly, were alcohol and tobacco. Commission reports and studies sponsored by NIDA just ten years ago would be considered overly permissive, even radical, by today's standards.

But DuPont, at heart a conservative, was preparing for a clampdown. While many states were decriminalizing possession of marijuana, NIDA quietly urged selected companies to improve methods of detecting individual drug use. Syntex had researched biochemical testing through its Syva division as early as 1966 but had lost interest in the field until NIDA opened the door to government money.

The first joint success was the immunoassay, a complex test procedure utilizing chemical binders for illegal substances. "Working together through the seventies, NIDA and Syva developed neat little EMIT urine tests for heroin, cocaine, speed, and PCP that are still used," noted Dean Lattimer, a general in the War on Urine Testing for *High Times Magazine*. The immunoassay met all NIDA's requirements: it provided sensitivity to very low concentrations of drugs; it was a procedure that could be easily taught and performed; and it was relatively inexpensive. The mere fact that it wasn't particularly accurate didn't seem to bother anybody. Roche Diagnostics developed a competitive, equally flawed, screen—Abuscreen—alongside Syva.

NIDA's role in promoting the immunoassay became a prestigious and eventually a financial coup for DuPont. At first, like the test developers, he intimated that the procedures would be confined to medical applications. In his preface to a 1973 Urine Testing Guide, he wrote: "Urine screening for drugs of abuse has become a necessary adjunct to treatment [of addiction]." When it later became apparent that Reagan was about to trounce Carter in the 1980 election, Carter administration appointees hoping to survive shifted to the right. It was no longer healthy to confer with NORML. In urine testing, diagnosis took a back seat to the possibility of mass surveillance. The repercussions of Watergate wore thin, and tight restrictions on FBI, CIA, DEA, and other intelligence-gathering agencies were loosened. Open vials of cocaine, which had once enjoyed high status in Washington, were now kept out of sight. The atmosphere changed rapidly.

DuPont, despite a basic antidrug attitude, was guilty by association with the trend toward liberalization. And at that time, he could find no niche in the New Order. He seemed to be soft on drugs and resigned (read: was squeezed out) from NIDA. He quickly signed on as head of the American Council on Marijuana (ACM, later the American Council on Drug Education), a quasi-scientific fear-mongering group.

Outlasting three Presidents, DuPont had developed survival instincts and a keen nose for shifting political winds. His "born-again" zeal on the dangers of drugs restored his hard-line image and caught the attention of the White House. The Reagans welcomed him back and urged him to resurrect the tests that he had helped create. He could be tough on drugs and gain power at the same time. What was once considered a conflict of interest had among the supply-siders become good efficient government.

DuPont forged the link between government, private agencies, and industry. The combination of large-scale funding, new technology, and propaganda precipitated the rapid growth of the Testing Mentality. Speculative equipment houses and laboratories began training personnel and opening satellite facilities, some before the urine tests were even commercially available.

Ironically, the most prevalent of the illegal drugs—marijuana—

proved to be the most elusive in terms of immunoassay detectability. Without a pot screen, EMIT had as much of a chance in the market as a breathalyzer that couldn't recognize alcohol. The reason was obvious: marijuana, although relatively benign, had millions of users. It was really the symbol of the sixties counterculture and, through the decriminalization movement, gained dangerous widespread support. Alaska made possession of up to four ounces of pot legal in the confines of one's home. Head shops were legitimate business. Cheech and Chong "pot" movies were big box office. But one of the hard-core tenets of the National Party Line is that pot leads to harder, more dangerous drugs. Therefore, stop pot and you nip drug abuse in the bud. The detection of marijuana usage became the primary focus of all research. Estimates are that fully ninety percent of all positive test results occurring today across the nation are for marijuana.

Researchers pursued the complex metabolic path of cannabis with the gusto of small-town dogcatchers, but even unlimited grant dollars couldn't expedite an accurate test. Finally a compromise was reached. Instead of searching for a primary THC metabolite— the one responsible for the high—an assay would look for a more accessible but inert chemical. Called THC carboxylic acid, it doesn't produce the high, but remains in the body for weeks after exposure to the drug. The accuracy would suffer, but tests for the presence of marijuana, however old, were enough to satisfy the developers.

This logic paralleled that of drug detection in the thirties, when opiate testing was based not on finding opium but the more easily detected quinine, the most common "cut" for heroin. Screening for THC carboxylic acid means the equipment is not searching for the chemical that impairs job performance. As we shall later see, it is mistaken for metabolites of other substances, which are quite legal.

Whatever scientific objections were raised got shouted down by the sales division. In 1980 excited public relations staffers at ACM and Syva revealed the EMIT cannaboid test. The Bladder Cops were now armed and dangerous. For the first time, the power brokers took notice. And they smiled. The EMIT assays, conceived as an adjunct to medical practice, were now being pedaled as the ultimate snitch.

What followed seemed more like a circus than the workings of responsible government. The ACM and NIDA, hand in hand, hawked the immunoassay as the final solution to the Drug Menace, which itself was being touted as the chief threat to "traditional" social values. This symbiotic relationship between the urine test and the chief social evil allowed one to feed off the other. In a more rational era, all this would have been laughed off as pseudoscience. According to Dr. Oscar Janiger, a noted Los Angeles psychiatrist who has worked with drugs and addiction for over forty years, "No respected scientist regards the urine test as anything more than quackery."

Enter the three-martini lunch. Lavish banquets and conventions were instrumental in selling EMIT, in getting potential buyers hooked. Chemical cheerleaders wined and dined PTA groups, prison boards, corporation executives, rehabilitation counselors, and, of course, the military. Very few were in a position to question the basic science involved. Conferences took on the flavor of pep rallies. Can do, gung ho, U.S.A. all the way! A light to cast on the darkest evil scourge had been found.

Eureka! It worked!

The entire medical diagnostic market by 1986 had total sales of $2 billion, six years after the THC test was launched. This includes all types of equipment, from CAT-scans to microscope slides. Urine-screening devices, the youngest segment of that market, is easily the fastest-growing, representing sales of over $100 million. Wall Street analysts predict a potential market in excess of $250 million annually by 1990. The *Washington Post* estimates sales of ancillary drug-testing paraphernalia could add another $150 million. And these are conservative estimates, made before Reagan announced his drug-free workplace in September 1986. Since then, as testing skyrocketed, analysts have doubled these projections.

Syva's EMIT is currently the industry leader. An aggressive marketing staff and favorable political climate helped it ring up over $40 million sales in 1985, and almost $60 million in 1986. All this despite persistent negative evaluations by respected scientists. Hoffmann-LaRoche is second. Its Roche Diagnostics sold $20 million worth of Abuscreen, its radioimmunoassay. A company spokesman predicts they will triple business by 1990.

But some folks are never satisfied. In an effort to boost sales, Syva established a consulting arm, called Performance Diagnostics. Armed with Syva's client list, the division was "formed to help companies evaluate the presence or extent of the drug and alcohol problem in the workplace." But it was really a front, another way to push the product. Dr. John Morgan, Professor of Pharmacology and Medicine at Mt. Sinai Medical School, observed, "This service by Performance Diagnostics often included the recommendation of EMIT testing" (Morgan, *Journal of Psychoactive Drugs*, 10/84). To the surprise of no one.

Corporate giants are often successful in new markets if they go in with enough money, but urine testing isn't just the domain of the big boys. It has attracted more than its fair share of entrepreneurs. After Reagan declared war on drugs, it seemed that everyone with a semester of high school chemistry was cashing in. Many have found success. The American Institute for Drug Detection in Rosemont, Illinois (which despite an academic-sounding name is a for-profit company), was founded in 1983 on a shoestring budget. Two years later it has tested over 100,000 specimens for major firms, including Exxon, General Mills, and my old jogging partners at the Chicago Police Department. This one small company experienced a 1985 sales increase of 450 percent over 1984. Profits for 1986 were expected to rise even higher. Keystone Medical Corporation, a subsidiary of Medical Diagnostics, sold nearly one million urine tests in its first year of operation, earning $4 million. And there are scores of others. Urine has literally and figuratively become the Gold Rush of the eighties.

Big money was made while researching urine testing, a lot of it off the taxpayers. During four administrations NIDA pumped millions into Syva and similar research programs. But the ones who really profited, both financially and in experience, were those in on the early development. Like Michael Deaver, who allegedly made millions on his friendships in the Oval Office, so too is the urine-testing industry saturated with influence selling.

Dr. Robert E. Willette was NIDA's head of Clinical Research Technology. As a chemist, he oversaw development of EMIT from 1974 to 1981. When EMIT was on the brink of commercial success,

Willette left the public sector and started his own consulting company—Duo Research in Annapolis, Maryland. Duo specializes in laboratory inspection and performance evaluation. For a sizable fee, a Duo team recommends improvements in technique, accuracy, publicity, and profitability. Above all, Willette exaggerates urine-test accuracy: "Chemical testing can be as close to 100% reliable as science permits." Maybe someday, but not now, not with these tests.

Peter B. Bensinger, former director of the Department of Drug Enforcement, formed a partnership with Robert DuPont with the creative name B and D Associates. Together they effectively counsel corporations into establishing get-tough drug policies. Business is booming. Bensinger is probably the most outspoken proponent of mass testing. He has appeared on the *Today* show, and his articles appear regularly in national op/ed pages. The media regard him as the unofficial industry spokesman. Question on urine? Call Bensinger. It will be his job to destroy the premises of this book.

Robert T. Angarola, former general counsel to the White House Office of Drug Abuse Policy, is an attorney with the Washington firm of Hyman, Phelps & McNamara. He is also a urinalysis consultant. Angarola carried the Administration's hardball approach to his private-sector clients: "The constitutional right to privacy protects people only against *government* [emphasis added] intrusion. Individuals acting as private citizens are not bound by these constitutional restraints. And this applies to private employers." Sounds like Edwin Meese? Talk of giving such free reign to employers appeals to Angarola's clients. These include Syva and Kidder Peabody, a brokerage house that started its drug-testing program in late 1985. Angarola's job is to head off lawsuits by disgruntled employees. To avoid them, he urges workplace candor; a worker who knows about his company's drug policy won't mind having his privacy violated. So if you understand how the guillotine works, you won't mind putting your head on the block.

In the small world of drug testing, these four—Angarola, Bensinger, DuPont, and Willette—are affectionately referred to as the Gang of Four. Dr. John Morgan explains, "They are the ones responsible for a good deal of drug testing's success, and some of the fear that goes along with it." Remember these names. These men are among the most competent and knowledgeable about drug testing—scientifically and politically. They are well-informed: they have to be. Their livelihoods depend upon their credibility. Unfortunately their expertise represents the greatest threat to the civil liberties we seek to protect. Know your enemy.

12.

Deep Inside Urine Testing

The problem of cross-reactivity—one substance confused with another—is the single most significant error in urine testing. It also happens to be the most common. Each popular screening kit lists up to one dozen legal products that could mistakenly give positive results. And those are just the ones the manufacturer recognizes. Dozens more reportedly cross-react, according to independent testers.

Cross-reactivity is not a chemical fluke; it does not occur occasionally or randomly on one isolated test out of a million. Rather, it is a built-in "acceptable" flaw in the urine screen. EMIT, which had been observed to mistake Advil or Motrin (both ibuprofen) for cannaboid, may turn up a false positive whenever ibuprofen is found.

If one hundred employees use Motrin regularly, they could *all* show up positive for THC right along with someone smoking ten joints the night before.

At first the Drug Industrial Complex denied that a cross-reactivity problem existed. Sample mishandling was responsible for errors, they claimed, because their test could never be so blatantly incorrect. Only after years of criticism from toxicologists did the manufacturers reluctantly come clean. The cross-reaction list keeps growing, as do the lines of irate innocents.

Accuracy is obtained only when the urine sample is at proper ambient conditions—optimal temperature and pH level. Urine should be within 5.5 to 8.0 pH *and* 20 degrees Fahrenheit of room temperature, or the results will be distorted. Naturally the urine-testing equipment itself doesn't measure pH or temperature, and many labs don't bother with these extra pretests. After all, when you test three hundred vials a day, any extra step adds cost to the process.

If a person voids urine outside the range of any important measurement, the machine can register a false positive. In other words, too hot, too cold, too alkaline, or too acidic urine will produce bad results. Considering that many samples are refrigerated, that there are often stoves and radiators present, you can see that temperature range has to be carefully monitored. Also consider all the spicy, salty, or acid foods and beverages one might have consumed the day before a test. Under any of these conditions, the Syva Autolab could be inhibited from optimal performance. As far as the government is concerned, the U.S. Attorney General says that both temperature and pH level will be checked *at the time the sample is given* (to make sure it hasn't been tampered with). But nothing is said about measurement when it gets evaluated clinically. A lot can happen between the voiding and the verification.

Another problem common to *all* drug screens is the inability to determine dosage or frequency of use. A concentration level in the urine does not necessarily correlate with the quantity of the drug ingested. In the eyes of the qualitative tests, high concentrations are equivalent to trivial ones—so long as both are above the pre-determined cutoff point for a positive result.

The person smoking ten joints a day is for test purposes lumped in with the passive smoker inhaling secondary marijuana smoke at a rock concert. A THC concentration of 1,000 nanograms per milliliter is identical to 50 nanograms per milliliter. (A nanogram is one *billionth* of a gram. Ten thousand nanograms would weigh about the same as a grain of sand.) As early as January 1977, even before an acceptable cannaboid assay was marketed, the *American Journal of Psychiatry* revealed that passive inhalation of marijuana shows up positive for EMIT. NIDA denied this, claiming that tests register only active drug use. Pot smoke wouldn't have enough THC to hit the cutoff point. Later, as the evidence piled up, NIDA turned unusually silent.

Richard L. Hawks of NIDA cited studies exploring the passive-inhalation problem. "These sorts of clinical studies put three smokers in a car or small room with a nonsmoker, and you test [the nonsmoker's] urine. They show that it is very difficult to get a sample that comes up to the 20 nanograms per milliliter point." (*Chemical Engineering News*, 6/8/86) Difficult, but not impossible. And the more smoke inhaled, the better the chance for a positive test result. Hawks glanced over the implications of condemning the innocent. "At some point you have to say the person wasn't doing it passively," he added.

NIDA seems to imply that if you go to a Grateful Dead concert and it runs the usual eight hours, it's just tough on you even if you don't smoke pot. You shouldn't have gone there in the first place.

The Surgeon General warns that secondary tobacco smoke leads to health problems for nonsmokers. He should also warn that secondary pot smoke leads to moral judgments and possibly lost jobs.

One school-bus driver got nailed for just this reason. Months earlier he had complained to his supervisors that the kids light up while he's shuttling them around. The supervisor placated him, "Kids will be kids, and don't worry, we don't think you're a doper." A month later the bus driver was given a surprise EMIT as part of a new policy. He tested positive for THC. The ACLU is appealing his abrupt termination.

False positives have resulted in many horror stories. The *Los Angeles Times* reported (12/16/84) the sad but true story of two Navy doctors who were labeled morphine users after a single drug test. The doctors protested their innocence and were given an opportunity to prove themselves with a second test—which also turned up positive. Several weeks later, the Navy concluded that poppy seeds in "normal dietary use" cross-react as morphine. No coincidence that both doctors regularly enjoyed poppy seed bagels at the hospital cafeteria.

The director of the Air Force drug-testing laboratory in Texas testified that the staggering false-positive rate in 1984 was the result of technicians using the lab oven to cook their lunch. One day tacos were heated, and some grease got into the screening equipment. The screen wrongly diagnosed taco grease for marijuana residue. Over 70,000 tests had to be reevaluated, at the taxpayer's and victims' expense!

Some interesting cross-reaction theories have been presented. Dr. James Woodford, a toxicologist in Atlanta, hypothesized in 1983 that melanin—the pigment associated with human skin color—cross-reacts with marijuana metabolites. He implied that a racial bias was inherent in EMIT and Abuscreen. Since blacks have more evident melanin, they were inherently vulnerable to additional false-positive conditions. While this suggestion of bias turned out to be a little far-fetched, it said a lot about the controversy surrounding urine testing. Shades of things to come!

The methods used in biochemical analysis are extensive—and with good reason. All human cells eat and excrete, just like humans themselves; there's a good chance that particles of any ingested drug will show up throughout the body (though not always in its original form). Understanding drug screening, then, first requires some understanding of human metabolism.

In spite of the inventiveness of drug users (or abusers, depending on your politics), there remain three ways of taking drugs: eating, inhalation, and injection. (Well, there is a fourth, but most folks don't know about taking cocaine rectally in homemade glycerine suppositories.) All of them achieve the same end result—converting a tangible substance into particles absorbed by the bloodstream. Altered by body chemicals, the new substance is called a *metabolite* of the original. If eaten, the compound is digested and active components (proteins, vitamins, drugs) enter the blood via the digestive tract. Smoked or snorted compounds enter the lungs or get attached to the throat membrane, passing into blood vessels. Injected drugs go right into the veins without the intermediary breakdowns. Needless to say, this is dangerous, because of the possibility of shock and the need for sterile needles.

For example, marijuana, when smoked, enters the lungs where it converts into over twenty identifiable compounds. The most active—and the one responsible for the high—is known as Delta-9 tetrahydrocannaboid, or THC in street parlance. The metabolic conversion is rapid, although the effects may take some time.

TABLE OF CROSS-REACTIVITY

Drug/Metabolite	Cross-Reactive
Amphetamine	Phenylpropanolamine (found in OTC cold medications: Nyquil, Vicks Nasal Spray, Neosynephren, Sudafed)
	Methamphetamine/Phenmetrazine/Phentermine (found in prescription diet medications)
	Dopamine HCL
	Ephedrine (found in prescription asthma medicines)
Barbiturate	Mephobarbital
	Barbituric acid (rarely prescribed compounds)
Cannaboids	Ibuprofen (Advil, Nuprin, Motrin, Mydol, Trendar—extremely common pain relievers)
Cocaine	Amoxicillin (unconfirmed)
Methaqualone	None reported to date
Morphine	Codeine (in any prescription form)
	Dihydrocodeine bitartrate/Levorphanol/Oxycodone (found in prescription analgesics)
	Poppy seeds
	Hydromorphone (found in prescription antitussives)
Doxylamine	(found in OTC antihistamines and sleeping pills)
Phencyclidine (PCP)	Dextromethororphan (found in some prescription cough medicines)
	Diazepam (found in Valium)
LSD	Methysergide maleate
	Ergonovine maleate
	Tryptophan (all the above are derivates of LSD; rarely medicinal)

Note: Cross-reactions depend upon concentration and duration of chemical in the human body. Reported cross-reactions are not associated with any manufacturer's screen. That is, cross-reactive compounds are not specifically linked with EMIT, Abuscreen, or Thin-Layer Chromatography. This book cannot guarantee the validity of cross-reactions, based on our limited testing and on potential improvement in screening accuracy. OTC means over the counter.

(Sources: U.S. Congress Office of Technology Assessment; Syva; Roche Diagnostics; Byrd Labs)

Within a minute after inhalation, traces of THC appear in the blood. The user gets the desired effect in twenty or thirty minutes, when the psychoactive metabolites peak in concentration. With the highest-grade marijuana, sensimilla, these effects are more rapid, intense, and longer-lasting.

Heroin goes through fewer conversions, since it is a power compound. There are three primary heroin derivates: heroin-morphine, morphine, and morphine-glucuride. It's safe to say that the longer a drug stays in the body, the more metabolites it spawns. But this process has a limit.

What is ingested must eventually be excreted. The remaining metabolites of the drug—inert after the high has passed—are evident in all routes of excretion. Sweat, tears, breath, saliva, urine, and feces all contain traces—legal evidence—of the drug used. Metabolites not excreted via traditional exits can be found in hair, skin, and fingernails. Nail clippings, casually discarded, might someday be used against you.

Urine is the specimen of choice since it contains the most metabolites of a drug taken. In comparison, blood and plasma contain a far smaller range of marijuana derivatives than urine. The reason: chemicals transplanted by the bloodstream collect in the kidney. Urine filtered through the kidney picks up this chemical silt and transfers it to the urinary bladder. From there it's an easy trip into the toilet. Or specimen bottle. Then on to the laboratory apparatus. This is like panning for gold, where traces give away the hidden lode upstream.

It is possible to screen fluids other than urine, but the results are inconclusive, even when compared to flawed immunoassays. Saliva testing is useful only in measuring recent contact with an illegal substance; cannaboids in the mouth are active for less than twelve hours after smoking. Breath testing, likewise, requires recent usage, probably because the lungs absorb particles so efficiently that little trace remains in the exhaust. But don't let this calm your paranoia. Science is working on ways to perfect additional intrusive measures.

For a drug screen to be effective, it must search not for the drug in its ingested form, but for its metabolites. And not just any metabolite, but those present in the fluid used as the specimen.

A barbiturate's derivate in the saliva is radically different from the one in the urine. Using a urine-dependent barbiturate test on blood would turn up negative, even if there was some barbiturate metabolite in the blood.

The Drug Industrial Complex boasts "accuracy" as a drug screen's main selling point. The term "accuracy" in diagnostic lingo is more subtle than the everyday definition. For a test to be statistically accurate means it satisfies certain criteria. A few definitions are necessary.

Efficacy and *effectiveness* refer to the reliability of tests in laboratory or real-life environments, respectively. In practical terms, *efficacy* is high if a test under perfect conditions can locate a specific metabolite ten times out of ten in a given set of samples. On the other hand, if in real life that same test locates only seven of ten samples correctly, its *effectiveness* is low. In other words, efficacy is an absolute measurement while effectiveness deals in probabilities. Lab tests are generally conducted under optimum conditions. But real life is sadly just that, real life.

By way of analogy, imagine an experimental engine that starts up every time it is evaluated at the plant. General Motors' engineers would be pleased with the motor's efficaciousness. If that same engine didn't start in cold weather, its effectiveness would be low in the customer's garage.

The dichotomy between laboratory conditions and real life is well known. TV commercials bathe you in a product's perfection, only to end with the caveat, "Actual results may vary." The urine test puts more at stake than a miles-per-gallon rating; careers and reputations hinge on the results.

Two more important terms: the FDA evaluates all diagnostics on *sensitivity* and *specificity*. *Sensitivity* is the ability to detect a drug's presence at small concentrations. *Specificity* is the ability to differentiate among the target chemicals.

The Food and Drug Administration requires that all diagnostic tests provide certain information about accuracy. This includes a "lower limit of detection," the minimum concentration below which the test is statistically inaccurate. (These are typically small quantities, billionths of a gram.) Also required is a "cutoff point" between a positive and negative result, a comfortable margin above

SENSITIVITY AND SPECIFICITY CHART

		Drug in Urine	
		Actual Presence	No Verifiable Presence
Screening Test Result	Positive	True Positive (1)	False Positive (2)
	Negative	False Negative (3)	True Negative (4)

(1) You fail. Immediately request confirmation using a different test.
(2) Worst possible error. To be avoided at all cost.
(3) Best possible error. To be achieved.
(4) Congratulations, you pass *summa cum laude!* Now get back to work.

the lower limit of detection. For example, the Abuscreen kit from Roche Diagnostics has a lower limit of detection for LSD of 0.025 nanograms per milliliter (ng ml). Its cutoff point is almost twenty times higher—0.5 ng/ml. Roche is implying, yes, we can detect a very, very small amount of an illegal drug in urine, but to give the subject the benefit of the doubt, we require a substantially higher level for a positive result. A test which cannot detect the presence of a drug above its cutoff point is flawed. This results in a *false-negative error* (see above chart).

What effect does this have on the person tested? Practically, none. You can't take smaller hits of cocaine and hope to fall below the cutoff point, escaping detection. But a cutoff point substantially above a lower limit of detection might mean the test isn't as accurate as the manufacturer suggests.

Specificity is the degree to which a test can differentiate between similar compounds in the sample. A test confusing lettuce proteins for PCP will get low marks in the specificity department. A test that can distinguish between doctor-prescribed codeine and illegal heroin (both opiates) will get high marks for specificity. A urine test that confuses one drug for another is said to *cross-react*. The result is a *false positive error,* saying something is there when it really isn't. This is the type of error that is playing havoc with the industry's reputation.

Dr. Lawrence Miike, Senior Associate in the Health Program of the U.S. Office of Technology Assessment, recently testified before a Congressional panel on the accuracy of urine drug tests:

> A manufacturer's recommended "cutoff level" between a positive and negative reading is based on the potential inconsistencies from test to test of measuring drug concentrations below that level, even though the test may generally measure lower concentrations of the drug. Many of the drugs that might cross-react with a particular test will give false-positive readings below the cutoff point and so would not be read as positive if the laboratory uses the recommended cutoff point to distinguish between positive and negative results.

In English, this means mistakes are made by the test and the laboratory that processes it.

Sources of Error

Now let's apply these standards. Imagine a company with one hundred employees, all drug-free. If they are each given a urine test with a 95 percent *specificity* level, five of these employees are statistically expected to turn up as drug users when they really are not—victims of false positive error. *The test is attributing drug abuse where none exists because it cannot accurately differentiate chemicals present in the urine sample.*

Now consider the converse situation. If a company is unlucky enough to have a workforce of one hundred heroin addicts, a urine test with a 95 percent *sensitivity* level statistically would be expected to register five people as nonusers, a false negative answer.

Error rate may look innocuous when percentages are written in a technical paper. Statistically, in large-number studies, negative and positive errors tend to balance out. Detection, on the other hand, is a far different ballgame than a general study. Test a hundred thousand people and automatically five thousand innocents may unfairly lose their jobs. Multiply this by the millions expected to be tested and you see the damage done by any margin of error.

You can debate forever which is the worse situation. Employers contend that the false negative is more serious since it permits actual problem workers to escape detection. The rank and file argue the false positive is arguably more vindictive, since it carries penalties. In a society which believes in innocence before guilt is proved, we must agree this is the worse of the two possible errors.

But the government doesn't see it that way. Generally urine drug tests have, in FDA parlance, an acceptable rate of error: 5 percent or less. Technology has advanced by giant steps in the fifteen years since tests were first used. Even non-laboratory, over-the-counter drug screens report lower detection levels of fewer than 5 nanograms per milliliter. But the tests remain locked at the 5 percent error rate.

The Drug Industrial Complex unfairly claims very high success rates for its tests. "Our test is state of the art, as accurate as it can be. Any built-in errors exist not for want of trying to remove them," remarked one chemical engineer. But he's wrong; the urine tests in daily use are not the best they can be. Clients have accepted a tradeoff: *a higher-than-ideal error rate in exchange for reasonable cost.* Claude Buller, President of CompuChem, which performs over 250,000 tests for the Department of Defense (DOD) every year, estimates that a truly reliable screen (one that avoids the false positives and negatives that trip EMIT) would cost nearly one hundred dollars per sample. Most companies now spend less than fifteen dollars, some as low as five. The ninety-five-dollar differential is the cost of accuracy that employers are reluctant to pay.

Even in 1976, when the technology was being developed, a scientific study noted that "some [urine tests] have been prepared with very high specificity—where cost was no object." It's almost as if the Complex suggested a compromise: "Okay, a *really* accurate test is possible. But it's going to cost a fortune, and you won't pay for it. So we'll give you a less accurate urine screen—not the best, but good enough—at a reasonable cost. Then, if you really want better information, you can pay later for confirmation."

This is conjecture. But industrial history suggests that higher risks are appealing when costs can be reduced. Look at tests of air bags versus safety belts in preventing auto fatalities. Air bags cost $800 per vehicle, the price of a superior passive-restraint system. The automakers and government have decided that human life just isn't worth the extra money.

The Immunoassays: EMIT and ABUSCREEN (RIA)

There are more than a dozen scientifically accepted screening techniques, and new ones are being developed as you read this book. They vary in cost and reliability, but all have the same aim— to identify drug users.

Despite the abundance of competition, only three tests are used in almost all civilian and military applications. They are technically referred to as the *enzyme-multiplied immunoassay technique (EMIT)*, the *radioimmunoassay (RIA)*, and *thin-layer chromatography (TLC)*. Of the two immunoassays, EMIT has become the standard in corporate America; RIA has won military support. Each test has strengths and weaknesses, as well as optimal applications.

A review of the chemistry is useful here. Both immunoassays are produced by chemical reactions on the molecular level. In the manufacturing process, a controlled substance (the illegal drug to be detected) is bound to a naturally occurring compound—usually a protein. The resulting complex molecule is known as a *conjugate*. The conjugate is injected into an animal (a *live* animal). Within three weeks, the animal's immune system produces antibodies to negate the effects of the alien conjugate.

With all the emphasis on constitutional rights and privacy, nothing has been mentioned in the popular press about the animals lost in the manufacturing process. Hundreds of animals die yearly because they are convenient chemical machines, walking antibody factories. Somewhere in the great American West, Syva raises sheep exclusively for its EMIT THC assay. Sheep livers (where the antibodies are produced) are similar to human livers; both attract similar cannaboids. The sheep are injected with conjugates to create the desired biological brew in their livers. After a few years, the sheep die.

The practice isn't limited to sheep. Roche Diagnostics uses antibodies from rabbits (for its LSD tests), goats (amphetamines, PCP), and donkeys (cannaboids, morphine, methaqualone). A virtual barnyard sacrificed behind a wall of silence. Where is Animal Liberation when you need it?

The animal antibodies are the heart of the immunoassay, since they attract the illegal substance. Getting the antibodies out of the beast is hardly humane: blood is drawn regularly. The blood is processed into something called *antiserum*, which when mixed with urine will seek the targeted drug.

Think of the immunoassay as a lock-and-key reaction. The antiserum is the lock, and the illegal drug is the key. If an antiserum is developed from marijuana, the two should react in urine and form a marijuana-antiserum complex. For those who remember basic chemistry, the reaction looks like this:

$$Anti\text{-}Serum = (AS)$$
$$Marijuana\ Metabolite = (\Delta\text{-}9\ THC)$$
$$(AS + (\Delta\text{-}9\ THC) \Leftrightarrow (AS\text{-}\Delta 9\ THC)$$

If the new complex (AS-Δ9 THC) exists when the urine is tested, the reaction is positive. And sometimes even when it doesn't. From the equation we can better understand cross-reactivity. A false positive occurs when the antiserum binds with a similar, but fundamentally different chemical.

There are numerous explanations for false positives. Stale or diluted antiserum may bind randomly with anything floating in urine. Maintaining a consistent level of antiserum throughout several production runs is a constant headache for testmakers. While true accuracy may vary from batch to batch, the guidelines—cutoff points, sensitivity levels—remain the same. It's even possible that a particular batch of antiserum may not be capable of detection at the FDA-approved concentration level.

This is one fear of independent research scientists. Even the Special Action Office for Drug Abuse Prevention, which championed the whole procedure, was apprehensive about consistency:

> No two antisera will be exactly the same. An antiserum obtained from an animal at one bleeding will differ from that obtained at a second bleeding. For example, one antiserum may not recognize morphine glucuronide as well as another, or one may recognize dextromethorphan better than another. Thus antisera vary in their ability to

differentiate between the drug, the cross-reacting drugs, or the metabolites.

Read through the jargon and you'll find a flawed test at the inception.

Industry engineers say quality controls are sufficient to prevent dilution of antiserum. A Roche Diagnostics spokesman assured me that all Abuscreen reagents are titrated to very small margins. Batches are prepared every twelve or eighteen months (the sera have expiration dates). A potential source of lab error is use of stale reagent serum.

Of the two immunoassays, EMIT was first available in 1972, produced by the Syva Company in Palo Alto, California. As of this writing, thirty assays are available. They test the licit and illicit: anything from acetaminophen (Tylenol) to tricyclic antidepressants, including the major naughties—cocaine, heroin, marijuana. Actually, over one hundred different drug or metabolites can be detected. (See chart that follows.)

According to Syva literature, the test is processed as follows: the EMIT kit for cannabis contains antiserum enzymes that attach to the THC metabolite in urine. If no cannaboid is located, a chemically tagged drug links with the reagent. Once all reactions have occurred, the physical properties of the sample fluid are changed. For testing instruments, the most accessible indication of chemical change is light absorption. As the handbook directs:

> EMIT test instruments measure changes in the amount of light the sample absorbs, which is related to the amount of drug the sample contains. The more drug present in the person's urine, the greater the response produced. On the other hand, if there is no drug present, the response is minimal.
>
> To determine the presence or absence of detectable drug, the sample's response is compared to the response of a calibrator which contains a known amount of drug. If the sample's response is less than that of the calibrator, the sample is considered to be negative. Conversely, if the sample's response is higher than or equal to the cal-

EMIT® d.a.u.℠
TEST PERFORMANCE

Assay	Drug or Metabolite Detected
Amphetamine Assay	Amphetamine (Benzedrine®, Dexedrine®) Methamphetamine (Desoxyn®)
Barbiturate Assay	Secobarbital (Seconal®, Tuinal®) Phenobarbital Pentobarbital (Nembutal®) Allylbarbital Butabarbital Amobarbital (Amytal®) Talbutal
Benzodiazepine Metabolite Assay	Oxazepam (Serax®) Clonazepam Chlordiazepoxide (Librium®) Demoxepam Desalkylflurazepam N-Desmethyldiazepam Diazepam (Valium®) Flunitrazepam Flurazepam (Dalmane®) Lorazepam Nitrazepam
Cannabinoid 20 Assay	Major urinary metabolites of Δ^9-tetrahydrocannobinol[3]

Assay	Drug or Metabolite Detected
Cannabinoid 100 Assay	Major urinary metabolites of Δ^9-tetrahydrocannabinol[3]
Cocaine Metabolite Assay	Benzoylecgonine
Methadone Assay	Methadone (Dolophine®)
Methaqualone Assay	Methaqualone Methaqualone metabolites Mecloqualone
Opiate Assay	Morphine Morphine-3-glucuronide Codeine Hydromorphone Hydromorphine Levorphanol Oxycodone
Phencyclidine Assay	Phencyclidine (PCP) 1-[1-(2-Thienyl)-cyclohexyl] piperidine (TCP)
Propoxyphene Assay	Propoxyphene (e.g., Darvon®, SK-65®)

ibrator's, the sample is considered to be positive for the drug.

Sad that people's reputations hinge on the cloudiness of their urine. *This above-or-below-the-line approach offers no clue to the amount of drug present, only an indication of its presence.* Syva throws up its hands and says that biological functions, physiological states of the testee preclude a quantitative measure of drug concentration. But failing to provide a level leads to more severe problems. Is a concentration of 4 nanograms per milliliter equally severe as 4000 ng/ml? "Drug detection programs only distinguish between recent use and no use," testified Dr. Miike. "People with very high levels of drugs in their urine will be treated the same as people who have levels of drugs in their urine that are barely detectable."

Syva's main selling point is that EMIT does not require extensively trained personnel or laboratory conditions. In fact, EMIT recommends in-house use as part of a cost-effective drug program: "[EMIT kits] do not require specially licensed personnel, subjective interpretation of results, or special handling techniques and safety precautions; they can be run by any trained staff member" (Syva, 1982). Common sense implies that an amateur trained by a traveling salesperson for only a few hours is bound to make more mistakes than professionals in fully equipped laboratories.

Syva makes three toxicology systems. All look very impressive, high-tech—lots of lights and dials. The basic model is the Syva Autolab System. The other two models have additional advantages (speed of processing or portability) but the fundamental technology in all systems is identical.

Scientists, Syva-sponsored and not, agree that EMIT is extremely sensitive to small concentrations of drugs. But that is no guarantee that external conditions can't alter the results. EMIT works less than optimally when the urine sample is more acidic or alkaline than normal. In fact, pH concentration may throw off critical enzyme reactions.

(For those of you who have nodded out on all this but just want to beat the test, pay extra attention to this point.)

Dr. John Morgan observed, "A false positive test could occur in some individuals because they excrete unusually large amounts of endogenous lysozyme or malate dehydrogenase." That means your body could betray you without the presence of any targeted drugs. Stale urine, like stale reagent serum, also leads to bad test results. As does improper temperature of the sample.

I could recount bad results forever. The point is, while EMIT is accurate to some degree, it ignores a number of factors, which makes for bad scientific procedure.

The second type of immunoassay is the radioimmunoassay (RIA). Sold commercially as Abuscreen, it has been manufactured since November 1972 by Roche Diagnostics, a division of Hoffmann-LaRoche, the drug giant.

RIA works on a principle similar to EMIT, but instead of linking a drug to an enzyme chain, the bonding ingredient is radioactive iodine. Again, the degree of chemical bonding determines the presence of a targeted drug. An instrument registers the amount of radiation present, which corresponds directly to the presence of cocaine metabolites. Roche markets the test as a rapid, simple procedure that can be adapted to automated processing for large-scale screening. And no wonder. The Department of Defense uses RIA on *all* its troops.

Let's consider the Abuscreen for cocaine metabolites. As the test enclosure details, "The Abuscreen RIA is a specific and sensitive in vitro [outside the body] test to detect the presence of benzoylecognine [the primary urinary metabolite of coke]. While the sensitivity of the test [lower limit of detection] is 5 ng/ml, for the identification of positive samples a cutoff value of 300 ng/ml is supplied as the positive reference standard."

The Abuscreen package is prettier than the EMIT. Each kit contains up to five reagents, conveniently color-coded: morphine is green, pot is brown, cocaine is yellow.

Since the test relies upon radioactive coding, Abuscreen users must be trained in a lab certified by the Nuclear Regulatory Commission. Licensing isn't that hard to come by and RIA may not be monitored much more closely than EMIT. But some regulation may make it appear the test results are more accurate. As the advertising says, Abuscreen is used as the primary test system for the Department of Defense and, previously was used by the Los Angeles Olympic Committee: "Because of their social, political, and personal responsibility to the people being tested, organizations such as these are increasingly selecting Abuscreen as the product of choice after extensive critical evaluation."

But Abuscreen is guilty of the same sins as EMIT, and has some unique quirks of its own. For one, Abuscreen is reported to have greater cross-reactivity than EMIT. Second, the urine sample must be voided as recently as eight hours before the test, or else it must be refrigerated immediately. Any delay results in decomposition, with a corresponding reduction in accuracy.

Each immunoassay has its advocates. For purposes of criticism, they are roughly equivalent. That is, they are equally error-prone. Any comparison between EMIT and Abuscreen must stress that they are only screening devices, not intended as the final word (or they'd be in court every week). Both companies put large disclaimers on the label recommending that any positive result be confirmed by a second test. *Any* second test. The immunoassays have marginally different sensitivities. RIA is preferred because it can *quantify* concentration. EMIT, on the other hand, screens a larger amount of drugs.

Confirmation takes many forms. Dr. Robert DuPont remarked on the "Today Show" that two EMIT tests on the same sample is sufficient for verification of abuse. One company required all EMIT-positive employees take the same test again, and duplicated the errors of the first. Other labs confirmed EMIT with Abuscreen and vice versa.

By the fall of 1986, the FDA was flooded with reports of bad confirmation programs. It ordered all manufacturers to recommend confirmation of positive results by a second, *more specific* test. But that is where Syva, Roche, and the FDA liability ends. They are untouchable through the courts.

Simply because something is popular does not mean it is any good. Unless you measure success like a Hollywood mogul—by box-office appeal. Ronald Reagan was elected because he acted presidential, belying his credentials. Similarly, the immunoassays are used because they *appear* acceptable.

In September 1986, the *Journal of Analytic Toxicology* evaluated EMIT and RIA under field conditions, and compared the results to more reliable Gas-Chromatography output. Mass-Spectrometry, EMIT and RIA agreed with each other 91 percent of the time. EMIT had a 4 percent false-positive rate, and a 10 percent false-negative rate; *it was wrong 14 percent of the time*. This was more than *twice* the manufacturer's estimate! RIA fared better: 99.7 percent of RIA positives were true positives, only 0.3% false positives and no false negatives. The article concluded that RIA initial testing followed by a "well-controlled GC/MS confirmation procedure" is an acceptable method of eliminating false error. (This study considered only the test itself. Laboratory handling, examined later, will add considerably to the margin of error.)

Thin-Layer Chromatography (TLC)

The third system used in urine testing is Thin-Layer Chromatography (TLC). TLC is not a new or developing technology; it has been around for thirty years, mostly in hospital applications. Standardized by the late sixties, TLC was adapted to urine screening when the immunoassays started getting attention. The TLC manufacturers push it as a reliable alternative to EMIT.

TLC's only advantage is the ability to screen a number of substances at once. For example, if urine contains barbiturate, heroin, and marijuana traces, a single TLC should ideally flag them all. Achieving similar results with EMIT would require three separate tests.

Every drug has a color spectrum and velocity which allows it to be identified absolutely, in much the same way that fingerprints are unique to people. TLC identifies a drug by these two characteristics.

Sounds simple, right? The theory is elementary, but not the procedure. First, the urine sample must be "cleaned," all particles and impurities extracted, the pH balanced, and so forth. The remaining fluid is a concentration of urine-dependent chemicals. This "clean" urine becomes the specimen to be chromatized. The urine is spread on filter paper coated with a thin layer of silica gel (hence the term "thin-layer") and is submerged in solvent. The filter is porous, so it draws the solvent throughout it, like a thin sponge. The solvent separates drug metabolites from the urine.

Assume that there are THC marijuana metabolites in the urine. When the solvent reaches the "clean" urine on the thin layer, the THC is carried along the filter for some quantifiable distance. (Drugs travel in a solvent at varying speeds, according to the molecular weight and volume.) After a half hour or so, the THC will have migrated up the filter far enough to be identified. The filter is then removed from the solvent and sprayed with more chemicals, which bring out color. Colored lines reveal the distance the THC has traveled. The sample filter is compared to a reference, which contains lines of demarcation for each drug analyzed.

The migration period and fluid preparation are more time-consuming in a TLC test than in either of the assays. Unfortunately, the extended processing time does not guarantee more accurate results. The process isn't finished until an "expert" technician compares the sample to a reference chart, adding to the possibility of human error. Clinically, TLC has a hard time competing with EMIT. It has a low-volume output and cannot be automated. Just about the only attractive thing about it is the price, which is low; therefore, it is generally favored by cost-conscious companies and the occasional fly-by-night laboratory.

Chemically, TLC's principal drawback is its sensitivity levels, or lack thereof. Urine must have substantially higher drug concentrations for accurate readings. The Toxi-Lab system, manufactured by Marion Laboratories, Inc., has cutoff points as much as seven times higher than EMIT's comparable assays. TLC also falls into many of the cross-reactivity traps which trip up the immunoassays.

TLC manufacturers try to compensate for their product's shortcomings with promotion and education programs. Marion Labs offers a three-day initial training workshop for new users and a two-day advanced course. Marketing efforts have paid off in customer loyalty. A recent survey reported 95 percent of Toxi-Lab users found the system reliable; 93 percent were confident with the results; and 92 percent found it easy to use. Of course, this was a company-sponsored poll; the results should be treated skeptically.

Together the three screens account for more than 75 percent of all urine-testing procedures. That includes confirmatory testing. What is surprising is not the lack of competition, but the alacrity with which employers have responded to them, in spite of obvious flaws. Granted, the customer is always right, but in this case the customer, being neither a physician nor chemist, has little or no knowledge about the product.

The Office of Technology Assessment summed the errors neatly:

> TLC and even the two immunoassays are widely viewed as being insufficient as conclusive evidence of use in urinary drug-detection programs. In the emergency room situation, a single patient is involved, and the probability that the drug has been identified correctly with 95 percent or more accuracy is good enough to assume that the correct drug has been identified. However, the mass-screening situation is fundamentally different. For any one person, a positive screening test has the same degree of accuracy as in the emergency room situation, but when many, many people are tested, there have to be some persons who will be falsely identified as having drugs in their urine.

We have to continually remind ourselves that we are dealing with probabilities and not absolutes. In the world of probability, what you do with the results of a particular test becomes crucial to judging the margin of error you are willing to tolerate. In a general survey of a town's schoolchildren, it might be interesting to note, say, that 42 percent have used marijuana. A plus or minus 5 percent margin of error wouldn't really undercut the generality. Conversely, if we were in Malaysia, where mere possession of heroin could mean the death penalty, and we routinely tested one hundred people for drugs, five of the innocent would be hanged. The significance of a good many of the statistics is dependent on the ultimate use of the results.

Urine tests are used to investigate little old you. Incidentally, the screens don't just look for illegal substances. They can trace virtually *any* psychoactive drug, prescribed or not, and some bodily functions. Privacy, the sanctity of the doctor-patient relationship, and medical-record confidentiality are compromised by a nosy test—and a lab technician whose report goes straight to the boss.

This isn't fear-mongering. In their mad quest to eradicate drug abuse, the Enforcers gain access to information they are not entitled to know. At a glance, the lab knows which workers are pregnant, under psychiatric care, asthmatic, or epileptic. Librium, Valium, Elavil, Darvon—take your pick, they all show up. Yet this part of the screening procedure is hushed up. A democratic citizenry aware of this capacity would certainly be less willing to give urine testing its blessing.

Better Technologies
The popular urine screens detailed above might lead you to conclude that truly accurate drug detection is impossible. But better, more specific detection methods are available. High cost, however, makes them accessible only to research labs, hospitals, and universities.

The most respected clinical procedure is gas chromatography/Mass Spectrometry (GC/MS). It also happens to be the most complicated to understand and operate. Similar in theory to TLC, it directly identifies chemicals by breaking them into smaller molecular structures. A specimen is bombarded by electrons until it breaks down into component molecules. These are measured by computer, tested for velocity, atomic weight, and a couple of other atomic standards. Very complicated, very technical.

Unlike the popular screening methods, GC/MS is the only one that approaches absolute reliability. It has a ridiculously high accuracy level, somewhat near to 99.98 percent. One urine-testing consultant, fed up with EMIT-type errors, noted, "GC/MS is the only method which works, and *always* works. It should be the only one permitted by law."

But you pay for it. Hewlett-Packard manufacturers GC/MS systems for $100,000 to $150,000. And that's just for the equipment.

Add $50 per hour for the technicians, and another $20 for the chemicals, and you can see why EMIT is so popular.

There are other means of high-tech identification, some of which define the limits of modern science. Light absorption (LA) and nuclear magnetic resonance (NMR) can identify specific subatomic characteristics of each drug in the urine sample, no matter how minute the quantity. These machines are allegedly 100 percent reliable. Maybe NASA can afford to use them on a few would-be astronauts, but they would hardly come within the budget of your local welding shop.

It seems a shame to waste such fine equipment on urine. The FDA seems to agree. It uses GC/MS, LA, and NMR for loftier purposes, like testing for carcinogens in breakfast cereal.

New Products

Highly specific methods of detecting drugs in urine do exist. That labs and corporations have chosen to avoid them for economic reasons reveals a basic truth about the process. Enforcers are concerned not so much with accuracy as with surveillance of their workers *at a reasonable price*. If Reagan or Exxon truly wanted a drug-free workplace, they'd shell out $100 per test for a GC/MS. The compromise—accepting immunoassays or TLC as the standard—makes the entire drug-testing philosophy hypocritical.

Lofty ideals are reduced to the cheapest materials, the first language of American business. By compromising standards, dozens of companies have come up with their own fundamentally erroneous screens.

Medical Diagnostics, a subsidiary of Keystone Medical Corp. in Columbia, Md, has unveiled the KDI Qwik Test (sic). Basically a litmus test for abuse, it requires a single drop of urine and presto!— instant chemistry. What takes a lab thirty minutes with heavy-duty equipment, Mommy can do on the kitchen table. Test the dog, test Daddy, have the neighbors over for a friendly test-in!

The urine is dropped on a pad of chemically treated paper, which responds to the presence of cocaine, morphine, PCP, methadone, crack, and whatever fashionable drugs are making headlines. If the paper recognizes a "naughty" substance, a tell-tale ring will magically appear: the mark of disgrace. Of course, Keystone warns that the Qwik Test is only a screening device; no decisions should be based on it alone. Don't be surprised to find these $7.50 junior G-man surveillance kits available sometime at the local K-Mart.

The latest craze in the world of urine detection seems to be on-site evaluation. No more big lab fees, no more shipping urine across town via pill-popping bike messengers, to be analyzed by white-coated ether freaks. Less accuracy, but do it yourself and save them bucks. Abbott Laboratories is taking a lead from Syva in developing an on-site employer-operated urine test for cocaine, PCP, and barbiturates. Called the TDX system, it will use a fluorescent bulb to determine whether a drug is present or not. Gro Lites could soon be joined by Glow Lites.

Not every company is betting on urine. The Diagnostics Products Corporation, anxious to avoid the repulsive bladder by-product, is bringing out a kit that screens saliva. The rationale: most people consider observed urination embarrassing. A test requiring someone to spit into a cup is a lot less humiliating. Right?

American Drug Screening in Dallas is pushing a test kit aimed at parents to use on their kids. Or vice versa, depending on which generation is more suspicious. It's called "Aware." Get this: For a mere twenty-five dollars, you get a specimen jar, instructions, a form, and a mailing label. Parents (or kids) are expected to mail the jar of suspect urine back to the manufacturer, who will run it through an EMIT machine and let you know if someone you love is smoking pot, doing PCP, barbs, cocaine, or Valium.

Aside from shattering family bonds, the "Aware" method is clinically bad news. Urine decomposes quickly if unrefrigerated. Mailing the stuff means a minimum of two days at room temperature or higher. By the time the sample arrives, the only thing it's ready for is the toilet, where it should have gone originally. No laboratory can con valid results out of stale urine. Nonetheless, ADS plans on selling 100,000 Aware kits next year. Be-Aware!

Of course, overnight delivery firms could step in and solve the deterioration problem. TV ads proclaiming "We put U back in urine" seem a natural.

One of the most frightening machines to emerge from the drug testing scene comes right out of Orwell's 1984. Named the Veritas 100, it is a patented computerlike device which measures brain wave data as influenced by drugs. The waves are converted into positive or negative results.

Like an EKG, the machine records impulses from electrodes wired to the temples, comparing it to standard brain references in the database. Its inventor, Dr. Thomas Westerman, a New Jersey ear, nose, and throat specialist, is himself a little unsure how the Veritas works. "We are probably measuring the influence of psychotropic drugs on the balancing mechanism, the eye-ear spinal reflex system, and the brain," he said (*Washington Times*, 6/20/86).

As weird as this sounds, this is the first machine to understand that people get high in their *brains*, not their bladders. So why not a more direct peek?

National Patent Analytic Systems, which makes the machine, contends that each illegal drug has a unique brainprint. They claim the Veritas 100 picks up on anything from alcohol to Valium with an accuracy level close to 99 percent. The scientific community is skeptical, to say the least. "Not only is it scary, it is next to impossible to differentiate between drug effects with their limited technology, which it claims to do," said a biological engineer. "Even if brain waves do vary, it is unlikely that any machine can indicate the exact drug responsible."

Urine, blood, saliva are all tangibles. When you start fooling around with brain waves, you get into highly sensitive, almost metaphysical, areas. What sort of information is being extracted? Where is the line drawn between an individual's privacy and science's ability to invade? For the time being, the Veritas 100 is the closest thing yet to the Thought Police. But National Patent Analytic likes the idea of a Thought Police and has a good track record of making the ludicrious sellable. Breathalyzers cleverly disguised as flashlights and radios have been pushed on many police forces. Why not brain scans for inquisitive employers? They get data without the mess. Unproved as yet, each Veritas 100 costs about $11,000.

Science marches on. British police have recently screened 5,000 murder "suspects" with a "genetic fingerprint" that they claim isolates genetic clues in blood samples that help identify murderers. Dr. Kevin Kelly of the University of Aberdeen, a biochemist who has performed the test and who recently coauthored an article on the subject, says, "It's technically difficult to do, but it has enormous potential. It's a real breakthrough!"

The procedure has met with little opposition in the rural areas where heinous murders have occurred. The technique, developed by geneticist Alec Jeffreys at Leicester University, focuses on the DNA that is present in the chromosomes of all human beings. The test is supposedly accurate even on dried blood as much as five years old or on semen residue three years old. No court challenges have yet occurred, and the British Home Office is already accepting genetic fingerprints as evidence. The current thinking is to do massive samplings of everyone within a radius where a crime has taken place. In one case, 5,000 men have been asked to "volunteer" blood and saliva; almost all have been convinced to cooperate. No murderer has been found yet, but the search continues.

So far, all the tests we have described, no matter how off the wall they might sound to the average urinator, will soon be available through conventions or trade catalogues. But visionaries in the field consider this level of urine screening too slow, cumbersome, and easy to beat. A Minneapolis firm named E.K. Tech, Inc. which made a name for itself in electronic scramblers and descramblers, is at work on the bravest of the new worlds we are about to enter. Hidden cameras will videotape toilets at the workplace. When flushed, the camera takes a picture, the urine passes into a dehydration chamber, and then to some sort of analyzer. Within minutes, a computer will not only be able to tell a person's recent drug history, but get this, *whether or not the person has had sex during the past twenty-four hours*.

Persons valuing civil liberties better be prepared to mount resistance right now or they should start learning how to hold their excretions for life.

13.

Golden Showers Come Your Way

As we've seen, all of the commonly used urine tests are inaccurate to some degree. The minuscule (5 percent or less) margin of error guaranteed by the manufacturer, however, is a distortion of true performance in the field. Technically it may be possible to achieve near-perfect detection, but only under rigidly controlled laboratory conditions, where all the variables—reagent strength, temperature, pH, and concentration—are controlled. Change anything in a real-life application and your 95 percent specificity plummets to 70 percent or less. One forensic scientist observed, "Duplicating the [manufacturer's] error rate in daily operation is impossible. Period. We've had assays bottom out at rates of 20 percent or more that were false positives when confirmed by GC/MS. These were clean specimens, but the lab didn't see it that way."

Maintaining those processing conditions that optimize test performance is next to impossible. So if the tests are inaccurate to begin with, laboratories only make the problem worse. Most drug urinalysis is done independently, in high-tech assembly-line operations, which assume full responsibility for the results. Sample mishandling, contamination, and poor reporting procedures have created nightmares undreamed of by the EMIT folks. Again, cost plays an important role. Underpaid technicians are judged on the number of assays they churn out. Remember, EMIT spelled backward is MONEY.

There are two kinds of urine-testing labs. The first is an offshoot of an established Drug Industrial Corporation that figures it can play both the demand and supply sides of the hysteria fence. The scheme works something like this: the Major Drug Manufacturer produces any number of controlled (though not necessarily illegal) substances. If their drugs are any good, if the distribution system and ad campaign are well funded, people are going to buy a lot of them. Now, the Major Drug Manufacturer doesn't live in a vacuum; it knows some drugs are prone to heavy abuse, probably some of its own. Opportunity knocks. *Not only can it cash in by making a drug, it can also get paid for detecting the people who use it.*

The practicalities are simple. The Corporation has enough experience in the biochemical world to develop a urine test or to set up a lab using prefabricated screens. It also has name recognition—and big bucks to support the venture.

The second type of urine lab is more humble. Private investors, venture capitalists, and other get-rich-quickers become "experts" by purchasing a variety of detection equipment—EMIT or TLC (ToxiScreen) if they don't want the trouble of NRC certification for radioactive RIA. A site is selected, technicians are hired and trained. The "laboratory," really a marketing company in disguise, seeks companies interested in farming out drug-screening programs. A well-funded lab might sponsor parties, conferences, and junkets, doing all it can to put the fear of uncontrolled addiction into the hearts of employers. The liquor flows freely. (An important point, since alcohol abusers, and those on the wagon are easily the most ardent opponents of marijuana and other illegal substances. Scapegoats are easy targets for those relying on denial mechanisms regarding their own drug habits.) Labs also have cooperative programs with test manufacturers or drug consultants, sharing trade advertising and administrative expenses.

What do the laboratories do? If they are a full-service operation, they collect the sample from the worker (occasionally sending someone to observe urination), label it, and have the urinator sign a disclosure form approving of urinalysis. (Direct observation is considered essential for accuracy, because "sample switching" occurs. However, it's controversial. It's difficult to urinate with your genitalia covered. The majority of companies, wishing to avoid embarrassment, voyeurism, and sexual harassment suits don't require direct observation.) The specimen then goes to the lab, where it likely goes through an assay-type test. A clerk gets the test results from the technician, notes and occasionally confirms positives, and reports back to the client. Self-serve labs do everything but collect urine. The entire procedure is more administrative than chemical. The big task is keeping track of all the samples, forms, and clients.

Laboratory errors are generally of three sorts: chain of custody, technician error, and contamination. Chain of custody refers to the progression of the sample through the lab maze: how it is labeled, who controls shipment, who makes sure specimens aren't mixed up, that the right name goes on the right jar. A technician going over one hundred samples gets bored fast, and sloppiness goes hand in hand with boredom. Many are part-time students who study their textbooks while the machines run. Contamination refers to the integrity of the sample and the equipment. Residue from a true-positive sample remaining on processing equipment could result in false positives for many, many subsequent "clean" samples.

Even straightforward jobs get screwed up. An expanding market has meant some unscrupulous activity. When the first shot in the War on Drugs was fired, the carpetbaggers ran to the front lines. They built many fly-by-night laboratories, which used minimally trained technicians to evaluate everything from blood to urine. To maximize returns, a lot of labs have been cutting corners, doing without basic equipment. Such is the profit motive in an unregulated environment.

With such shoddy procedures, errors in laboratory evaluation have become legion. Urine samples have been misanalyzed, tainted, lost. *U.S. News & World Report* (10/20/86) revealed that sloppy procedures are nearly epidemic: "Some [labs] identify a sample only by its position in a rack holding hundreds of indistinguishable specimens."

With conditions like these, you're just asking for trouble. But still the labs operate with impunity. "Give us a chance, we are in our infancy," rationalized Steven Hale, a technician with a Midwest laboratory. "It's natural that mistakes are made. We learn from them. And we're getting better."

Mistakes are part of human nature. But when lab results are used as weapons, any mistake becomes ammunition.

Criticism has come from all sides. Even manufacturing companies that make error-ridden urine screens have bad-mouthed the laboratories. Dr. Harold M. Bates, a chemist with Metpath Laboratories, told the *National Law Journal* (1/7/86):

> The real room for error is not with the technology, but with administrative errors . . . When the volume of work goes up, the error rate goes up. That's the scary part. My company makes millions of dollars doing drug testing, but I wouldn't want somebody taking my urine. I think it's an invasion of privacy. I would always be afraid somebody might . . . mix up samples.

The severity of the "lab problem," as it came to be known, peaked in 1985, when the *Journal of the American Medical Association* profiled a Center for Disease Control study. (*JAMA*, 4/26/85) From 1972 through 1981, the CDC and NIDA jointly ran a proficiency-testing program for thirteen independent labs. To give you an idea of the result, just read the title, "Crisis in Drug Testing." The program was conducted as follows:

"In this program, ten drug-spiked samples were mailed quarterly to each participating laboratory (each laboratory received 40 samples per year). The participants in the program tested the samples for the requested drugs and submitted a report for grading on each quarterly survey by the cutoff date."

The CDC was very generous in classifying labs. To earn a "satisfactory" rating, a lab needed correct results only 80 percent of the time. Anything lower was "unacceptable." That implies the CDC was willing to sacrifice twenty workers out of every hundred to bad test processing. With high unemployment rates, new labor comes cheaper.

The study marched on for nine years. Like restaurants that serve superior food only to reviewers, the CDC along the way suspected its specimens were getting preferential treatment. To run a fair test, they needed anonymity:

Early in the program, allegations were made that some laboratories were not subjecting samples to the same testing procedures as their routine samples. These claims prompted two CDC studies in which data were collected through an alternative mode—the blind test. This mode of testing requires the use of a dedicated surrogate office to introduce the test samples into the laboratory without the laboratory's knowledge.

All laboratories reported accurate results only when they knew the samples were spiked. *But unknown, blind tests led to disastrous conclusions.* False negatives for samples containing illegal substances were as high as 100 percent in some cases!

Error rates for thirteen laboratories on samples containing barbiturates, amphetamines, methadone, cocaine, codeine, and morphine ranged from 11% to 94%, 19% to 100%, 0% to 33%, 0% to 100%, 0% to 100%, and 5% to 100%, respectively, Similarly, error rates on samples not containing these drugs (false positives) ranged from 0% to 6%, 0% to 37%, 0% to 66%, 0% to 6%, 0% to 7%, and 0% to 10%, respectively.

Needless to say, the CDC and anyone bothering to read *JAMA* were shocked. (Remember, the CDC *is* the U.S. Government.) They caught the labs red-handed and red-faced. They reached the same conclusions that urine-testing opponents had been screaming about for years: that labs generally take poor care of urine samples and don't live up to their promises of accuracy: "Laboratories are often unable to detect drugs at concentrations called for by their contracts." This is a traditional business technique known as forcing the data to conform to the ad copy.

When the Industrial Drug Enforcers read this attack, they downed their Valiums, rushed to the nearest bar, and rallied their forces. They decided to play down the findings and cast doubts on the tactics of the CDC study. This traditional business technique, known as shifting the blame, is standard operating procedure by the tobacco industry facing similar studies. "It's unfair using the performance of only thirteen labs to condemn hundreds," they pleaded. "More lab studies will show just how wrong you are. We need more studies."

Unfortunately for them, more studies were on their way. The next year, researchers were confirming and extending the CDC's conclusion left and right. The Armed Forces Institute of Pathology sent anonymous spiked urine to CompuChem in Raleigh, N.C., for EMIT and RIA processing. The results were equally alarming. Less than half of the true positive samples were detected by EMIT. RIA, on the other hand, performed admirably, turning up 99 percent of the spiked samples. CompuChem defended itself, shifting the blame back to the army pathologists, like good little Drug Industrialists. The pH level of the spiked urine was unusually low, pH of 4, they argued, and is unlikely to be discharged by humans; their EMIT equipment couldn't handle the aberration. The Institute of Pathology didn't buy the excuse, but CompuChem executives weren't upset. EMIT grows more popular every day with their industrial clients.

A famous study conducted by Northwestern University discovered a national average false positive rate of near 25 percent. The *Los Angeles Times* reported a UCLA study which found that of 161 prescription and over-the-counter medications, 65 produced false positives in the three most widely used urine tests.

Why all the errors? Mostly because procedures and workmanship vary. Diagnostic laboratories are unregulated by federal authority, and only a handful of states have basic proficiency or equipment requirements. All it takes to start a lab is a $3,000 piece of equipment, some white aprons, and some promotion. So labs are accountable only to the needs (and anxieties) of the marketplace. The free market trades sensitivity for bad technique.

Even carefully trained lab personnel can make errors. Syva, which markets EMIT as an in-house program ("it can be run by a nurse, or trained member of the personnel staff"), prides itself on producing "professionals" in a few hours.

Dr. John Morgan is skeptical. "The Syva Corporation wishes to supply on-site EMIT for relatively untrained personnel to engage in difficult biochemical manipulations. There are no data confirming that such personnel can do this work adequately and the EMIT test has consistently failed field condition analysis. [I am] convinced that such use of EMIT is improper." (*Journal of Psychoactive Drugs*, 12/84, p. 316)

Dr. Arthur McBay, head toxicologist in the Chief Medical Examiner's Office of North Carolina, has been equally critical. Addressing a conference of forensic scientists in Cincinnati, he asked, "Is there anybody in the audience who would submit urine for cannaboid testing if his career, reputation, freedom or livelihood depended on it?" No one answered. (*Chemical News*, 12/83)

National Health Laboratories, Inc., is a chain of thirteen outlets in the Northeast, performing all kinds of diagnostic medical testing. Large and filled with lots of imposing equipment, each site serves hospitals, physicians, and, lately, private employers. NHL's fastest growing department is, not surprisingly, urine testing. One technician estimated a 175 percent increase in the number of samples evaluated within the past two years. The majority of those tests are pre-employment, company-sponsored screens.

Prices are competitive. For twenty-five dollars, NHL will evaluate a urine sample for ten drugs and confirm all positive results with a second test. But the choice of procedures leaves much to be desired. Thin-layer chromatography is used on all initial urine samples, and positive tests are confirmed with EMIT. One scientist remarked, "That's like reading someone's palm and confirming by reading tea leaves." Real accuracy is available, but it costs. Gas chromatography/mass spectrometry testing goes for ninety-five dollars per sample.

The National Health folks work hard at maintaining an air of decorum about their work. They report no chain-of-custody problems of the sort that have haunted their competitors. All specimen bottles are sealed, clearly marked, with tamper-proof labels put across the top. When pressed, though, they'll admit there was one problem not long ago. Not a technical problem, mind you, but a clerical one—an innocuous transcription error. Someone listed a negative result as a positive one. And there was some trouble. But the procedures have been improved, and no further errors have been reported.

Those brought up on science fiction movies know that a teenie-weenie error in the lab by the end of the movie has a fifty/fifty chance of destroying Earth.

The solution to the lab problem is a simple one, but it has escaped serious consideration—thanks, no doubt, to the lobbyists. Labs have operated openly in an unregulated environment. Clearly such freedoms result in sloppiness that natural economic laws haven't gotten around to fixing yet. (In fact, there's an unconscious bias toward believing a lab is more on the ball the more positives it reports, whether or not they're correct.) Labs have no incentive to improve their urine-testing track record because clients are willing to pay, regardless of the level accuracy or chain of handling. Close inspection, regulation, licensing, proficiency testing, and technician certification would all improve the labs' performance.

Some tiny steps are already being taken. NIDA is starting a voluntary quality-control program. "Voluntary" in this situation does not mean the same as "voluntary" when applied to a worker facing the test, certainly not to a new job applicant. That "voluntary" is spelled m-a-n-d-a-t-o-r-y.

Few workers are aware of the errors resulting from laboratory handling. Information is hard to come by. The media only reveals the inflammatory anecdote or the National Party Line. The groups that have taken sides on the issue—scientists, lawyers, consultants—are too polite to air their disagreements openly, no matter which side they're on. The Drug Industrial Complex is very reserved. (After all, we are talking about bodily excrements!) Opinions must be substantiated in print by at least thirty column inches before they can be considered.

But battles are being waged in the pages of academic journals. Beneath the dull graphics and schematic representations, facts are refuted, hypotheses challenged, and reputations are slandered. Actual name calling and challenges to duels are missing, but you can decipher them between the lines. To its readers, the *Journal of Psychoactive Drugs* can be just as exciting as the *National Enquirer*. When one drug-screening giant's product was roasted—through technical expository testing, of course—the company responded with its own twenty-pager, attacking the methodology of the original piece and the credibility of the author with the strongest language libel laws allow.

Reagan's Executive Order tries to regulate the urine-testing environment on the federal level, but it's doubtful that any meaningful change in *private* laboratory operating procedures will come about. Until labs are monitored, the unhappy worker faces two sources of error: one in the imperfect test, the other in the processing.

At this point you should be mad enough to urinate on the shoe of the next person who demands a sample. But wait, we have better ways of "Just Saying No!"

Not all the opportunities are found on the wrong side of the urine tracks. Jeffrey Nightbyrd embodies the entrepreneurial spirit of the eighties while within him still beats the heart of a sixties rebel. Jeff is Texas, free enterprise, populism, and Yippie prankster, all in the same enchilada. Throughout the decades, he's found a way of combining his politics with street smarts for making a living.

He's been through various and innovative careers. As Jeff Shero, a leader of Students for a Democratic Society, he founded *The Rat* (in New York City), one of the best of the gritty underground sixties newspapers. He has contributed to the *Village Voice*, where he won an award for distinguished reporting. He published *The Rag* in Austin and was a columnist for the *Daily Texan*. More recently, he has been working on pioneer telecommunications, where he has been called the Ted Turner of low-power television.

But none of these ventures have prepared him for the tremendous publicity surrounding his latest product, drug-free urine. "I'm a civil-libertarian entrepreneur out to make money," he said.

It began in 1985. Nightbyrd, a genial Texan whose easy drawl complements a quick wit and fierce sense of independence, noticed that an increasing number of people in Austin were being subjected to urine testing as a condition of employment. "I thought, my God, what's happened to the Texas spirit with all these people lining up to take urine tests like sheep at a shearing. That's pretty antithetical to the Texas motif. I thought it was the most intrusive, totalitarian, Big Brother thing I could imagine."

Nightbyrd was incensed, but like everyone else felt helpless to stop it. Only after thirty construction workers on a local high-rise project were given a surprise EMIT and subsequently fired did he decide to take action. "One of the workers complained, 'It's a fascist country when they judge a man on the quality of his urine, rather than on his work.' " Nightbyrd explains, "A bunch of them claimed they were innocent, but that didn't do them any good. Later I got to know their lawyer and learned the drug test was a sham." The contractor was behind on his construction schedule and had speeded up work to compensate. The result was compromised safety and an unusually high number of accidents on the job site.

Instead of taking responsibility, management shifted the issue from contractor safety practices to drug abuse. "It was easier for them to accuse the workers of being stoned or drunk than admitting they screwed up," Nightbyrd said. "The EMIT test was a magic wand, taking the burden off them and putting it on someone else."

Jeff knew the tests were wrong and that something should be done to stop it. The legal system was no help, and protests would be ineffective since too many people could lose their jobs. "It occurred to me the only way of stopping drug testing was by beating the test. And one way of beating the test is by substituting drug-free urine for your own." From this humble idea came a potentially lucrative business.

The first steps were tentative. Nightbyrd came up with a name for his prospective company—Byrd Laboratories—and took out a quarter-page "marketing probe" in a local paper. He had what's called a phantom product, only an idea. Response to the ad would determine if production was feasible or not. "I spent $100 and wrote a pretty witty ad for an Austin paper. It offered 'Success In Urine' for only $5 and included a complete guide to passing corporate and government urine tests. I also offered 100% pure urine samples for $45.95. I had to say 'For Experimental Purposes Only' so I couldn't be accused of anything illegal. Then I waited."

He didn't have to wait very long. Within a day of publication, he was deluged with phone calls. "I got anywhere from 50 to 100 calls a day. They ran the gamut. Some wanted to know if this was a joke. Others wanted to know if franchises were available. I got lots of sob stories, people who lost their jobs." And he got orders. He was convinced he had come up with a breakthrough.

The next step was building an inventory. In a week he wrote

and printed the ground-breaking pamphlet, "Success in Urine Testing." Then he approached a senior citizens' home for his urine supply. "They were surprised, but very receptive. Here I was offering to pay them for something they were flushing away. It worked out well for both of us." The urine was collected in a large drum, bacteria inhibitors were added to keep the product fresh, and every batch was tested by EMIT to make sure it was drug-free. On the administrative side, Nightbyrd ordered jars and labels for the fledgling company. He established an account with Federal Express for next-day delivery. A slogan, "Purveyors of Fine Urine Products," was added, and business was off.

After several months, though, Byrd Labs was having quality troubles. "Liquid urine has a couple of serious problems. It has a short shelf life, it's unaesthetic, expensive to mail, occasionally leaks, and it's hard to regulate the supply." The solution lay in research and development. Graduate chemistry students were hired to work on a freeze-drying process, but the results were dismal. "When you freeze-dry urine, you end up with a lot of awful smelling, gummy stuff on the sides of the freeze-drying chamber." Freeze drying was out, and Nightbyrd was back to sloshing liquid urine around town.

Jeff complained to his sister, a medical student, about his experiments. "She knows her chemistry pretty well and wondered why I was wasting time freeze-drying it. 'You're not going to drink the stuff, after all.' She suggested a powder would be perfectly suitable. So we went back into the lab and came up with a dehydration process that gave us a fine, compact, easily reconstituted powder." The powder was packed into small vials along with the instruction "Just add water."

The powdered urine boosted sales. And Jeff became a darling of the media. He was profiled in the *New York Times* ("Texan Is Selling Drug-Free Urine to Meet 'Unanticipated Demand' "), the *Los Angeles Times*, and the *San Antonio Light*. He swore he was going to be the country's first urine millionaire. And the War on Drugs became a war of words: "Oil put Texas on top, urine will keep it there," and "Test your government, not your urine." When asked where he got his urine, he answered, "From nuns, choirboys before their voices changed, spinster librarians. I wanted bird watchers, but the Audubon people weren't interested in the money."

And then came the Urine Ball.

The Urine Defense Fund, an offshoot of the Texas ACLU, needed money to fight drug-testing discrimination. And Jeff Nightbyrd needed a venue to promote his product. A symbiotic relationship was born. Jeff organized the Austin event, billing it as "wet, wild, rock & roll variety show." The highlight of the evening was a phone call to the White House, where 1,000 people shouted into a telephone, "We won't drop our zipper for the Gipper!" Byrd Labs had record sales that night, selling nearly two hundred bags of powdered urine at $49.95 a shot.

The White House doesn't take such telephone calls lightly. The FDA, acting on orders from the top, harassed Byrd Labs until the specter of sticky litigation made them decide they had no jurisdiction.

Business continues to grow. "Right now I'm selling between $2,000 and $3,000 a week. I'm the classic entrepreneur. But I'd like to be thought of as a Renaissance man."

Jeff's publicity and success have brought on competitors, but after three hours of reminiscing over Woodstock and some rounds of Lone Star, we struck a deal. By mentioning the battle cry of the Urine Free America Movement—"Just Say No!"—you, the reader of *Steal This Urine Test* are entitled to a 25 percent discount on two vials of pure Texas urine (this is guaranteed drug-free and is no put-on). For experimental purposes only. Although they are usually $19.95, you can get two vials for only $14.95 from: Byrd Laboratories, 225 Congress #340, Austin, Texas 78701, (512) 480–0085.

One reason I want to give this effort a strong plug is because several newspapers, including the *Boston Phoenix*, the New York *Village Voice*, and the Minneapolis *City Pages*, refused to accept ads, claiming the product was an attempt to defraud the test administrators. These knee-jerks forget the urine tests themselves are the only fraud involved.

14.

Steal This Urine Test

Introduction

Finally, the heart of the matter—beating the urine testers in their own stalls. Above all, this chapter is activist. It urges you to fight against evil tactics. But it has an equally important goal: to clear up rumor, misconception, and street lore which can be hit or miss in terms of reliability. Misses can be especially risky, putting jobs and reputations on the line. For example, the most common street "remedy" for beating urine tests seems to be drinking lemonade. Lemon juice, an acid, supposedly tricks the EMIT machine into turning up a false negative. However, our research and medical consultants have convinced us that the body metabolizes the lemon's acidity too quickly to make it a viable chemical adulterant. Anyone using the "lemonade method" might next have to beat the unemployment line.

This book is written for persons with limited access to necessary survival information, who find themselves trapped in a bathroom stall against their will. What you are about to read are facts and methods proven reliable in getting around or actually beating urinalysis. Every technique has been verified. Toxicologists have reviewed our chemical dilutant and adulterant procedures. Most importantly, major laboratories have tested spiked samples under the typical conditions that your specimen would face.

Urine test manufacturers claim that their tests are virtually 100 percent accurate, that they are impossible to beat. Don't be intimidated by such bravado. These are marketing ploys, attempts at convincing potential clients of their product's virtues, and at the same time striking fear in the hearts of workers. The word "virtual" is your key to success. It admits imperfection without coming right out and saying so. In fact, "virtual" can mean anything from 95 percent accuracy to 30 percent or less.

Mind Over Bladder

You can confront any obstacle by summoning up the proper determination—in this case, mind over bladder. Are you going to let a spongy, primitive organ determine the rest of your life, or are you going to use your brain?

There is a Zen master in India who can draw milk into his body, using his penis as a straw. A San Francisco woman uses her vagina to smoke seventeen cigarettes a day. (She can also blow soap bubbles.) Intense concentration is required to perform such feats. We are not going to ask you to go this far, but you should be aware of the potential of self-discipline. There is still lots to be learned about internal relationships among organs, especially between the brain and the genitalia.

This isn't to say you can influence what your bladder excretes (other than by controlling what you ingest). Pulse, respiration, and nerve reactions can be slowed down by meditation, but internal metabolism keeps plugging away at its own sweet pace. You can't "wish" drugs out of your urine.

The best defense, said a great American philosopher, Vince Lombardi, is a good offense. Learn to fight. Although the stall door may be bolted shut, in your mind you must have the enemy surrounded and in serious trouble. For you, the Enforcers must be up the proverbial yellow stream without a paddle. Combine biology and ideology. Be positive in your mind and negative in the vial.

One way or another, YOU WILL BEAT THE TEST!

Manifesto of Free Choice

Distrustful as they are about the Enforcers' motives, some folks are equally wary of opposition tactics. Two wrongs don't make a right, they say. But civil disobedience is a great American tradition. Mind over bladder, sleight of hand, chemical masking, defensive fake-outs, and other forms of chicanery should be regarded not as ancillary to survival, but as a justifiable civil duty to perform, your "necessity defense." Serious violations of privacy rights make it necessary to defend those rights by any means. But defend them you must. Mark Twain once said, "Our rights remain rights only as long as we have the prudence not to test them." Sarcastically, he was saying the powers that be can do anything unless we act to stop them.

By beating the test you become part of a movement whose goal is to stop this and all government intrusions into our private lives.

You are using your vital fluids to sign your name to the manifesto of free choice! The pledge of resistance!

Urinators of the world, unite! You have *nothing* to lose.

Everything considered up to this point has prepared you to do your duty. Reason and research have destroyed the Testers' arguments of constitutionality, democratic fairness, technical accuracy, and the myth of invincibility. Understanding how the tests work, what your legal rights are, and what political options exist are as equally important as understanding how to score well on a urine exam. Many people get A's but invariably miss the point of the subject. You are urged to take the higher philosophical road— knowledge will expand your opportunities, not simply get you through the foxhole of life.

True education, as Socrates taught it, was a subversive act. The philosopher's philosopher would have known how to respond to mass, random urine testing. The knowledge you gain here may be considered equally subversive, since it challenges the status quo of the National Party Line.

No third party should have access to your medical information unless it's expressly given to them by you. *Any biochemical test gives out your medical history as surely as if you had given your consent.* If you use drugs (over-the-counter, prescription, or otherwise), do not be coerced into surrendering privacy simply because "they asked me for it."

Don't fall for propaganda. If you plan on beating the test, don't consider yourself a misfit or criminal, but a defender of freedom. You are not aiding criminals or spreading the "evil plague." Most of the drugs the Enforcers screen for are legal. The government's game is to divide and conquer.

Even if you don't use drugs or any substances that may cross-react, it's still imperative that you maintain a community conscience in order to defeat a practice you personally abhor, and to safeguard against similar invasions to come.

The attitude "what have I got to hide?" plays right into the hands and equipment of the Enforcers. The point is, in a free society you should never have to ask that question. After all, this is the question that also crosses your mind while tied naked on a chair in a dark cell with torturers poised to do you bodily damage. This is the questions good Germans asked themselves in the 1930s.

If Presidents have the privilege to say, "No comment," in an egalitarian society, why can't you?

Like It Or Not, Homework Helps

Beating the urine test is no different from beating any other exam. You have to begin with a certain amount of—ugh!—study.

1. **Learn which test is being used.** Learn as much as you can about your employer's plan of attack. As we pointed out in an earlier chapter, accuracy varies from test to test. Typically, one of three tests is used as the initial screen. Thin-layer chromatography (TLC), arguably the weakest test (also the cheapest), requires a strong concentration of drug in the urine sample, and results are based on the subjective interpretation of the technician. EMIT is marginally more accurate, since it automatically targets specific drugs in the sample. Abuscreen is the best of a bad lot, earning the highest rating from the Centers for Disease Control survey.

State-of-the-art gas chromatography/mass spectrometry (GC/MS) does the chemical equivalent of finding a needle in a haystack. But don't worry, GC/MS is almost never used as either the initial or confirmation screen, despite its accuracy. The reason: cost. But it is the standard confirmation test as far as science is concerned.

Knowing the type of test is important. Not because the tricks to get around them are all that different, but because each is limited in what it searches for and the concentration required. The following chart lets you know exactly which test searches for which target drugs.

EMIT, ABUSCREEN, AND TOXI-LAB DETECTABILITY
FOR SELECTED CONTROLLED SUBSTANCES

	EMIT	*Abuscreen*	*Toxi-Lab*
Drug/ Metabolite Detected	Amphetamine, Methamphetamine	Amphetamine metabolites	Amphetamine
	Barbiturate metabolites	Barbiturate metabolites	Barbiturate metabolites
	Benzodiazepine (Valium, Librium)	No information	No information
	Cannabinoid metabolites	Cannabinoids, THC, Carboxylic Acid	THC
	Cocaine metabolite benzoylecgonine	Cocaine metabolite benzoylecgonine	Cocaine metabolite benzoylecgonine
	Methadone	No information	No information
	Methaqualone, Mecloqualone	Methaqualone	Not yet available
	Opiates	Morphine	Morphine
	PCP	Phencyclidine (PCP)	PCP
	Proxyphene (Darvon)	No information	No information
	Not yet available	LSD	Not yet available

(Source: Syva, Roche Diagnostics, Marion Laboratories,
U.S. Office of Technology Assessment.)

If you suspect that some prankster from the CIA has recently doused you with LSD, don't worry about EMIT. Syva hasn't come out with that specific test yet. On the other hand, pay attention if RIA is used. Similarly, if you use phenobarbitol or ethyl alcohol (booze) don't hassle on an RIA test. But be prepared for EMIT. Also, *nothing* currently screens for Ecstasy or any designer drug. Psilocybin (found in certain mushrooms) and mescaline (found in peyote) are also not tested. Neither is nicotine.

2. Find out who is conducting the test. If the urine is collected by a designated in-house employee, you have a better chance of learning about the screening process than if a tight-lipped independent lab is getting its buckets filled. Solidarity among workers counts for something. Learn who gets access to results, what happens to people who flunk, what appeal, rehabilitation, and treatment policies exist. Is your company out for blood or just control?

One important point: many urine testers cheat in your favor. We have heard that scores of paid observers sabotage specimens and results. In some cases, departments, entire companies, and perhaps one major federal agency put out the word that no one is to be penalized regardless of policy or test results. Military officers discreetly advise suspect troops to take a day off when a surprise test is forthcoming. Some informers have witnessed urine testers eyeballing the sample in front of the subject, saying "it looks okay to me," and dumping it down the toilet with a big wink. But be careful. Not everyone is on your side.

3. Find out who is processing the test. Are the urine samples being evaluated in-house or by an independent lab? If you don't recognize the collector as a company person, processing is probably done in an outside lab. Also, if your company is running fewer than one hundred tests, it's a safe bet they've subcontracted the job.

How does someone get to be a designated urine collector? In small companies, management posts the job or approaches trusted workers and asks if they would like to earn a few extra bucks as a watchdog. Why not, they think, the extra money can help, and it's not all *that* disgusting. In a larger organization, a Fortune 500 type, the medical staff is assigned additional duty. Whoever the collector is, the role is all-important. Know how much you can maneuver. There are many ways of gaining confidence and information. Asking the watchdog to collaborate is risky. Expect some resistance and threats to report you to the top, but they rarely will.

They don't have the best job in the world. The Health and Human Services Agency lists responsibilities for the Federal Urine Collector (the FUC): "The male [or female] collection site person should accompany the individual into the public restroom . . . The collection site person remains in the restroom but outside the stall until the urine specimen is collected and handed to the collection site person by the individual. The collection site person should flush the toilet." On top of this, they have to measure amount, temperature, and note any unusual activity. The bathroom scenery doesn't change much. Plumbing is plumbing, and the FUC doesn't come out a hero in the lunchtime jokes.

In-house screening almost certainly means EMIT, and that lets you get away with sample adulteration and false negatives more easily, because the folks running the equipment aren't always professional technicians. They don't know what to look for.

If it's an independent lab—take-out service—processing can involve any of the three standard methods. Narrow the possibilities. If you're in the military, you are, in all likelihood, being tested with RIA. The majority of federal agencies screen with EMIT. Private-sector companies split between EMIT and TLC—which is fine, since both are equally beatable.

If in doubt about the procedure, ask around. The personnel office is a good place to start. Be discreet; they're under no obligation to talk. Make friends with the secretaries or someone from the infirmary. Pose questions vaguely: "Oh, I read in *Reader's Disgust* that some urine tests are better than others. I was just curious about what we use here. . . ." An open-ended question will get them talking, even bragging about the procedure without arousing unnecessary suspicion. Call local labs.

4. Keep informed. The Drug Industrial Complex isn't stupid. When a certain drug becomes fashionable, it's only a matter of time before they devise a test for it. Learn what the weasels are up to.

Two good ways of keeping abreast are by reading the medical

journals or contacting the manufacturer directly. Writing as a curious citizen will get you some brochures and propaganda, but little else. Here's a better way. On real or dummy corporate stationery, type a formal-sounding letter to both trendsetters in the field:

- Syva Company, P.O. Box 10058, Palo Alto, Calif. 94303. Or call the technical service lines: (800) 227-8994, or (800) 982-6006 in California.
- Roche Diagnostics Systems, Division of Hoffmann-LaRoche, Nutley, N.J. 07110. Telephone (800) 526-1247 or in New Jersey, (201) 751-6100.

They'd love to hear from you. That's why they have toll-free numbers. Use them. In fact, use them often to answer any questions you have. Pretend you are a potential customer. Or just call them up and ask them the ball score! Tell 'em you represent the Contras softball team and want to challenge Syva's house team. But even if you can't determine which system you are going against, you can still beat the reaper.

Prenotification or Random Screening
Now that you've done your homework and know the name of the enemy, you have to prepare your first line of defense. It's based on test administration. Try to find out whether the impending test is given randomly—as a sneak attack—or occurs with prior warning. At first, you might think there's no chance of beating a surprise test. That's why so many employers give one—without due cause or objective fact. Mass random testing, though, is not without its Achilles' heel, because that's what generally has been losing in the courts, especially state courts.

Prenotification means you unwittingly have a friend in the company testing program giving you the most precious gift, time. Prenotification may be disguised as an annual checkup, a blood drive, or any situation where you suspect urine may be withdrawn without arousing your suspicion.

Prenotification can also come in the form of a formal announcement, or a sweet letter in the employee's in-basket. Pacific Refining Company sent a policy statement to all workers:

> The Corporation reserves the right to conduct screening as deemed appropriate. The format for screening shall be dictated by the prevailing circumstances and may vary by location and method. These programs and policies are not set out as a result of suspicion, rather they are formulated with the idea that if properly conducted, will benefit all employees. [This is how the expression "the velvet noose" originated.]

Surprise testing for some is prenotification for others. If everyone in Sector 5 gets tested on Tuesday, Sector 6 can expect it shortly. Time to go on *yellow alert*.

Of one hundred companies surveyed in our research, prenotification was given by only twenty-two, a distinct minority. The time lag between announcement and testing varied from one to four weeks, and was rarely less than a week. This is ample time to do what you must.

In the tradition of all drug busts, surprise is seen as no less essential in mass screening. This is how it might come down on 80 percent of you:

> Good morgen and good news to all you fine workers on the fourth floor. Lunch hour has been extended an extra half-hour. At exactly 1200 hours, you are to report to the infirmary, where professionally trained personnel will assist you in voiding the contents of your bladder. No one may leave the premises without special permission, and no-shows will be disciplined. There is no suspicion of guilt, my friends. This program is exactly the same as is being carried out in thousands of factories across our great nation, with the blessing of our beloved President. I know all of you join us here at Ramjac Corporation in our effort to maintain a safe, productive, and happy environment. Continue work as usual and thank you for your voluntary

cooperation and this show of good will toward your fellow workers.

Now as panic sets in on the job floor, you must remain calm, completely in control. If you can, go to the toilet right away; each specimin is less concentrated than the last.

In addition to knowing what the tests look for and don't, trigger those little synapses in your brain and recall what drug you may have been exposed to and when. As the Stones say, "Time, time, time is on your side." But retention time varies from substance to substance. See the chart below.

Of course, duration varies from person to person. These numbers are nothing more than educated estimates for a person of average weight and size. Retention depends on any number of variables: metabolism, body weight, amount of drug consumed, body fat, and so on. A good rule of thumb: always allow a day or two beyond any reasonable estimate. Your mileage may vary.

Given ample prenotification of impending doom, *abstinence* doesn't do much for sexual organs but it'll make the bladder born-again. If that's too tough, try the next best thing: switch your vice. If you smoke marijuana and are certain they're going to test for

DRUG RETENTION PERIOD

Compound	Approximate Retention
Amphetamines	20–25 days
Barbiturates	10–14 days
Cocaine	2–4 days
Ethyl Alcohol	1–2 days
LSD	20–40 days
Marijuana	14–30 days
Methaqualone	14–21 days
Opiates	10–14 days
Phencyclidine (PCP)	10–14 days

(Note: Length of retention varies because of many factors, including body weight, metabolism, body fat ratio, and the quantity and concentration of drug. The author cannot guarantee the validity of the retention period.)

that, do something else. Have a drink. A shot of Grand Dad makes a nice change and may help the heart. So doctors say. Alcohol (see chart) has a short retention period and, though most companies can (and say they do publicly) test for booze, they choose not to, for reasons discussed in Chapter Ten.

If you can't abstain from recreational drugs for, say, five days, perhaps you are not just a user and should seek private help. However, if you're on prescription drugs or have a physical condition you wish to keep secret, there's a plan for you coming up also. Stay tuned.

If you're not sure just what is in your bladder, you might want to conduct a parallel EMIT test on yourself, a dry run just to see what might turn up. You can find your local urine lab in, where else, the Yellow Pages. It's worth twenty or forty dollars to know exactly where you stand. The point here is: know your enemy and know yourself.

I ♥ H₂O

Whether forewarned or not, the following are two excellent disciplines you should try cultivating if your company already has a program or you suspect one is on the way.

1. Drink lots of liquids. The human body is 90 percent water. Everything you find attractive about Mel Gibson, Kim Basinger, and Richard Gere is just lust for a fancy water container. Chemicals are constantly sloshing around inside you. Increasing nonalcoholic fluid intake will dilute everything inside you.

2. Purge your system. Urinate as often as you can before leaving for work or before the actual test. *The first urine of the day contains the highest concentration of contaminant particles.* Most food, drink, or controlled-substances lodge in the kidneys overnight and have the best chance of being flushed away with the first urine. Each subsequent voiding reduces the concentration level proportionately. Depending on the amount of water you drink, afternoon urine is 50 percent to 75 percent less concentrated than the first voiding. Think back to this morning. Your first urine was thick, opaque, and odorous. All these variables declined later in the day.

Some people can't "go" with someone watching, especially under pressured conditions. The testers, to speed up excretion, might encourage you to drink as much water as you can. DO IT! Suck that faucet dry!

The urine tests, naturally, don't target water contaminants like dioxins, PCBs, heavy metals, or fecal coloform—pollutants regularly poisoning our water supply.

3. Adjust your sleep cycle. Since subsequent urine is less chemical more water, getting up earlier will let you squeeze in more trips to the bathroom before T-time. We especially recommend this if you're taking a confirmation test—it pays to squeeze and rinse a little harder. If necessary, stay up all night and drink water.

4. Use your glands. A good sauna flushes out impurities through sweat, and lets you feel good in the process. THC and other metabolites are retained in fatty tissues. Any exercise to reduce body fat may help you beat the test.

Intense watering does not hide the presence of any illicit substance. You are aiming to dilute all traces to a level below the cutoff point needed for a positive result. This is mandatory, elementary defense.

The Consent Form

To protect themselves from lawsuits, testers will ask you to complete a urinalysis *consent form*. Basically, this piece of paper says you understand and approve of this and any pending biochemical analysis: "By my signature below, I hereby declare that I give my consent to submit to urinalysis in accordance with the policy of the above-named company." Further, you will be asked to provide complete information regarding all medications and drugs you have been exposed to recently.

1. To sign or not to sign? Signing the consent form could mean forfeiting your right of privacy, although I doubt it. Anything signed under pressure is coercive, and should be legally invalid. True, a nasty judge could see it the other way, but to date this has not been an issue. But large companies have few qualms about firing nonconsenters (recall Barbara Luck). If you hate your job, want to quit, and want to do so on the grounds of moral objections to urine testing, make a stand now and don't sign. Otherwise, sign away.

You might change the form a little bit, though. Write at the bottom, "Signed under fear of job loss," or "I object to tests on constitutional grounds."

The form will also require that you list any and all medications you've taken in the past week. Cross out the word "week" and write "month." If the supervisor screams, just say, "I read an article recently and learned that the medication I took three weeks ago for the flu can show up even now."

2. Listing drugs. Listing all prescription medications you've used over the past months can present a real dilemma. This is private medical knowledge. Why just confess? *I would not list any sensitive medication.* That is, do not list psychiatric drugs or anything that the boss might use as an excuse to can you. Check out, for example, the problem faced by epileptics. Phenobarbitol is the treatment drug of choice, yet it is one of the primary EMIT target drugs. Many companies have a policy of not allowing any job-impairing drug use.

Checking the charts, you will see that several prescription drugs are routinely screened. If you own up to the treatment, you make yourself vulnerable. People have been fired for having epilepsy, diabetes, asthma, and undergoing psychiatric care. Even though the Vocational Rehabilitation Act clearly protects epileptics from such discrimination, you might have to tell that to a lawyer. And the lawyer will have to make the case in a divided court against company lawyers on retention. Retention means the company pays the lawyer by the year not by the case (i.e. your case costs them nothing in legal fees).

However, you should list certain legal drugs if you feel you have been exposed to targeted substances. Use the cross-reactivity chart (page 187) to your advantage. List one cross-reactive drug for every targeted one. Be frugal. Listing too many could draw unnecessary suspicion. And don't use the poppy seed bagel story; it's too well-known. But common over-the-counter pain relievers, such as Advil, Nuprin, and Midol are used by millions. They cross-react with marijuana, one of the toughest substances to purge from the system. Put one on the list. Put one on even if you don't know how to spell marijuana.

If you don't have the seventy-two-hour grace period needed to eliminate cocaine metabolites, list ampicillin or amoxicillin as prescription medications. Having some in your medicine cabinet could help later. Any new antibiotic may be okay to list on the consent form—it may cross-react as cocaine. Few companies would risk a suit challenging you.

The next time you have a cold with a bad cough, insist that the doctor give you a codeine-based cough syrup. Do not finish this bottle, even if it's the last high in the house. When you fill out the consent form, cough a lot and jot down that you have the flu and are under a doctor's care. A bottle in the medicine cabinet is a terrific alibi for an opiate. And your personal doctor will substantiate the initial prescription.

For your personal protection, as well as to build resistance to the procedure, it's important to get a sympathetic doctor, of which there are legions. Find one to back up your claims. I have yet to meet a doctor who doesn't believe urine tests used for everything other than diagnosis or treating illness are a corruption of medical practice.

3. Finishing the form. Be forewarned, the testers are going to try talking you out of listing cross-reacting drugs. "Oh, don't worry about all those medications," they'll say, "we're not going to test for those." Be skeptical, be firm. Insist on your right to list any subtances you want. Then add a line like, "That's all to the best of my knowledge," and sign the damn thing.

Of course, all this scribbling may catch the eye of the test administrator. Our man in Austin, the Texas Nightbyrd, advises subtle informed resistance through a conversation: "Well, Jennifer, you seem to be quite knowledgeable about these tests. Perhaps you are a little paranoid about failing?" "Mr. Boyle, my job here at Zignat Plastics is so important to me that I took the time to educate myself about the testing procedure. Did you know the error rate for positive results is over 25 percent?!"

This shows you take the test as seriously as your job.

If the company doesn't provide a consent agreement and still wants a urine donation, immediately inform them that you won't submit. This won't get you out of it, but it will get your initial objection on the record. Consent to testing only if you can create your own form, with a list of applicable medications and cross-reactive drugs.

The Urine Exchange

Nothing that we've said up to this point negates the importance of advance preparation. Don't think you've got it made in the shade if you've fudged a consent form and have a packet of powdered urine in your pocket. You also need privacy!

When urine tests first became a fixture in the workplace, workers were free to give specimens unobserved. As more and more people cheated, professional voyeurs were planted in the bathroom to make sure no hanky-panky went on. But the courts have been calling direct observation a degrading practice. Our research shows that fewer than one third of all companies closely observe urination. Most don't follow the golden stream from the body into the jar. According to Ed Meese's "Blue Water Edict" of March 1987, Federal Urine Collectors (FUCs) remain in the restroom, but don't enter the stall.

Even if you are under close scrutiny, a heart-to-heart talk with the FUCs might shame them into standing outside the stall, or at least get them to turn their backs for five minutes.

Blushing Kidneys. Something like 5 percent of the public finds it impossible to urinate with someone nearby. More find it difficult to void under direct observation. It's a documented medical condition, known as "blushing kidneys." Although a minority are afflicted, who is to say you're not one of them? A doctor's note or plaintive insistence of "Please, I can't do it if you're watching" will do wonders for ensuring privacy.

Sleight of Hand. Be creative when you're in the bathroom. Use your body to disrupt line-of-sight observance. Hand placement can conceal a lot of activity, but block with anything else that's available, too. Males might say they only urinate sitting down. Like a good magician, distract the observer. Ask them to run the faucet; say that the sound of running water coaxes your own activity. Practice, practice, practice! People from large families with small bathrooms become expert in hiding their genitalia very quickly.

Observers, though they may not show it, are as embarrassed as you are. The longer you take to urinate, the longer the line behind you grows. Apply enough pressure and they'll give you the latitude you need to perform your little alchemy.

Why all the contortion? Because you want to make some subtle substitutions, replacing your urine with clean stuff.

1. Warm and Dry. Assume a temperature reading will be taken from the specimen. Don't swap an ice-cold brew for tepid pee. This reminds me of a famous sixties antiwar story. At a draft-induction center, one guy managed to substitute beer for urine. Just before he handed it to the nurse, he said, "Oh, excuse me," and drained the specimen jar with gusto. To everyone's disgust, I might add, he asked if they had any more around. This ploy earned him loonie status, and he missed his exotic two-year vacation in Vietnam.

Getting pure urine is the first step to making an effective substitution. Know your source. A relative, a minister, an infant, anyone who can be counted on for "clean" urine should be tapped. The sample should be as fresh as possible. If you need to keep it a few days before the switcheroo, stick it in the refrigerator (please, in a plastic container with warning stickers—you don't want herbal-tea freeloaders surprised). After a two-month period of abstinence, you can make your own pure urine samples galore. Freeze them indefinitely in plastic baggies until needed.

For those without a drug-free friend, the country's biggest urine pusher, Jeff Nightbyrd, offers two vials of guaranteed drug-free urine powder plus instructions. (See Chapter 13, "Golden Showers Come Your Way," for special discount and ordering instructions.)

WARNING: Do not substitute animal urine. Do not make "urine" from water and yellow food coloring or Jell-O. These are easily detected and bomb out in processing.

You are not going to have a friend at the processing lab. Technicians are the enemy. They enjoy nothing more than declaring a sample positive for drug abuse. Don't give them any more ammunition than they need. The substitute must have all the features of freshly voided urine. Otherwise you're just asking for trouble.

If the swap has been refrigerated, get it as warm as possible, to room temperature or beyond. The government wants its samples to be between 90.5 and 99.8 degrees Fahrenheit, but it's only relative warmth they're after. Most FUCs don't measure temperature unless the sample is unusually cold. Private collectors are even less likely to measure temperature, since the collected samples are usually refrigerated. But don't be stupid: no one, not even a FUC, is going to accept a specimen with frost on the glass.

2. Houdini in the Washroom. The substitute urine is clean and warm. Now you need a device to get it into the bathroom. At a pharmacy, purchase a Bard Dispoz-a-Bag® Drainage Bag or similar product made for temporary use by ambulant patients. Cost: under $4. They come in different sizes. In our trials the large leg bag worked best because the extra volume and shape allowed for flatter distribution along the midsection where you'll end up wearing it. It has a short tube and cap, but you can add a short piece of rubber tubing and a valve for easy filling.

When a test is imminent, fill and seal the bag with clean urine. Squeeze all the air out, seal, and put it on—remembering it can't withstand more than eighteen hours at room temperature. So if the test doesn't go down, take the bag home and put it back in the fridge, or freezer. You can repeat this as many times as needed.

Here's the correct procedure for concealing the bag. Pull down your skirt or pants. Secure the bag to your abdomen, exposing as much of the latex to your skin as possible. The more surface area taken up, the flatter the bag will lie, and the better concealed it will be. *Using the abdomen, not the leg, will let gravity do its thing.* Tape it in place. If you don't want to tape it to your body, it might rest easy if you wear panties or jockey shorts. Women shouldn't push it inside panty hose because when you take them off to pee, it'll fall out, unless you cut a pee hole for the hose. You can also purchase incontinence pants for about ten dollars. These give a firm fit, additional warmth, and need no tape. Fancier colostomy or urostomy bags are available, but why pay the higher price (over thirty dollars)? If you need, buy a spool of surgical tape.

Now, snake the output tube from the bag to your crotch. The tube and the on/off cap should be within easy reach, but hidden from sight. It should also feel comfortable—strange at first, but comfortable. After a few hours, you'll forget about it. When the time comes for you to "urinate," discreetly reach into your clothing, locate and turn on the release valve, or take off the cap. The "clean" urine will empty into the jar, apparently your own product. When the bag is empty, or you feel you have given enough, turn off the supply, zip up, shake your rear end, and smile. A few drops on your shoe or the seat adds a measure of authenticity.

This method works well for two reasons. First, urine observers are on the outlook for bulk—glass jars, things concealed in pockets and so forth. While some will occasionally ask you to remove a coat, frisks and strip searches are *verboten*. And someone would have to get awfully close to see the small hose at work. Men standing with their backs to the observers and women sitting with their skirts up are shields enough. The drainage bag is form-fitting, especially when taped flat. No one but you knows it's there. Second, your abdomen serves as a heating pad, radiating body warmth directly to the sample. In an hour the bag will be near enough to body temperature.

As good as the bag trick is, it may not be right for everyone. A good variation: purchase a few reservoir-tipped condoms (nonlubricated, please). Fill one, pull a second over it (to prevent bursts), and tape it as close to your crotch as possible. When the time comes to urinate, with a presharpened fingernail, puncture the reservoir tip, and go with the flow.

To give you an idea of how easy concealment is, those of you who watch porn movies might be surprised to learn that many ejaculations are staged. They are faked with a carefully concealed tube and hand pump. Sorry to ruin your fantasies, sports fans, but we're talking reality.

Women have an anatomical advantage, the option of inserting a urine-filled condom within the vagina. This ruse has been successfully used in women's prisons. Again, use sharpened fingernails or a concealed pin to get things flowing. Even at extra-close range, it's virtually impossible to tell the source of the yellow stream. Some court cases, though, have permitted body cavity searches of inmates.

These techniques should be tried and perfected at home. Novices should use water in their dry runs.

3. **It's All Over Now, Baby Blue.** Diluting urine in the specimen jar is invariably more effective than diluting it in your bladder. In fact, dilution was so rampant that Edwin Meese ordered all federal

toilets filled with blue dye before a urinalysis. The toilet was one source of dilution the FUCs hadn't thought of earlier.

If a surprise urinalysis is forced on you, don't panic. You're in luck if you're looking into clear water. Dip the specimen cup and fill half full of toilet water. Dry the outside. Fill the rest with your own urine and shake. Rub the jar with your hands to warm. Presto, the sample should be dilute enough to fall below the cutoff point.

Complete privacy means opportunity galore. Rinse and fill the specimen jar with hot water to increase the temperature; then dump it clean. Never use scalding water, since that may put it outside the acceptable temperature range and could even crack a thick, cold container. Don't be alarmed if you don't have a thermometer. Your finger is a reliable dipstick.

Although the Health and Human Services Administration insists that toilets be dyed blue, low-level sources inside government washrooms assure us that in most cases the dye is dumped only in the bowl, leaving you fresh, clear water in the tank. Avail yourself of the porcelain oasis. But be careful—removing the tank top makes a lot of noise. And don't flush if you are ordered not to. The thin copper or plastic spout in the tank contains fresh H_2O. Push down on the big float to activate the fresh-water spout. Avail yourself. Take that, Blue Water Meanies!

If you're a moderate drug user, or your last use wasn't last night, as little as one third cup of water can make all the difference between negative and positive results. Conceal water in your mouth, in a rubber between your legs or under your arms. Be resourceful. Don't use spit! Saliva contains some tell-tale metabolites.

4. Color Bias. Although the color of urine varies from person to person and hour to hour (depending on diet, metabolism, etc., it's nearly always yellow), there is an unconscious Enforcer bias that rich yellow urine is the real thing. Dilution diminishes the color, so it's semi-important to compensate. No problem. Taking vitamin C capsules will give your urine a darker shade of yellow. When you then dilute it, it will balance back to innocent mellow yellow. The vitamins increase the odor, which also compensates for the added water.

Even random, surprise searches mean long lines and lag time.

There is always *some* warning before you're in the stall. Use this time as if there had been an atomic bomb warning. In other words, get your act together right away.

Use a good buddy in your department. When the bomb drops, ask him or her to rush to the front of the line, surveying the exact procedure. How much privacy and time are available? Is the water tinted? Is a secondary water source nearby? How closely does the observer watch? Is the FUC a stranger? Women should object right off if a male watches. All the women collectively! A religious leader complaining to the company will immediately end direct observation. Amen (and women!).

Mixers and Additives

As this book heads to press, anti-Enforcer scientists are working on the ultimate chemical additive—a super urine test-buster. The additive does all the work; controlled-substance metabolites will be broken apart into compounds unfamiliar to EMIT, RIA, or TLC equipment. All you have to do is add and stir into your own sample. A pending miracle in the Age of Convenience! The Nobel Peace of Mind Prize!

Already straight science is on to some promising alternatives. A new experimental drug known as Ro 15-4513 negates the impairing effects of alcohol. The *New Republic* noted, "Take it and you promptly feel sober as a judge—but still fail the Breathalyzer test when you exhale. Ro 15-4513 blocks the intoxicating effects of alcohol—the fun parts." (*New Republic*, 5/4/87). The point is, new developments happen daily.

Until the ultimate additive is invented, you're limited to more primitive means of beating the urine test.

No sweat! A number of chemical additives can be mixed directly into the urine sample while in the stall, masking or changing evidence of drug use. Their advantage is portability—small quantities are needed. Additives should be used only when it's too risky to try a full-fledged clean urine substitution. Tape condoms or a vial of additive between legs or under arms. A good container is a latex finger cot (finger condom). If using a vial, tape it upside down, so when you remove the cap, the contents flow out.

1. **Salt.** Three tablespoons of iodized salt dumped in the sample and quickly stirred (or, as James Bond prefers, shaken) will deceive EMIT tests for *all* substances. The salt, an electrolyte, increases the conductivity of the specimen, and makes it harder for the binding reagents to find their target metabolites. Just make sure *all* the salt goes into solution. Nothing is more incriminating than a small pile of insoluble salt at the bottom of the jar.

2. **The Medicine Cabinet.** Common household hydrogen peroxide is excellent. Use one-fourth cup. The oxygen molecules inhibit reagent reactions, and the rest breaks down into plain water—undetectable. The disadvantage is the comparatively large amount needed. Ammonia or chlorine bleach works nearly as well, and you need less. Three tablespoons of concentrate have disguised positive results. Don't use powdered bleaches with the little blue dots, or you'll see them floating inside the jar.

Additives should be clear, very strong, and soluble. Sure you can use a half cup of Drāno to mask a specimen, but it will look very weird, something like an underwater volcano bubbling over with lemon lava.

If you don't care about positive results and *really* want to get the Enforcers, substitute hydrochloric acid, sulfuric acid, or just plain battery acid for urine. It won't disguise any drugs, but it will sabotage their mechanisms. Repairs to their delicate equipment could run to thousands of dollars and slow things down considerably. You know how long it takes when you send your VCR out for repairs? Well, this is much worse. Only be careful. Acids are very powerful and should be carried in a safety-glass container and handled with extreme care. NO SKIN CONTACT.

3. **Internal** Additives. As noted earlier, there's a good deal of street lore about drinking acids (i.e., lemonade, cranberry juice), alkalines, or salt, perhaps changing the pH level of your urine while it is still in the body. This home cure recognizes an important factor: that EMIT-type tests are accurate only within a "normal" pH range. Exceed that range, and you inhibit the test reagents and increase the odds of a false negative.

But body chemistry nearly always balances an extreme pH. While earning an A for effort, this approach can't be recommended. All tampering (except drinking lots of water) should be done in the vial, not the body. Don't drink your car's battery acid in desperation!

Pay As You Go

You're pulling a switch. Everything is going smoothly. The salt is dissolving just as it should, you're keeping quiet—looks like you'll be done in half a minute. Then SMASH! The stall door bursts open. The FUC stands before you, pointing the finger, grinning. "Hold it right there!" he says.

Be brave. Look, if you're caught with your pants down, as they say, pull them up. Face the technician in the white suit. Hold your vial up with a painful look. And quickly remember, *these people are not well paid, and do not like their work at all*.

You have some options. Crossing the palm with a fifty-dollar bill might work wonders. So might begging for mercy. Or persuade the technician to urinate in your vial. The best move may be to make the most reasonable request, "Just close the door and I'll be out in a minute."

If White Coat is caught in a dilemma, keep pushing the fifty. Sooner or later, he's going to take it. Don't overpay; fifty dollars is standard gratuity for such custom service. But don't insult him either—ten dollars and he'll turn you in faster than a false positive.

Bribery is a fine art. Underground, I always kept some big bills handy, just in case. When cornered, I learned an important lesson which I can pass on: most Enforcer types would rather be rich than famous. Which was worth more, my life or a couple of hundred? And which is worth more to you, fifty dollars or your livelihood?

And Now a Short Message to Keep the Lawyers Happy

I wrote *Steal This Book* in 1971, sixteen years ago. To this day folks still stop me on the street, wanting to know the two best ways of flying free, which I only hinted at in the book. Many question me about one guerrilla technique or another.

They miss the point completely about this kind of information. Enforcers will be the first in line to get their copies of *Steal This Urine Test*. The developing technology on both the rebel and Enforcer sides is a constant struggle. One side thrusts, the other parries. Then the other side thrusts back. You have to be in the battle constantly to beat them. That's why I recommended at the beginning of this chapter that you get on the mailing list of testing companies and be informed about new developments.

Scientists who helped us research additives and dilutants know certain techniques work, but are not sure why. What seems to work in theory often doesn't in practice. The opposite also occurs—results without a known reason. This is especially true in a science as new as biochemical screening.

Important Caveat: The information we are providing is state of the art. Don't blame us when the state changes. Just upgrade your art.

15.

Beating the Bladder Cops

In September 1986 I launched a series of live radio talk shows on New York's listener-sponsored WBAI-FM. The show originated from the Village Gate nightclub and was designed as a kind of urban "Prairie Home Companion." With a title like "Radio Free USA," obviously there was more controversy and avant-garde culture involved than homily. It was Greenwich Village striking back at the Empire and, I am told, the only talk show with a live audience and music. *RFUSA* was intended for syndication to brave noncommercial and college stations across the fifty captive nation-states. Our rates for satellite feed were very low by broadcast standards, and local sponsorship would take care of the economics. No one involved would make much, but we could survive and put on a professional show.

It seemed like an idea whose time had come. After all, there were literally hundreds of "viewpoint" talk shows, and in a truly open free-speech society you should expect political and cultural opinions similar to mine somewhere along the dial. Not so. It's hard to be anticorporate in a medium ruled by corporate sponsorship. Not impossible, perhaps, but very hard. Sure, college kids can be "radical," go on the air, play some punk records, and have their friends call in to curse (minus seven words) authority. But a professionally produced "Radio Free USA" aiming for two million listeners weekly was intended as opposition to standard fare. We were just as serious in our alternative programming as the communications industry is serious about making money.

If television was once described as a vast wasteland, radio must be the cotton-candy valley of Saturn. The shows—four three-hour pilots—got tons of publicity, earned record contributions for the station, and steadily won listeners when the seed capital dried up. Expanding popularity would have soon made the show economically feasible and we did everything we could to keep it on the air. But it's hard sitting through a four-hour Corporation for Public Broadcasting meeting, listening to some bureaucrat give a vaunted speech about funding "new, exciting experiments on radio" only to watch them award a million dollars to a series about birds. They never once mentioned "Radio Free USA." Many more people believe in free speech than actually do it. I suspect the ratio is about ten thousand to one.

No new lessons learned here. *RFUSA* moved to the back burners. Maybe you'll remember it in your will. Sour grapes, you say? Fine, but the real story is that access to large numbers in the media is consciously and unconsciously controlled by the National Party Line. I've appeared on many talk shows and can tell you the guest role does not mean free speech. No matter how hip the host appears, sponsors and censors still dictate the show's parameters.

In our premiere, we were the first to publicly *attack* (as opposed to discuss) urine testing. Not content to debunk the tests and give tips to beating the bladder cops, we took things one step further. **We urine-tested the audience.** A trained nurse collected forty-seven voluntary samples as part of our "Urine Free America" campaign which we dumped in a big bucket.

We sent our liquid contribution down to Ron and Nancy in a mock show of support. Bringing the gallon of urine to the Post Office the next day was interesting. When the postmistress saw the intended recipient (1600 Sesame Street, D.C.), shook the package, and heard a lot of sloshing, she deduced the contents were fluid. "Urine," we explained. Saying nothing, she pulled out a list of prohibited liquids you can't send His Royal FUC (Federal Urine Collector). Nitroglycerin, gasoline, sulfuric acid . . . The list is fairly exhaustive, but: "Nope, nothin' 'bout urine. Guess it goes through," decided the postmistress. Actually, she thought it was a good idea, disapproving of the urine-testing policy herself.

The media lapped it up! Hundreds of stories appeared, and soon

I was receiving scores of letters from local groups who were "flooding the White House" with their own samples. Thus began the public movement against Reagan's Bladder Raiders, joining other grass roots efforts to return the Constitution to the people. Here's the real address:

President Ronald Reagan (or Occupant)
The White House
1600 Pennsylvania Avenue
Washington, D.C. 20500

This part about "returning the Constitution to the people" is important if you are curious about the difference between this book and *Steal This Book*, and sixties versus eighties activism. Social protest must be rooted in history, but its form must be as contemporary as technology and communications permit. The sixties happened before the Vietnam War ended in disgrace, before two Presidents were driven out of office. The question generally posed to protesters, "Isn't it better working for change within the system?" became academic when the leaders who defined the system were discovered operating outside. Millions of Freedom of Information Act pages later confirmed what was being exposed publicly. For example, here's a dialogue leaked out of the National Archives to investigative journalist Seymour Hersh while he was writing *Price of Power*, an excellent study of the Nixon-Kissinger era. It was printed in very small transcript type in the *New York Times*, but nowhere else. I've condensed it somewhat, but all these words were actually taken from a recording made at the Oval Office in May 1971, between the President and his chief-of-staff. They are discussing demonstrators who were in Washington that day.

NIXON: We need some thugs to go in there and beat these guys up.
HALDEMAN: Yeah, strike breaker types, real murderers who can go in there with gusto and smash some noses.
NIXON: Like the Chicago Seven. Aren't the Chicago Seven all Jews? Rennie Davis is a Jew, you know.

HALDEMAN: No, not Davis.
NIXON: Abbie Hoffman! He's a Jew!
HALDEMAN: Yes, Hoffman, definitely a Jew.
NIXON: Then at least half the Chicago Seven are Jews.

In my autobiography, *Soon to Be a Major Motion Picture* (a title I consider my worst literary error), I depict my attackers as regular police. You can see the photo of me with my nose shattered. The above conversation was made public three years after I wrote that book. This conspiracy to commit felonious assault was one of a hundred incidents that emerged during and after Watergate. The same year Nixon and Haldeman had that little conversation, G. Gordon Liddy, working for the government, drew up a plan to drug and kidnap me to Mexico. Eleven states banned me by name from entering and speaking. Six federal and at least two major city intelligence agencies had me under surveillance, most of which was illegal. Their tricks included unauthorized wire taps, break-ins, and harassment of relatives. I routinely gave speeches where there had been several bomb threats.

Today I've spoken in all those eleven states, and there are no more threats. I cannot honestly say I've had a hostile reception even at the most conservative colleges imaginable. People don't shout "Go back to Russia," throw red paint, or shoot at you. If I'm being wiretapped or followed everywhere, they are awfully clever. Despite Reagan and the rise of the evangelical right, it feels like there's more tolerance in America. Perhaps, more indifference. Or more suspicions of unrestricted power.

Harsh economic times and changing demographics overpowered many lessons the citizenry was learning about government and protest. Tolerance of dissent increased throughout the seventies, but Reagan, Meese, Fitzpatrick, Buchanan, et al. have tried desperately to turn the tide. The backlash wasn't entirely unexpected. History moves in waves and contradictions. And when the force of Empire/Enforcer mentality peaks, natives in the colonies abroad grow rebellious and the young at home grow restless. The media has about a two- or three-year lag time in recognizing the change. It gave the sixties extra years.

Knowing where you are in the cycle is essential to successful social protest. In 1983 I was involved in one of several environmental battles. A grassroots organization, Del-Aware Unlimited, had come to the end of its long battle with the Philadelphia Electric Company and others out to damage the Delaware River for progress, nuclear power, and the preservation of established authority. I was hired as a dollar-a-year "hired gun" to make strategy that would keep the bulldozers out (they were coming in two weeks!) and preserve that stretch of the river. I was literally the last resort.

I took along Al Giordano, from New England, who was, in my view, the best under-thirty community organizer in America. Folks called us the Batman and Robin of Bucks County. Well, to make a long story short, we beat PECO, the politicians, apathy, and lots more down on the Delware. Today there is no pumping station in Point Pleasant, Pennsylvania, nor the Limerick Nuclear Plant that was to follow. In the campaign, Al taught me the strategy of "capturing the flag." After all, the Delaware was crossed by George Washington to battle the Hessians (the only attack he ever won, by the way). Valley Forge was only a few miles away from our protest site. We used every patriotic image we could cram into our campaign. Our protest song (as it should be in all environmental battles) was "America the Beautiful." Although I always believed in that song (I once said the only thing wrong with this country was the national anthem—a war song no one could sing—while a terrific pastoral ballad made it only to second place on the charts), it was very hard to sing it during the sixties as we were being shot, clubbed, jailed, and illegally wiretapped by the government. Especially hard while the mob sang all the patriotic songs. Today it seems appropriate. So goes the cycle. (Note: the Delaware River battle appears headed for a double-header.)

Al's up in Maine today running a voter referendum on nuclear power, which he will win this November. I took Al's lesson with me to the University of Massachusetts on November 24, 1986, when I spoke at a rally against CIA recruiting on campus and in defense of eleven students under fire by the university administration for the same act. Over one hundred of us occupied a building in an act of civil disobedience. Among our numbers was a Brown University sophomore who symbolized the voice of a new generation, a new attitude—Amy Carter. Eventually, fifteen of the fifty-eight arrested went to trial. We used a necessity defense—meaning we admitted breaking the minor laws (trespassing and disorderly conduct) to stop larger, more serious crimes—CIA covert activity in Central America and elsewhere. That trial, our subsequent acquittal by what the Northampton District Attorney called "a very conservative, middle-America jury," is not the subject of this book any more than is "the Battle to Save the Delaware," but the notion of who is and who is not acting in the best interests of our country is very much to the point. Self-image and how you present yourself to the public at large are also critical.

Acting as my own lawyer, in the closing arguments to the jury I said, "You have seen the defendants act with dignity and decorum. You have seen our lawyers try hard to defend our position . . . the judge is here, the prosecutor . . . the public, the press. I ask you, is it we, the defendants, who are operating outside the system? Or do CIA activities in Nicaragua and elsewhere mean it is they that have strayed outside the limits of democracy and the law?"

Seventeen years earlier, my closing remarks in the Chicago Conspiracy Trial, before the judge sentenced us, included the statement, "When the law is oppressive and the court tyrannical, the only dignity and decorum left is to speak out with contempt." That was the sixties. Defiance was proper for a trial that was clearly rigged. The Chicago Eight and the Northampton Fifteen acted with dignity and decorum appropriate for their separate times and forums.

"Capturing the flag" implies you are as good an American or better than the Enforcers. It is a strategy essential to winning in the eighties. Inside/outside the system is a useless separation. The correct stance is one foot in the street (civil disobedience if necessary) for courage and one foot in the system (for brains, to learn how the institutions actually work). Having both feet inside will not lead to change because you then totally identify with the status quo—you are part of it or aspire to be. Two feet outside won't work either, because it takes no brains to sit-in or lie down and get carted off to jail.

Creativity, mobility, courage, moral outrage, intelligence, and the "will to win" are how the people defeat superior forces in the field of social change.

River wars on the Delaware River or the St. Lawrence, where I live, are not all that different from keeping Enforcers off your own little yellow stream. The environment, either external or internal, presents issues all Americans can get behind.

At least sixteen groups I know of, from Boston to Austin to San Jose, have staged public urinations as acts of defiance. Everything so far has been in good taste. These *are* the eighties! Standard rally programs have included civil liberties speakers, music, information leaflets, comic skits, and end with an on-site collection. People bring samples in plain brown bags, or use public washrooms if there's a mass attack of "bladder shyness," or quickly do it with or without ceremony.

From be-ins to pee-ins in twenty years—is this progress or regression? *Steal This Book* has plenty of organizing tips that remain fresh, but a fertile mind and a full bladder are your basic weapons.

Never forget that the whole idea of urine testing is ridiculous. Satire and truth are the best tactics. Facts can triumph over hysteria. Apathy, ambivalence, and false modesty about bodily functions are your worst enemies. Don't give in to hysteria. But don't let the opposition define your stand as "pro-drug." Don't feel compelled to slam drugs in a simplistic way, either.

Be firm. Experience has taught me that soft-liners often only make the battle more difficult. Examples are those who could not call for troop withdrawal for fourteen years in Vietnam, but could only propose the permanent division of the country in two. Another example are those voting against aid to the Contras, who begin each argument with five minutes of "Sandinista bashing." Balanced in this way, the focus shifts back to where the Enforcers originally wanted it. The soft-liners inevitably use the same premises and language as their opponents. This gives legitimacy to Enforcer arguments and the battle becomes protracted. More dead bodies. The issue clouds, making it easier to sit on the fence.

Here the issue is clear. **This battle has nothing to do with drugs and everything to do with fighting against a repressive police state.**

Don't get out-public-relationed by focusing on the wrong issue. *You control the debate.*

Take the campaign to the front door of corporations who are testing workers. Some politicians have done this and veered from scripture. Representative Charles Schumer petitioned the chief executive officer of every Fortune 500 corporation to stop urine testing. The crux of his campaign was a letter detailing the accuracy and privacy issues.

Trying to hit every company is overly ambitious. And wasteful. Concentrate resources on flagrant abusers. Like dominos, if one falls, the rest follow. IBM makes a great target. It was just forced out of South Africa by the anti-apartheid movement. Altered logos reading IPM look great on picket lines. Kidder Peabody has taken the lead in publicly promoting mass-surveillance of their employees. Hit 'em with signs saying, "Don't Kidder Me, Pee-Body," or "Don't Pee on My Body, Kidder." (A la "Don't Tread on Me" J. P. Jones.) Don't be too worried about wit. You're out to put the issue on their agenda, not make the board of directors laugh.

Distribute leaflets advising workers about the tests and their rights. As Meese said, get them in the lunchroom, the locker room, and nearby taverns. Locate a legal action committee prepared to handle court suits. This is harder in small towns, but the ACLU or National Lawyers Guild (see appendix) in New York City will give you local contacts. Avoid a split between "hard hats" and "hippies." Union halls, military bases, and college campuses are potentially centers of resistance, since they are also centers of urine testing. Take it to 'em, before they come for you.

Feel free to copy and distribute the "hook," the material on how to beat the test detailed in the previous chapter. After all, that's why I'm doing this book. Give the people the information they need, and use that to expand their vision of participation in decision making.

Successful opposition depends on the strength of one's convictions. Stanford diver Simone LeVant challenged the National College Athletic Association's (NCAA) urine-testing program, contending that it violated the 1972 Privacy Amendment of the California State Constitution. She won her case and was exempted from having to submit to urine testing when she participated in the national championships. Her lawyer, Robert A. Van Nest, called the ruling, "broad and sweeping. It is a complete repudiation of the NCAA's drug-testing program." Simone LeVant earns our Hero of Labor Award. She scored a perfect ten on her dive, but many more acts of defiance are needed to stop just the NCAA. Working on your own campus to eliminate drug testing of athletes makes a great starting point. Pressure the administration to defy the NCAA. It sounds screwy, but many universities are run by their athletic departments.

The question of why athletes were the first to feel the Enforcer's wrath is pivotal. Athletes are role models for youth, and thorns in owners' sides. In an era where unions had to fight to limit cutbacks, professional players' associations were making big gains. High salaries, free agentry, pension agreements, and the right to strike are some of the concessions won. Owners struck back by moving the spotlight to drugs and urine testing, an excellent revenge ploy. This put a new and difficult chip on the bargaining table. Major amateur campus sports, those that feed into the big-money games, are hardly amateur—except for 95 percent of the players. That's why they are attacked as well. Which of these questions would Peter Ueberroth rather deal with? Should college players, since they bring millions to their schools, be paid for their work? Or should athletes be drug-free as models for the young? In the resistance movement it's important to support *any* athlete who is under fire or who bravely takes a stand.

Graffiti the nation! Use yellow, since not only is it the color of you-know-what, but it is also the color symbolizing sympathy with hostages. Use these slogans and others like them: "Our bladders are hostage," "Just say no—to urine testing," "Ban the Bladder Cops," "Do it on Ronnie's leg," "Free our bladders!" Spray-paint Mr. Reagan's likeness on fire hydrants, and thousands of dogs will gladly join the campaign.

Using the legal section of this book, press your city council, student government, state legislature, and union board. Lobby wherever deliberative decision-making bodies gather. If you buy advertising space to promote your group, balance the list of endorsers. Include known personalities on all sides of the political fence. If you can't, I would advise not publishing a list of endorsers at all. *Your strategy, to be successful, must cross political lines.*

Hail resisters, people like Barbara Luck and Julie Baer, who have the integrity to say no, even if it means denying themselves economic opportunity. Hail those who take it to the courts and win, like the Firehouse Sixteen of Plainfield. Don't let the resisters get picked off without a display of solidarity. They are doing as much for you as for themselves.

Get to the doctors. Okay, some doctors worked for the Nazis. Some work for the American Tobacco Institute and claim no cause-effect connection between smoking and cancer. Everyone has their price. If you had to pay a quarter-million dollars tuition and wait fourteen years to cut people open, you'd probably be ready to follow any National Party Line. The truth is, many doctors sincerely want to heal people. They know urine tests are an embarrassment and worse to their profession. Dr. George Lundberg, in the *Journal of the American Medical Association,* called it "chemical McCarthyism." Sign 'em up. Get them on the talk shows. People listen to doctors. What other choice do they have, Jerry Falwell?

Byrd Labs is not the only supplier of pure urine. Several firms positively, absolutely guarantee delivery of clean urine overnight. Get guerrilla chemistry students to synthesize urea as a powder. Be generous! Give the stuff away, especially to athletes, outside plant gates, and in offices where programs are under way. Tell the public why.

Did you know Howard Hughes collected all his urine and had it stored under lock and key? Hughes was no fool—he knew this was coming down, and probably felt safeguarding the evidence was better than flushing it away. And who knows, the Enforcers may be out to bug your toilet.

When we talked about the drug experience, we stressed it was not the drug that mattered, but your relationship to it. Now, in the guerrilla war on the Enforcers, it's your relationship with your own bladder that counts. You simply cannot tolerate an "enemy within." You either have to win the organ's allegiance, or do what any guerrilla force must of necessity do with a traitor—**rip it out and send it to the enemy as a warning!**

Now you're getting serious. This tactic is not for all of us—only those committed enough to rise to the highest call of battle, those willing to go the full twenty miles. Find a doctor who'll see things your way, who'll remove a perfectly healthy organ to prevent it from succumbing to temptation and becoming a squealer. Sure, your bladder may be quiet now, but just wait until Meese's boys make it an offer it can't refuse.

Yes! Yes! Better to rip it out now! Even without a doctor, it's an easy operation. Hey, so I never got to med school like my parents wanted, so I have to wing it, but it's in there someplace, a balloon-like spongy thing. Get a sharp knife and go for it! (Demerol will help.) Just cut above and below, stitch up loose ends, stuff the guts back in, and sew up your stomach. No more squealer, and you got yourself a brand-new beach ball! You'll not only live without your big-mouth bladder, you'll sleep better at night. You can get one of those pretty colostomy bags. Tie it around your stomach and install a filter. It's 100 percent foolproof vinyl. Or you don't even have to bother. The bladder is only another exhaust pump. Without it, you'll just squirt a few extra times in movie theaters, on the bus, in the welding pit. You'll be combining biological necessity with ideological commitment everywhere you go! And then, bladderless, what options abound! The complete resister!

Now we're getting down to the nitty-gritty, talking massive resistance to the War on Drugs. Welcome to the Revolution!

Fight fire with fire, ridiculous with ridiculous.

Aiding and Abetting

Doing this book properly meant interviewing more than one hundred people from all byways of life. It's impossible to list everyone, but some deserve special mention for their knowledge, courage, and commitment, at a time when such are rare qualities.

Attorney Loren Siegel, of the American Civil Liberties Union, a tireless defender of civil rights, was a key source of legal information. Attorney Paul Samuels, Director of the Legal Action Center (NYC), has spearheaded the legal fight against biochemical surveillance. Jim Little, Executive Director of Veritas, and Dr. Darryl Inaba, of the Haight-Ashbury Free Medical Clinic, both profiled in the book, forced me to think deeper about my own ideas on drugs. Jeff Nightbyrd, of Byrd Labs, is on the front lines battling drug screening with his rebel research, public education campaigns, and pure urine substitutes. Dean Lattimer, senior editor of *High Times Magazine*, fought the battle early on and helped with leads.

Edward Brecher and the editors of *Consumer Reports' Licit and Illicit Drugs*, along with Dr. Andrew Weill and Winifred Rosen's *Chocolate to Morphine* authored the two most helpful books available. Andrew Weill, along with David Smith and Oscar Janiger are probably the most informed, unbiased medical people I can recommend on this subject.

Gerry Lefcourt and Len Weinglass—I'm indebted to them for limiting "time spent" in various jail cells to a minimum over the years. Lawyers, not doctors, got me to fifty. Dr. Todd Florin, Dr.

Ken Porter, Bob Fass, Monica Behan, Walli and Sam, Nina Kraut, Al Giordano, Abby and Tony McGrath, Uncle Bert, A.J., and Dr. J. S. No all gave good advice. Lisa Fithian, who organized the first mass urination in Boston, is one of the few young activists prepared to take on the Bladder Cops and the CIA.

Many people gave inside information about testing policies within corporations and government agencies, but requested anonymity for obvious reasons. The same goes for those who supplied urine samples to test or inside information on the current drug scene. Elli Wohlgelernter did valuable research in the early stages of the book, which helped immensely. Jay Levin of the *L.A. Weekly* and Paul Krassner of the *Realist* both gave good brain. Also, some gratitude has to go to the other defendants in the Trial of the CIA. Who knows, if we hadn't successfully beat the rap, we might all be refusing urine tests in the Hampshire County Prison today.

My brother Jack was one of my few political advisors who considered the project important. My kids Andy, Amy, and America all helped raise me. Florence, my mother, taught me that "serious" and "funny" were close relatives.

Jodi Sue Ross provided distinguished moral support and love for the project.

Gerry Howard edited the book with calm and intelligence, keeping one eye on the details and the other on the Dreaded Deadline. Bruce Shostak, his assistant, was always available to soothe the savage beasts. Alan Kellock, publisher of Viking Penguin, believed in a project apparently too controversial for seven other publishers. If there'd been no Alan, no book.

I must tell you of my favorite rejection scene. The publisher of a major house, with eager staffers present, flatly declared, "The project is wonderful, but Abbie, you're simply not an expert." "Oh," I answered, "like Nancy Reagan, you mean?" The room cracked up. Everyone knew the rules of the game. Nancy, without adding one bit of truth to this serious subject, could still command a million-dollar advance. An advance for a book neither she nor her husband would write. That sum is easily thirty times more than any true expert could expect to receive. Perhaps the advance should be more. Nancy just received an honorary doctorate from Georgetown University for her "outstanding contribution to our understanding of drug abuse." In 1968, the whole world was watching. In 1987, the whole world is laughing.

Finally, my friendship and thanks to Jonathan Silvers, who was as much an "and" as a "with" author. Our collaboration was complete in every way. Jon's brain and heart went the full distance. We have emerged ready and eager to slay other dragons in the Enforcers' dungeons together.

APPENDIX AND BLADDER

Recommended Reading

Books and Articles

Abel, Ernest L., ed., *The Scientific Study of Marihuana*. Chicago: Nelson Hall, 1976.

——, *Marijuana: The First 12,000 Years*. New York: Plenum Press, 1980.

"Addiction and Rehabilitation." *Playboy*, May 1987, Volume 34, Number 5, page 149.

Albert, Judith Clavir and Stuart Edward, *The Sixties Papers*. Westport, CT: Praeger Press, 1984.

Brecker, Edward, ed., and Consumers Union, *Consumer Reports' Licit and Illicit Drugs*. Boston: Little, Brown, 1972.

Brill and Winick, ed., *The Yearbook of Substance Abuse*. New York: Human Sciences Press, 1985.

Cramer, Richard Ben, "Citizen Ueberroth." *Esquire*, February 1987, Volume 107, Number 2, page 69. (An in-depth look at the self-proclaimed Drug Czar.)

Flanagan, Joan, *The Grassroots Fundraising Book*. New York: The Youth Project, 1982.

Helmer, John, *The Deadly Simple Mechanics of Society*. New York: Seabury Press, 1974. (See also John Helmer's *Drugs and Minority Oppression*, an examination of drug-related prejudice.)

Herner, Jack, *The Emperor Wears No Clothes*. Seattle, WA: Queen of Clubs Publishing, 1985.

High Times Encyclopedia of Recreational Drugs. New York: Stonehill Press, 1978. (Out of print, but available for $40 through: Cape Ann

Antiques, P.O. Box 3502, Peabody, MA 01960) Get their unusual catalogue on drug antiques, including many out of print books. Price $5.

Hoffman, Abbie, "How to Fight City Hall." *Parade,* June 24, 1984. (General tips for activists that can be applied to any campaign.)

————, *Soon to Be a Major Motion Picture.* New York: Perigee/Putnam, 1980.

————, *Steal This Book.* Worcester, MA: Jack Hoffman Sales, 1971 reprint. (P.O. Box 15, Worcester, MA 01613, $10.00. Allow four weeks for delivery.)

Lee and Shlain, *Acid Dreams.* New York: Grove Press, 1985.

Levin-Epstein, Michael, ed., *Alcohol and Drugs in the Workplace.* Rockville, MD: Bureau of National Affairs, 1986. (An excellent and comprehensive view of the issue, including corporate case studies, histories, and essays by active participants and observers.)

Mungall, Constance, ed., *Yes We Can!: How to Organize Citizen Action.* Ottawa: Synergistics Consulting Limited, 1980.

Parkhurst, William, *How to Get Publicity.* New York: Times Books, 1985.

Rangelagh, John, *The Agency: The Rise and Fall of the CIA.* New York: Simon and Schuster, 1986.

Schaef, Ann Wilson, *When Society Becomes an Addict.* San Francisco: Harper & Row, 1987.

Sloman, Larry, *Reefer Madness.* New York: Grove Press, 1979.

Smith, Dr. David, *Love Needs Care: A History of the Haight-Ashbury Free Medical Clinic.* Boston: Little, Brown, 1971.

Smith, Dr. David, ed., *Substance Abuse in the Workplace.* San Francisco, CA: Haight-Ashbury Publications, 1985.

————, *Treating the Cocaine Abuser.* San Francisco, CA: Hazelden, 1985.

Solomon, David, ed., *L.S.D.* New York: G. P. Putman's Sons, 1966.

————, *The Marijuana Papers.* New York: Signet Books, 1966.

Weil, Andrew, and Rosen, Winifred, *Chocolate to Morphine.* Boston: Houghton Mifflin Co., 1983.

Wood, Dr. Garth, *The Myth of Neurosis.* New York: Harper & Row, 1986.

Books by Saul Alinsky, the father of modern community organizing, and those by Ralph Nader and Don Ross might also be helpful.

Periodicals

Common Sense for America
NORML
2001 S Street NW
Washington, DC 20009
(A quarterly periodical.)

Employment Testing: A National Reporter of Polygraph, Drug, AIDS, and Genetic Testing
University Publications of America
44 North Market Street
Frederick, MD 21701
(800) 692-6300
(A biweekly compilation of political, social, and medical events.)

High Times Magazine
211 East 43 Street
New York, NY 10017

The Journal of Psychoactive Drugs
Haight-Ashbury Free Medical Clinic
409 Clayton Street
San Francisco, CA 94117
(Rates for individuals and institutions, and catalogue of related books available on request.)

ALSO RECOMMENDED

Reefer Madness (the movie), available on videocassette from Kartes Video Communications, 10 East 106 Street, Indianapolis, IN 46280. $19.95 or an easy rental.

National Treasury Employees Union v. William Von Raab
The most important appellate decision to date supporting compulsory urine testing. The opinion elaborately applauds and documents testing.

Federal court cases may be located in the Federal Case Supplement for the appropriate year. Any law school or university library and several legal aid societies carry these volumes.

Legal Services or Organizations

The following organizations have been instrumental in protesting drug screening:

American Civil Liberties Union
132 West 43 Street
New York, NY 10036
(212) 944-9800

Center for Constitutional Rights
666 Broadway
New York, NY 10012
(212) 614-6464

Legal Action Center
153 Waverly Place
New York, NY 10014
(212) 243-1313

National Lawyers Guild
853 Broadway
Room 1705
New York, NY 10003
(212) 614-6464

National Organization for Reform of Marijuana Laws (NORML)
2001 S Street NW
Suite 640
Washington, DC 20009
(202) 483-5500

Treatment Facilities

The following two centers provide expert treatment and advice:

Haight-Ashbury Free Medical Clinic
409 Clayton Street
San Francisco, CA 94117

Veritas Therapeutic Community
68 West 106 Street
New York, NY 10025

FOR THE BEST IN PAPERBACKS, LOOK FOR THE

In every corner of the world, on every subject under the sun, Penguin represents quality and variety—the very best in publishing today.

For complete information about books available from Penguin—including Puffins, Penguin Classics, and Arkana—and how to order them, write to us at the appropriate address below. Please note that for copyright reasons the selection of books varies from country to country.

In the United Kingdom: Please write to *Dept. JC, Penguin Books Ltd, FREEPOST, West Drayton, Middlesex UB7 0BR.*

If you have any difficulty in obtaining a title, please send your order with the correct money, plus ten percent for postage and packaging, to *P.O. Box No. 11, West Drayton, Middlesex UB7 0BR*

In the United States: Please write to *Consumer Sales, Penguin USA, P.O. Box 999, Dept. 17109, Bergenfield, New Jersey 07621-0120.* VISA and MasterCard holders call 1-800-253-6476 to order all Penguin titles

In Canada: Please write to *Penguin Books Canada Ltd, 10 Alcorn Avenue, Suite 300, Toronto, Ontario M4V 3B2*

In Australia: Please write to *Penguin Books Australia Ltd, P.O. Box 257, Ringwood, Victoria 3134*

In New Zealand: Please write to *Penguin Books (NZ) Ltd, Private Bag 102902, North Shore Mail Centre, Auckland 10*

In India: Please write to *Penguin Books India Pvt Ltd, 706 Eros Apartments, 56 Nehru Place, New Delhi 110 019*

In the Netherlands: Please write to *Penguin Books Netherlands bv, Postbus 3507, NL-1001 AH Amsterdam*

In Germany: Please write to *Penguin Books Deutschland GmbH, Metzlerstrasse 26, 60594 Frankfurt am Main*

In Spain: Please write to *Penguin Books S. A., Bravo Murillo 19, 1° B, 28015 Madrid*

In Italy: Please write to *Penguin Italia s.r.l., Via Felice Casati 20, I-20124 Milano*

In France: Please write to *Penguin France S. A., 17 rue Lejeune, F–31000 Toulouse*

In Japan: Please write to *Penguin Books Japan, Ishikiribashi Building, 2–5–4, Suido, Bunkyo-ku, Tokyo 112*

In Greece: Please write to *Penguin Hellas Ltd, Dimocritou 3, GR–106 71 Athens*

In South Africa: Please write to *Longman Penguin Southern Africa (Pty) Ltd, Private Bag X08, Bertsham 2013*